FIRST STEPS IN
COLLECTING

By

G. M. VALLOIS

Author of "Antiques and Curios in our Homes"

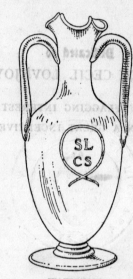

WATERFORD
TWO-HANDLED JUG

PUBLISHED BY
T. WERNER LAURIE LTD.
AT 30 NEW BRIDGE STREET, BLACKFRIARS
LONDON

Dedicated to

ALICE CECIL LOVEJOY

WHOSE UNFLAGGING INTEREST HAS

BEEN A GREAT INCENTIVE

Printed in Great Britain by Wyman & Sons Ltd., London, Reading and Fakenham

FIRST STEPS IN
COLLECTING

T.WERNER
LAURIE
Publisher

DERBY WARE.—"THE MANSION HOUSE DWARFS" AT BRAMBRIDGE PARK

From the collection of Lieut.-Col. Dampier, from a drawing by Miss Stanbury

PREFACE

PREFACE

THE very kind reception accorded to my last book, " Antiques and Curios in our Homes," makes me hope that it fulfilled its modest mission, which was to interest owners of some one, or more, treasures (be they of furniture, china, silver or what not) in their own possession, and lead them on by means of simple instruction and gossipy information on the different subjects, to regard with interest any examples they may encounter, that come to them from the long distant past, and to stimulate them to further and deeper researches. My books are not learned—there are plenty of those—but I aim at interesting my readers, and so enticing them towards more robust efforts, when the more technical and advanced books will, I hope, be sought for with ardour.

At any rate I fondly trust that after reading my chatty efforts they will know a few simple things, such as the difference between Chelsea china and salt glaze pottery, and be quite clear as to the relative dates of a Jacobean and a Heppelwhite chair.

To know something of even one of the handicrafts of the past, whether it is furniture making, pottery, china, silver, or needlework, it seems to

me essentially necessary also to know a good deal
of the condition of society, of education, of trade
and even of means of locomotion, in those far-off
days.   I have, therefore, quoted often from books
(not always obtainable) that throw light on these
matters, and I hope I shall prove to have whetted
the appetites of my readers, to search for themselves into our ancestors' manner of life.   It is a
fascinating study, and once really begun is seldom
relinquished.   Each year as we know a little more
and connect certain styles of furniture, or forms
of pottery, with some special period of history,
the more these inanimate things seem to speak
to us of the " long ago."

When we think what a Jacobean chair could
relate if only it could speak, it makes one's brain
whirl.

It lived through the great Rebellion ; mourners
of the martyred king, or exultant sympathisers in
his murder, sat on it, for all England was sharply
divided into two parties.   In 1660 it overheard jubilant triumph, or sour disappointment,
discuss the Restoration ; it listened to deep sor-
row, or, at the least, to horror-struck astonishment at the judicial murders of Judge Jeffreys',
on the Western circuit.

After that the advent of William of Orange,
that sly and astute man, and clever sovereign,
decidedly caused much discussion and heated
argument.

In 1715 and 1745 we may be sure the old chair

overheard many excited conversations as to the
chances of success for the Jacobites, and bitter
regrets for the deaths of the brave and the true
on Tower Hill, when those long cherished hopes
perished and died, and the star of the Stuarts set
for ever. The tremulous hopes of some, the fears
of others, and the wail of the bereaved must all
have been heard around.

Later, in 1793, sad faced *émigrés* from France,
who had themselves barely escaped the guillotine,
and perhaps left their nearest and dearest behind
them cold and lifeless, would sit on our old friend,
drink tea out of the Caughley or Turner tea set,
seen in Fig. 52, and try to take heart at the kindly
sympathy they met with.

At the time when Napoleon was an abiding
terror, and there were fears that after all he would
succeed in landing and swallowing us all, there
must have been numerous twitterings of fear to
be heard, followed in 1815 by the joyful news of
Waterloo ; and so through all his long life, our
old friend has listened—the Crimean war, the
Indian Mutiny and many another grim story
greeted his ears.

I sometimes fancy that the furniture and
fittings of a house like mine, all belonging to far-
off times, must, in the dead of night, perhaps,
communicate in some subtle way with each
other, and compare notes as to what they have
witnessed.

It now only remains for me to thank those who

have kindly helped me, some by giving me pictures of their beautiful possessions, and others with valuable advice, and reference to their interesting writings. Miss Whitmore Jones, of Chastleton, Sir Henry Bedingfeld, of Oxburgh Hall, Mr. Frank Falkner, Dr. Sidebotham, Mr. G. W. Rhead, Messrs. Wedgwood, of Etruria, Mr. C. E. Jerningham, Messrs. Twining, of "The Golden Lyon," and last, but not least, Messrs. Gill and Reigate, for whose kind generosity with illustrations which they allowed me to choose without stint, I am deeply grateful.

With regard to collecting some old treasures, if you do not already possess them, I have given you a few hints further on, and I wish you all success in the quest. If means are small never mind, do not be discouraged—many interesting things can be found with very little expenditure of money, and now and again, if the price of a hat, or a box of cigars, is dedicated to the altar of " collecting " I am sure in the end you will have more pleasure in what that money has secured ; very soon the hat would be shabby, or at any rate old fashioned, the cigars would have disappeared in smoke, but an 18th century chair, or a Staffordshire tea pot, will endure and be a lasting joy !

GRACE VALLOIS.

CONTENTS

PART I

LIST OF ILLUSTRATIONS

Those marked * in colour.

PART I

Part III

FIRST STEPS IN COLLECTING

PART I

HOW TO COLLECT OLD FURNITURE

BEFORE we can have success in our hunts for old furniture, it is absolutely necessary to have some slight knowledge of the subject ; this seems indeed an elementary necessity, but considering the light hearted *insouciance* with which the middle class collector, or householder who is *not* a collector, sets about " getting a few good pieces together," one is struck with their amazing simplicity.

Nowadays one has to be very wide awake to be able to secure anything that is really substantial and good, without giving a very large price for it.

In my first book, to which the public accorded so kind a welcome, I said a good deal about the history of furniture, and I must not be tedious by repetition, but as I describe each piece in this volume, I shall endeavour to insert a little more

I

useful instruction like " the powder within the jam." Perhaps some energetic and enquiring spirits will refer to that modest book as to a kind of useful first Primer.

This time I especially want to be a little help to those who wish to furnish a flat or house with furniture of respectable antiquity, or who wish to make a small addition to what they already possess.

I am thinking particularly of those, whose means being small, would limit themselves to an expenditure of £10 or at most £20 for one important piece, but would perforce consider a long time before laying out such a sum. It is well before laying plans to buy anything, to consider well how much you can afford for that particular piece, and adhere rigidly to that price. Of course this means slow and careful work, but then the pleasure of it ! To make really a collection of furniture, even of modest dimensions, is beyond most of us, but if we are setting up house it is quite possible to buy old and well seasoned furniture, instead of the gimcrack stuff of the present day. Thoroughly good furniture is made now, naturally, but it is very expensive, so, if your tastes are towards old things, they will not cost more if you go about the business carefully.

Another thing you must have in mind is scanty space, do not get your pieces too big ; in these days of " commodious residential flats," where the grand idea seems to be to have as little space as possible for one's money, there is but scant room for the solid old furniture made two hundred years ago for vast manor houses, spacious city mansions, and comfortable, roomy farm premises.   There is to me something distinctly incongruous in seeing a large Welsh dresser (never originally meant for anything but a kitchen) occupying the entire wall of a little jerry-built twentieth century dining room, and adorned with the necessary adjuncts of every day life, biscuit boxes perhaps, and a Tantalus stand. Sometimes the dresser is promoted to the "drawing room" so called, and thrusts its grand, simple old lines, among palms in pots, an ugly but convenient Sutherland table for tea, or, crowning atrocity, one of those three-tiered stands for cake and bread and butter.   These things may be convenient, but they do not go with the old dresser !

So let us—if our lines be in small places—not be too ambitious, and let us try to make our homes as harmonious as possible.

It is not necessary to have everything of the same period, that, to my mind, is dull and uninteresting.   An ancestral home is necessarily built up bit by bit, each generation has added something and left their impress in the old house. I like to see Jacobean chairs living amicably with Sheraton cabinets, and old four posters sharing floor space with 17th century Bridal chests, and 18th century Heppelwhite chairs.

That is as it should be, and appeals to me far more than a perfect 18th century house, where everything inside and out seems to speak of Adam.

For those who are complete beginners in the study of old furniture, I would advise to keep steadily in their minds the three broad divisions into which furniture naturally falls—that made of oak, of walnut, and of mahogany; satin wood comes later and was but little used until towards the end of the 18th century.

Up to 1660, always speaking very broadly, almost every article of furniture in England was made of oak; gradually walnut was planted and used, and we see most things constructed of that, till about the middle of the 18th century. Mahogany had been discovered earlier, but it did not come into really general use till about 1740 when, for a time at least, it superseded all other woods.

From many causes periods overlapped, and you will soon learn that it is rather difficult to apply hard and fast dates to any fashion or custom.

First of all, it is not much use, unless your purse is a long one, to go at once to an antique dealer, but more of this anon. The plan I always advocate is to visit the suburbs, and devote one's attention to those unattractive shops which give themselves up to the sale of first hand and secondhand household goods ; the kind of man in whose shop now and then you find a treasure is he, who, on some sudden compulsory move, is invited to enter a house and remove all superfluous belongings " at any price they will fetch." This price, alas ! is often only a few shillings !

As a rule this *débris* consists of miserable rubbish, cheap modern chairs, bedsteads destitute of one or more castors, pots and kettles of dubious utility, blue glass paraffin lamps, coal scuttles with bunches of roses painted on them as appropriate decoration, most certainly art flower pots, of a kind to give the artistic soul an indigestion, and above all, overmantels of all degrees of atrocity.

But occasionally amidst all this worthless flotsam and jetsam, there is a something that will reward patience. Perhaps a good solid " gentleman's wardrobe " as they are called, made of dark mahogany, closed with two doors above, behind which are sliding shelves, and

B

below three deep drawers. This is a great find, and if in good condition, well worth £4 or £5.

Chairs are not very often met with of any real worth, being fragile things they are more easily broken, and being broken or shorn of a leg and defective in the back, they have been broken up to light the fire. Alas! what old treasures of Chippendale, Heppelwhite, Mainwaring, etc., must have thus perished, it makes one shiver to contemplate.

With regard to these secondhand furniture shops and antique dealers of a modest sort, the same rule holds good; make friends of them and haunt their shops continually, for this reason; it is the custom in the trade for these small men to have a tacit understanding with the larger dealers, that they will not dispose of anything of value to outsiders, until they (the superior dealers) have had the refusal of it. By this means the small and insignificant trader becomes a kind of middle man and jackal for the antiquity dealer *par excellence.*

But bargains and agreements are mutable, fortunately for the small purchaser, and sometimes the humble suburban shopkeeper feels that he would like at once to realize a small sum on an article just come in, rather than await the condescending patronage, and very often grinding terms, of the great men of the trade—also he has discovered, that the private purchaser gives better prices, and so he occasionally hides from the observant eye of his commercial patron, some nice little bit of cut glass, some choice bit of old china, perhaps cracked but still respectable, some queer little wig stand—the use of which, to him, is quite incomprehensible, or, perhaps, greatest treasure of all, a Chippendale or Heppelwhite chair minus a leg, but having the said leg attached to its body with string, so that a few shillings will save the situation.

If you make your rounds early in the morning you may be the lucky bird to pick up a succulent worm, for the trader feels that often a " bird in the hand is worth two in the bush ! "

Be careful that anything you buy is solid and in good repair ; if it is only a matter of a little veneer missing, that does not greatly matter, for it can be replaced, but do not forget that the repairing of an old piece of furniture is always an expensive matter ; it requires skilled labour of the highest sort, and is charged for accordingly.

Do not buy a piece simply because it is old, some old things are very ugly, though substantial and well made, but if they are ugly and *not* substantial they are not worth having.

If you are furnishing begin by getting a few necessary pieces, and leave the rest to be acquired bit by bit, due consideration being given to each article ; as surely as you attempt to do the whole thing at once, so surely you will repent it and find you have bought rubbish.

A bed, a table, and a chair, as the children say

when executing a primitive drawing, are the first necessities ; beds, alas ! are hard to find, and in all probability you will have to content yourself with a good modern reproduction, at any rate at first ; you will see more on this subject in the chapter on beds.

For a dining table, nothing is better than a gate leg ; it accommodates a larger number in proportion than a rectangular one and always looks graceful.

Your chance for these is to find one at a provincial dealers, destitute of polish, and very often gone in the hinges, but if the legs are not seriously worm eaten, the hinges can be renewed, and the polishing done by cleaning with methylated spirit (do not use soda, it pales the wood), rubbing down with a heavy brick in a cloth, and then assiduous doses of elbow grease assisted by beeswax and turpentine.

For chairs, I must admit one always meets with some difficulty ; still, odd ones are to be picked up if the hunt is continued with diligence. If, however, you want to secure a few really good examples, it will be better to apply to a dealer, I mention this in the chapter on chairs. Let him know what you want and to what price you are willing to go, in the end it will be worth it ; why good chairs should be so difficult to trap I know not, but so it is, from a variety of causes probably, and your having applied to a dealer need not stop your hunts on your own account.

I have mentioned in Chapter II. the desirability of a set of farmhouse wooden chairs, or a good set of Windsors, for your dining room if means are limited. You have no idea how nice and uncommon these last would appear. I know an old inn in Bucks, where beanfeasts are of frequent occurrence, where there are 34 of these nice old chairs, four of them being carving chairs.

If you can light upon a " chest upon chest " or " tall boy " as some call them, it is always a good investment, especially if floor space is limited.

Washstands constitute a difficulty. Our ancestors were content with very small accommodation of this sort, as we can see from the pretty little corner contrivances that we now prize so highly, and to live with such meagre fittings for daily ablutions is not possible.

It is a bit of a puzzle to get something that will not look too incongruous, and yet be roomy and comfortable. In one case we got over the difficulty by having a plain, substantial, mahogany Pembroke table, turning down the leaf by the wall and covering the top with thick white oil cloth ; there is a particular kind made for this purpose. Then we got toilet ware of a chintzy kind of design, and it really suited very well.

A better arrangement is to have a wide knee-hole table, but these are very expensive, and unless you have plenty of old furniture it would be a shame to use a good piece in such a manner.

In fitting up the sitting room, in spite of ana-
chronisms, I would plead for a couple of commonplace, every-day, comfortable basket chairs, old
chairs are not usually comfortable, and why
sacrifice comfort to appearance. I should leave
the drawing room quite to the last and be very
slow in filling it ; two or three good things are to
be preferred to many doubtful ones.

Usually old furniture looks best upon a plain
paper, and if liked, shades of yellow, biscuit and
brown gives the best effects, green is not good and
blue worse, so if yellow tints are disliked there are
several shades of salmon pink and terra cotta
that do well.

I think I have spoken to you before about the
Friday market in Copenhagen Fields, where, occasionally, but it is indeed very occasionally,
treasures may be picked up ; you must, however,
be a very early and a very sharp bird to pick up
a worm there !

I have had one or two successes, but they
stand out as red letter days in a wilderness of
unrewarded hunts ; that arid desert, many acres
square, is swept by the discriminating eye of
many a son of Israel, which leaves but little for
our less acute sight.

I have seen one or two chairs there (pushed
behind beds and bedding that make one shudder)
that were undoubtedly good ones, but in a shock-
ing state of disrepair, so bad indeed as to be beneath the notice of the dealers ; one that I judged

to be a japanned Heppelwhite had lost a leg, another was in a state of senile decay. Nevertheless these cripples could be mended, and though not of commercial value, would be interesting possessions. I also saw another chair, with all four legs intact, but the seat had given way and showed a yawning void.

I think this, too, was of the Heppelwhite time, though it was enamelled hedge sparrow blue, a colour much beloved in the artisan class.

I could not be really sure whether it was good or not, for it was held in a suffocating embrace by a frowsy bed of a grey and speckled appearance. that suggested hideous possibilities. Still, I think it would perhaps have been worth buying, re-stuffing, and carefully removing the enamel. Do you know how to do this I wonder ? This is the manner of proceeding : get a small methylated spirit lamp, hold it close to the paint till it crackles and bubbles, and then scrape off with a knife or piece of glass. It is a tedious job, but quite satisfactory. Then rub in beeswax and turpentine. That is always safe, only let there be much rubbing and little beeswax and turpentine. One pretty little article of furniture I have seen several times at the Friday market, and that is specimens of the charming little 18th century mirrors. They are small and I imagine they are despised by the ladies of the coster class, who find their surface all too small to receive the reflection of their mighty headgear.

BIBLIOGRAPHY

A History of English Furniture *Percy Macquoid*
*Furniture of the Olden Time *Francis Clary Morse*
English Furniture Designers of
   the 18th Century   .   . *Constance Simon*
The Furniture of our Forefathers *Esther Singleton*
Dutch and Flemish Furniture . *Esther Singleton*
*Chats on Old Furniture .   . *Arthur Hayden*
*Chats on Cottage and Farm
   House Furniture   .   . *Arthur Hayden*
*The Chippendale Period in
   English Furniture   . *K. Warren Clouston*
The Verney Memoirs   .   . *Lady Verney*
Through England on a side
   Saddle in the time of Wil-
   liam and Mary   .   . *Celia Fiennes*
The English Housewife of the
   17th and 18th Centuries   . *Rose Bradley*
The " Connoisseur " Magazine
The " Burlington " Magazine
Ancient Coffers and Cupboards . *Frederick Roe*
An Illustrated History of Furni-
   ture   .   .   . *F. Litchfield*
Antiques and Curios .   .   . *Grace Vallois*
English Furniture of the 18th
   Century   .   . *Herbert Cescinsky*

CHAPTER I

BEDS AND DAY BEDS

THERE are now, alas ! but very few old four post bedsteads left to rejoice our hearts, but diligent search will be rewarded by finding still a few, but almost all belonging to the first 15 years of the 19th century.

As we look at them now, we wonder how our ancestors could sleep happily in such a confined and stuffy atmosphere, for, not only were their curtains sufficiently wide to draw all round the sleeper, but they actually were so drawn, and lest still one breath of air should penetrate to the occupant, " bonnegrâces " were added ; these were small supplementary fixed curtains that closed any possible aperture between the curtains that drew.

Naturally, as time went on, all these fortifications against the air of Heaven, more or less diminished, but closely drawn curtains, though shorn of the " bonnegrâces " and " cantonnières," another arrangement of somewhat similar intention, were still considered necessary. We, who in this generation sleep with all our windows wide open all night, regard such a condition of things

13

as preposterous, but that was the time—and
not so long ago either—when it was considered
that night air was deadly and to be guarded
against at all costs, even a very little of it being
provocative of a mysterious " tightness about
the chest," also likely to develop a " weakness
of the eyes." This opinion still holds good in
the lower classes—on asking why a child had
developed severe pneumonia, the answer I
received was " he was took so through the
winder being left open a mite last week, cos our
Polly forgot to bolt it ! "

Sleeping with windows open would, indeed, have
been considered by our great grandmothers as
a tempting of providence, which would assuredly
meet with a well-deserved punishment. So they
lived, slept, and at last died, in their well-
sheltered four posters (but apparently none the
sooner for the lack of filling their lungs with
the wholesome air of Heaven), the curtains closely
drawn, lest one whiff of pernicious fresh
air should reach them. Perhaps, after all, it was
really just a case of the survival of the fittest.

I am sure you will remember the delightful
picture of Mr. Pickwick surprised in bed by the
middle aged lady, who, all unconscious of his
close vicinity, begins to curl her hair and to
attend to other details of her toilet, which so
alarms Mr. Pickwick that he thrusts his night-
capped head between the curtains, closely
gathering them modestly round his chin, to see

if a favourable moment had arrived to break the shock of his presence on Miss Witherfield's seclusion.

Probably the first beds were no more than rough sacks of reeds or grass on the floor, covered with rags, or more ornate draperies, according to the status of the owner ; the next step, judging from the old missal illuminations and other monkish pictures, were frames of oak, with rough linen canvas, or skins of beasts strained from side to side, upon which the aforesaid sack was placed.

By slow degrees greater luxury was attained, feathers replaced the reeds, and a species of thick webbing, very much like what we have in the present day in upholstery, supported the large sack.

Very few beds of Tudor times still exist ; a beautiful one is to be seen in the Victoria and Albert Museum in perfect preservation. It reminds me, however, of a tomb, principally I think because the actual bedstead is placed *within* the tomb like posts, but not touching those at the foot. By the kindness of Sir Henry Bedingfeld, I am enabled in Fig. 1 to show you a perfect specimen of a bed, the date of which is unknown, but it must have been before 1487, for in that year Henry VII. slept in it. It is a beautiful specimen and has been well preserved. Observe the vast footposts grandly carved by hand in a spiral pattern—spiral turning by a machine did not come in till very long after.

The hangings of the bed are worth study, and are of a later date by nearly a hundred years; they are the work of the unfortunate Mary Queen of Scots, and of her ladies. It was the custom in those days for embroiderers to put their initials on some part of their work, and very often the date also. This work bears the initials of the tragic Queen, and also of Elizabeth Talbot, Countess of Shrewsbury, better known to all as "Bess of Hardwick." Queen Mary was in the custody of this dame from 1569 to 1584, the work must have been done between those dates.

The hangings and coverlet are green velvet, and the designs, worked in small panels of different shapes, are executed in gold thread. They represent flowers of conventional design and (what is most interesting) beasts and birds, intended to be represented as God made them, but lest the worker's skill should be inadequate to a clear understanding of the subject, the names are in many cases appended, such as " A Fyrete " " A Boare," " A Civette Cat," " A Frogge," etc.

The coverlet has the Queen's initials, M.R.S.A.F. (Mariæ Regina Scotia Anglia France) surmounted by the crown, and in another place there is George and Elizabeth Shrewsbury. A large number of the little panels have E.S. under them, and one, the Dolphin, has M.R. with the crown over it. Besides the many proofs of poor Mary's participation in the work, there is a sad and heart-

FIG. 1.—THE OXBURGH BED.

rending hint of the worker's fears of treachery and constant anguish of mind, conveyed in a motto which she has embroidered in the corner of the quilt, " Anguis sub herba latet "—" a snake lies hidden in the grass."

Poor Mary, guilty or innocent of the many sins laid to her charge, her charm for us will never die —wherein lay that charm ?   Not, apparently, in her actual features, for, according to the authentic portraits we have of her, she was by no means beautiful—but who can define charm ?   At any rate, in her case it was potent enough to ruin almost every man who came under her influence, and yet, with all the devotion of so many good men, she threw herself away upon the odious Bothwell ! Her lovers are by no means all dead now, we almost all come under her magic spell, and even now such hot controversy rages round the subject that it is hardly a safe one for general conversation.

I am the more obliged to Sir Henry Bedingfeld for allowing me to give you this illustration of the beautiful Oxburgh bed shown in Fig. 1, because his splendid seat in Norfolk is not one of those shown to the public. The room in which this bed stands has tapestry of the time of Edward IV. on the upper part of the walls, and fine linen fold panelling on the lower, whilst the floor is of fine red bricks, disposed in a pattern.

There are several good beds of the 16th and 17th centuries in the Victoria and Albert Museum, and I should like you to study them, for, although we cannot hope—naturally—to collect such things, we need to study the gradual steps by which each kind and variety of furniture attained its various developments.

Study well the Sizergh bed which, with its beautiful surrounding inlaid walls, is to be seen there. The whole thing is a gem ; the groundwork rather light oak, inlaid with holly and darker oak. Mr. Robinson puts the date of this room at about 1570. Another bed worth a visit is that at the Rye House, called the Great Bed of Ware. The Rye House is an odious place, given over to bank-holiday parties and that sort of thing, but it is worth putting up with that to see a bed that was considered a wonder, even in Shakespear's time. In " Twelfth Night " Sir Toby Belch refers to it :

" If thou *thou'st* him some thrice, it shall not be amiss ; and as many lies as will lie in thy sheet of paper, although the sheet were big enough for the Bed of Ware in England, set 'em down."

The bed is some twelve feet square, but there is no record of why it was made of such enormous dimensions. It was in the 17th century that the beds, and especially the bedding and hangings, came to be so sumptuous, and to cost so much.

Evelyn, whose diary is such a mine of wealth to us concerning the 17th century, writes under the date 1644 that a Cardinal travels " in great state with his owne bedstead and all the furniture."

This custom died hard, not so much as to the bed-stead, but for the furniture, as Evelyn calls it. It is not thirty years ago that arriving at the station to see some dear old fashioned friends off to the Continent, I beheld a truly Brobdignagian parcel among their impedimenta, sewn up in a sacking. Curiosity overcame politeness, as I saw four porters wrestling with the unwieldy thing that had no excrescences by which to hold it. " What *is* that mass ? " I enquired. " Oh ! don't say anything, my dear, it is B——'s feather bed, he never travels without it," was the reply.

To me one of the joys of Continental travel is the beautiful bed almost always found, even in the humblest inn. Most certainly our neigh-bours across the Channel would never consent to sleep upon the antiquated mattresses (some of them for comfort little better than sacks of pota-toes) on which we meekly recline when travelling in our own land. I cannot imagine what they would think of our really horrible habit of sleep-ing upon a mattress that has not been picked or cleaned for six, seven, eight and sometimes not for ten or twenty years !

As for the ancestral feather beds which are still treasured possessions among the lower middle class and the peasantry in provincial England, one shudders to think of them—" that was my grandmother's," they will proudly affirm, " and nothing ever done to it, except just to rub out the cover ! " and so the feathers and ticking, on which

several generations have been born, slept out
their lives and died, still remain untouched, the
" rubbing out " of the outside covering being
considered all that the most fastidious could
desire !

I wonder what any decent housewife, even of
the superior peasant type in France, or Italy,
would say to that greatest of all tortures of the
modern English bed—a straw palliasse—as hard
as iron, and with no more spring than a concrete
road. That was a nineteenth century instrument of torture, and was popular with all who
distrusted the luxury of a box spring. We are
improving a little in these matters, with our
chain and box springs, but still, even in wealthy
houses, the mattresses remain unpicked and un-
cleansed year in, year out.

To return to our 17th century bedsteads, grand
as they were, their magnificence was well supported by the sumptuous bedding and magnifi-
cent hangings. These, of course, varied in splendour. You must always try to keep before you
the fact that a great deal of entertaining was done
in the bedroom, and therefore the bed, being the
chief article of furniture, was bound to be somewhat handsome, and the ladies vied with each
other in working hangings. At this period the
ladies wrought those strange designs of birds,
beasts, fishes, trees, etc., in all kinds of greens
and blues and browns, that we sometimes
see and admire as " Jacobean embroidery."

In the " Verney memoirs "—that mine of wealth
for the student of the 17th century—we read of a
set of hangings being worked by poor Mary Abel,
the wife of young Edmund Verney, who was sometimes quite mad for weeks together. A charming relative, Doll Leeke, of whom we hear much,
writes to Mary's father in-law, Sir Ralph, concerning Mary's embroidery, that she is helping
her with the " rosemary stitch " ! One would
like to know what that was like, and she goes on
to describe the design, which she considers to be
rather too intricate. " There is certain birds
and flyes and other crepers which I know not,
and frute which I do not much like, but it is a
very fine thing, though they be left out." Miss
Bradley, who I see is in love with the Verney
memoirs as deeply as I am myself, remarks concerning this in her book, English housewives of
the 17th and 18th centuries, " The birds and
flyes and other crepers have become familiar
to us in that handsome Jacobean design, and we
do not like them the less, because like Doll, we
know not the originals."

A good deal of this work still exists. I, myself,
slept under a coverlet of this description in an old
inn in the Basque country. Traditionally, it
had been used for some of the company assembled
to do honour to the marriage of Louis XIV. with
the Infanta of Spain at St. Jean-de-Luz. No
doubt the neighbouring country was eagerly
sought for rich " plenishings " suitable for the

C

distinguished company. It was a sumptuous piece of work in the style somewhat of Fig. 55, but the chief glory was the border which consisted of a procession of parrots, very much developed as to eyes and beaks.

I should strongly recommend your studying the " Verney memoirs," and also Miss Bradley's book mentioned above. They are not only extremely instructive, but delightfully amusing. I always have a volume of the " Verney memoirs " at hand, and so cleverly is it written that we seem to know personally the various members of the family. Sir Ralph who (for us) had the agreeable idiosyncrasy of being unable to throw away *anything*, so that we even have a morsel of the brocade that Lady Sussex wanted matched for a " choate " for her godson. As to writing, it seemed too sacred for destruction, so that we have his " foul " copies of all sorts of interesting documents. Then we see plainly before us the first Mary Verney, his " Deare Harte," for whom he mourned for forty-six years ; also dear unselfish Doll Leeke, whom we fancy dimly would like to have been Sir Ralph's second " Deare Harte," and Lady Sussex is a never ending joy, with her practical good sense and strange spelling.

We hear a great deal about beds in these books, and among other things of the curious custom of those days to have in a house of importance a " mourning " bed, upholstered in black, and even with a coverlet and sheets of black, a most ghastly idea and calculated to prey upon delicate nerves : as this funereal article of furniture was necessarily expensive, and superfluous furniture was only possible for the wealthy, we hear of mourning beds being lent to families, in time of domestic afflictions. In these memoirs we read a good deal of the peregrinations of the mourning bed. " In 1644, Colonel Eure was killed and " Mrs. Eure writes to Sir Ralph." " Sweet " Nephew, I am now overrun with miserys and " troubels, but the greatest misfortune that " could suer hapen to me in this world was the " death of the galantest man that ever I knew in " my life. . . ."

" Sir Ralph replies full of sympathy, and offers " her the loan of the great black bed, and hangings " from Claydon, as the only consolation within " his means. This great black bed, with its " impressive amplitude of gloom, travels about " the family whenever a death occurs, till the " very mention of it gives one a feeling of suffo- " cation." One hears of it in the family as late as 1688 when young Sir Edmund dies and all are busy preparing requisite gloom.

The extremely rich beds of this period were naturally considered as heirlooms and valuable bequests. In " Gossip from a muniment room," we read of legacies of this kind. Dame Anne Newdegate in 1610 bequeaths " my bodie to the earth from whence it came desiringe either to be buried in Herfield Churche by my husband S^{r}

John Newdegate, or in Gamesworth Church by my dear ffather Sr Edward ffitton wth out anie extraordinarye cost, but in a comelie manner as is fitt wth some small memorie of mee, as my name, and my husband and ffather's Armes together in some windowe sett " She then divides her " gowns, petticoats, jewels " amongst her five children, " and to Richard the bedstead with the yellow velvet canopy and taffata quilt wch my uncle Francis Fytton gave me."

No wonder these pieces of furniture descended from generation to generation, for their cost ran into hundreds and sometimes, in exceptional cases, to thousands of pounds. In Mr. Macquoid's splendid book on old English furniture he gives a letter written in 1612, which gives us some idea of their opulence—it reads very quaintly.

" About this day sevenight, the Countess " of Salisbury was brought to bed of a daughter, " and lyes in very richly, for the hangings of her " chamber being white satin embroidered with " silver and pearl is valued at fourteen thousand " pounds. . . ."

Going on a little further in dates, we come to the time of William and Mary, and as to this period, we are greatly helped by the staterooms at Hampton Court, which contain fine examples of this period, of that of Queen Anne and of the Georges. There are the hangings and all just as the users slept in them, often doubtless illustrating the old line " uneasy lies the head that wears a crown."

William thinking moodily of his unpopularity— of how—no matter what he did for the English, they still regarded him (very naturally) as a usurper, and a foreigner. Mary, sadly thinking, in spite of her blooming youth, and love for him, how feeble was her hold on the affections of her taciturn husband, and how entirely she was powerless to detach him from the influence of the clever, squinting, Elizabeth Villiers, and perhaps in the silent watches of the night, remorse gnawed her soul for her treachery to her father. Poor woman, could she but have known it, when " struck for death " with small pox, that scourge of the time, she would perhaps have been comforted to see William's desolation after her death. Probably he loved her far better than they either of them realized. It has been said— perhaps with reason—that poor Mary's guilty conscience saw in her husband's infidelity a just retribution for her sin against her father—a sin the less to be excused, because, whatever the faults of James II. as a king and a man had been, to her he was ever the tenderest father.

And poor foolish Queen Anne, we know the same remorse haunted her, as she lay in the immense catafalque—it is really more like that than a bed—all upholstered in crimson, cream, green, and white, and with vast monumental urns at the corners.

Her miseries took a different shape ; her good-
natured Danish husband, the " Est il possible "
of poor James' solitary joke in his hour of humili-
ation, never gave her cause to doubt his fidelity,
but she lost seventeen babies, the last of whom
only lived to be a few years old, and then poor,
foolish George who had always been kind to her.
In these domestic afflictions she read her punishment, and would doubtless have named her unfortunate brother her successor, if death had not
been too swift for her.

At this period there was practically no wood
belonging to the bedsteads visible, and a plethora
of heavy brocaded curtains, velvet or linen, used
for generations without cleaning, and in the case
of " mourning " beds lent round from house to
house ; what a blow to our present sanitary
ideas !

Personally I think we were far happier when
we did not concern ourselves so incessantly with
sanitation. I do not mean that I want to go
back to stuffy bedrooms, and a bath about once
a year, as a last desperate remedy in some disorder, but I do think people bring a lot of misery
on themselves, with perpetual anxieties about
microbes and bacilli. When we knew nothing
about them we were much happier, and I believe
we lived as long.

Think of the microbes in those formidable four
posters at Hampton Court ; on those sepulchral
velvet-covered urns there must be poison enough

to destroy half London, one would say, if all one hears is true.

In William's and Anne's times, the height of the beds became enormous, that one at Hampton Court, which was used by William, is 16 feet tall. The cornice, according to the fashion, is much scalloped, and scrolled, and with the usual vase-shaped finials at the four corners; once evidently there were hearse-like plumes waving from these finials, but these have long since disappeared. The tester, or rather the ceiling of it, is dome-shaped, and altogether it is a formidable piece of architecture! Poor William must have looked like a little mummy in it!

The once beautiful rose coloured damask, trimmed with a gold galon, now hangs in forlorn rags about the mighty structure, and even the feet of the posts are covered with these once gorgeous materials. It is well to study here the original mattresses and bolsters which remain (little the worse for the passage of years) covered in cream coloured satin and fastened down with coloured silk tufts. The splendour of these satin covered accessories helps us to understand the cost of the bed in which the Countess of Salisbury "lyes in very richly."

The bed belonging to Queen Anne is more simple in shape, but still higher, being 19 feet high and eight wide. The cornice is much plainer but has the vase-shaped finials, which are covered with the same brocaded velvet that forms the hangings. It is wonderfully ugly, being a mixture of olive green, deep red and cream. The same kind of mattresses are on it, as in the last example.

As a rule at this period there was no carved wood visible, everything was covered with drapery, and the cornice and feet, if carved, were all the same, closely covered with material nailed and even glued on. There is a much smaller example of this kind to be seen in the Victoria and Albert Museum. It is in very good preservation. The hangings are of a kind of rep (rose coloured) which I fancy is the material we hear referred to as " camlet." There is a good deal of tarnished silver lace about it, which adds to the somewhat sepulchral appearance.

The first change towards showing carved work of walnut wood, was the emerging of the finials into the light of day ; these began in George I. and II.'s reign to show boldly as pine apples, vases, burning torches, etc. It is but seldom that we can see old beds of this period, entirely untouched and unaltered, because in the first place the hangings wore out, and in the second, the taste of successive generations differed and each owner of the heirloom altered it a little, but, fortunately for us, the Hampton Court beds remain untouched and in their original somewhat grotesque splendour. By degrees the bed posts emerged from their obscurity and gradually became things of beauty and the portentous height greatly diminished.

A quite modestly proportioned bed, used by George II. is placed next to that of William III. I daresay that warrior king was drawn to something that resembled, though distantly, his camp bed used in many campaigns.

I should like to see a " truckle " or " trundle " bed, which was so contrived that it could be rolled under the bigger one in the day time ; this was used by the gentlemen in waiting, or plain valet in attendance, as the case might be. A large number of these must at one time have been in use ; what has become of them all ? One may ask the same question respecting the stools, a pair of which accompanied the big beds, as an aid to mounting the stately structure. You see them at Hampton Court, but not often elsewhere, and yet what vast numbers must have been made. Every house of social importance in the 16th, 17th and early 18th century had a state bed for the reception of royalty and other distinguished company, but after about 1765, it was at any rate no longer general to have one of these imposing structures added to a newly built house.

Before leaving this gorgeous period in beds, let us glance a little at the draperies and coverings in use. Mr. Macquoid in his grand work, " A History of English Furniture " (vol. 2), gives us some enlightening extracts from letters of the time concerning the building and furnishing of Blenheim which took place under the redoubtable Sarah from 1705, when the Duke of Marlborough was at the height of his glory and popularity. It was not finished till 1720, when that popularity and power had grievously declined.

I do not apologize for quoting Mr. Macquoid's book so often, because I feel sure that these items from it will be greatly appreciated by those who are unable to study the book itself. Mr. Macquoid has been tireless in hunting up old records, letters and journals that throw light on domestic matters of all periods. At page 234, he gives us a short letter from Lady Wentworth to her soldier son abroad, that at once gives us a kind of rough idea of the opulence of Blenheim.

" My Dearest and Best of Children,

" I am much rejoysed at your fyne
" present, I wish you may often have such
" and better, till you are as ritch as the Duke of
" Molberry, whoe is billding the fynest hous at
" Woodstock that ever was seen, thear is three
" score rooms of a flower, noe stairs, only a little
" pair that goes to the uper roomes which are
" only for sarvents, and staitly wood, which he
" cuts out walks in, and fine gardens that are
" fower mylis about. It is beeleved furneture
" and al cannot cost les than three hundred thou-
" sand p^d why should you not be so fortunate
" as he ? "

The punctuation being such as it is, at first I thought the " staitly wood " referred to the " little pair " of stairs, but it is evident that it is the grand park surrounding Blenheim.

Every one knows Sarah of Marlborough was a shrew, and most decidedly she knew how to get the utmost value out of everything and everybody —with great skill and astuteness, she makes all turn to her advantage, witness the following :

" DEAR MRS. JENNENS,

" I have looked upon this damask by day " light, the pattern is not so large as he " stated ; but he has kept it so ill that it looks " full as old as what I have, which is better than " if it were a fine fresh Damask. But I think " it is a good argument to him to sell it cheap " for tho' I like it very much for this use, I " would not buy it for any other. But don't " part with it, for I would have the whole piece " on any terms that you can get it. I shall " want a vast number of feather beds and quilts. " I wish you would take this opertunity to know " the prices of all such things as will be wanted " in that wild unmerciful hous, for the man you " go to is famous for low prices. I would have " some of the feather beds Swandown, all good " and sweet feathers, even for the servants. I " am not in Hast for anything you are so good " as to do for me."

The redoubtable Duchess evidently spared no pains in her furnishing, nor did she spare her friends. Here is another letter to the same lady full of demands and instructions, and showing the parsimonious spirit which never left either of the ducal pair !

" This narrow Fring is enough to put upon
" the feet Base of the Bed, and if the broad can
" bee made to do the two side Bases, they are not
" seen at the same time that the Feet is seen, and
" if it is a little narrower, I think it no great
" matter. I say that because I fancy they may
" make it up of near half the breadth it is now.
" Six feet is wanted for the side Bases, and as
" much more as it will take up in putting on.
" It is to lye upon the Damask which require
" the less thicknesse. I shall want galloon of
" these sorts to lace the curtains, and to turn
" the chairs and window curtains. May I ask
" what they will do it for an ounce. You will
" observe the fine colour of the gold ; tis being
" the best duble quilt which makes it last
" so long, and look so well for this has been
" made this eight years at least . . . . This
" is the collour of the Damask, of which this
" bed is made, which I must match exactly,
" because it will be so fine Fourniture . . . .
" I shall want of it two window curtains, twelve
" chairs, and four curtains for the bed."

Mr. Macquoid gives an illustration of a bed,
which he says is the only one left of the early
furnishing and he thinks it must be the one concerning which there are these minute orders.
To continue—fashions moved slowly, and the next
decided period in the history of beds is that of
Chippendale.

Of the actual beds of that period not many

FIG. 2.—CHIPPENDALE BED.—EARLY STYLE
(By permission of Messrs. Gill and Reigate.)

FIG. 3.—CHIPPENDALE BED.—LATER.
(Ey permission of Messrs. Gill and Reigate.)

remain, the few that still exist of so-called Chippendale time are those belonging to the later years of that time and are (as a rule) only found in ancient mansions and at a few of our first-class antique dealers.   Such a one is illustrated by the courtesy of Messrs. Gill and Reigate in Fig. 2.   It is very ornate and grand, and you are most unlikely to see such an example, but I show it to you that you may accustom your eyes to the styles of the different dates.   It has hangings of printed linen, which in the early 18th century began to be held in great esteem.   The date of this bed I should think would be about 1755 to 1765.   Mahogany was then in constant use, and lent itself to the delicate lattice work on the posts, as well as to the more rococo work of the cornice. I have only met with one bed of this period in " private life."   It was in Yorkshire, and was the property of a maiden lady of small means.   She belonged to an old yeoman family, and though her means were very straitened, he would, indeed, have been a very bold man who had—however tentatively—suggested selling that old family treasure.

These pieces of furniture were unavoidably expensive, and they were not made in vast numbers like chairs. People who could not afford four-posters contented themselves with a structure equally comfortable, but less decorative, being a stout rectangular framework with a headboard. We had such a one once, it was very ugly, but vast and comfortable, the framework stained and pretending to be mahogany. It was in other days probably a servant's bedstead. Fig. 3 represents another bedstead of the Chippendale era, not so ornate as Fig. 2, and more likely to be occasionally met with. It is probably a good deal later in date than the last, as shown by the much simpler tester, this also has draperies of Damask in good preservation. Very often in old four posters you find the cornices more or less unavoidably repaired, the taking down and putting up of valances, sometimes not very carefully done, tended to ruin the wood work with multitudes of nail holes, and so by slow degrees the fabric weakened and had to be renewed.

In the early Chippendale beds the curtains were usually placed only at the head of the bed, leaving the beautifully carved foot posts to be seen in all their glory. This was a natural change from the earlier beds, like the Hampton Court ones, where the framework seemed to be nothing, and the covering and hangings everything. Between the two styles there were, as is usually the case, some variations, such as retaining the funereal hangings, but allowing to be seen coyly peeping from them, beautifully carved ball and claw feet.

I cannot impress upon you too much, that in the study of furniture you must never expect to find complete changes of style that you can comfortably and without hesitation assign to a certain fixed date. This is really never the case—

one style overlapped another—and in the country districts especially, fashions changed slowly, and were much behind those of large cities. This, of course, constitutes a great connundrum and makes it very difficult, well-nigh impossible in my opinion, to give hard and fast dates to furniture.

It is not very often that you find on Chippendale and Heppelwhite four posters that all the four posts are decorated. Those at the foot being very handsome and ornate, their owner did not wish them obscured by drapery, hence the curtains only at the head, and reciprocally—if curtains hide them, why should the headposts be carved, so as a rule the workmanship is all at the feet. Very much later, about 1810 to 1820, there came in the arrangement of all four posts being carved, very frequently a handsome headboard and a rich valance from the cornice and drapery behind the headboard, but no curtains. This was an ugly and senseless fashion, the beginning of the reign of the ugly 19th century furniture.

It has always been said by experts that there is far more furniture that owed its origin to Heppelwhite and his influence, than to any other maker of the 18th century. George Heppelwhite died in 1786, but we have no information as to when he began to work. He was an oldish man when he died, and it is known that he worked many years. After his death the business was carried on by his widow, Alice, and later on under the title of A. Heppelwhite & Co. Thus a large quantity of furniture was made not only immediately under the influence of George Heppelwhite himself, but also in accordance with his designs which were published after his death as " The cabinet maker and upholsterer's guide."

The only fault that has been ever brought against his designs is a certain lack of proportion, and this applies to his chairs and does not touch his graceful bedsteads, which we are now about to consider.

It is towards the beds of the middle of the 18th century that we may look as being possible—but alas ! I fear, far from probable, to be transferred to our own houses.

In our home we had the relics of two, one of the Heppelwhite time and another not so old, probably about 1800. They fell into crumbling ruins as far as the framework was concerned, and only the beautiful foot posts survived, these I found in the lumber room and have had them made as supports to china shelves, and very handsome and appropriate they look, but it was a sad pity not to have had them mended in time. My grandmother was an enlightened woman, loved old things, and abhorred the furniture of 1830, but I daresay in smaller London rooms she found the four posters rather overpowering. In Fig. 4 you see a very good example of Heppelwhite's style ; it is, you see, plain and graceful, and shows well the slender posts tapering to the top which became a great feature of the furniture of that

FIG. 4.—HEPPELWHITE BED.
(By permission of Messrs. Gill and Reigate.)

FIG. 5.—DAY BED, LATE CHARLES II.
(By permission of Messrs. Gill and Reigate.)

firm. They very seldom, if ever, over decorated anything, as Manwaring did, and as, in his later work, did poor disappointed Sheraton. Heppelwhite was most partial to a pointed leaf as decoration, and here you see it filling its appointed place most happily about ten inches above the mattress ; a circle of them forming a cup in which to hold the fluted pillar.

My " relics " of the Heppelwhite bed are unusually fine, having his favourite design of wheatears, supplemented also with the leaves of the wheat, waving conventionally round the post ; about 14 inches from the framework below, near to the origin of the wheat, is a circle of balls, about as big as very small plums, then a collar of spirals slightly rounded, then another circlet of balls, then the post again slightly thicker, surrounded with acanthus leaves, and lastly, reaching to the floor, a solid octagonal block. The whole effect is very good, really rather ornate, but having the pleasing effect of simplicity. My other pair of posts, frankly, I cannot place, they are a bit of a puzzle, from their appearance I should not have considered them to be older than 1800 to 1805, not so much from their design, which is a most elegant and rather ornate spiral, alternately composed of running acanthus and a rounded rib, but because of the general effect, the colour of the wood, the shape of the post, and even the " feel " of the mahogany. Family records, however, prove that the bed was in existence before that,

D

at least ten years, so again we have the extreme difficulty of dating correctly much of our furniture.

For those who, in furnishing, would like to have a four poster, my advice would be to seek in provincial towns, and it will be necessary to make your wants known to all, dealers as well as others. This publicity will naturally have a tendency to make the price go up, but that is, I think, unavoidable in this case. It is only in this way that you will hear of specimens for sale —generally the owners will never have thought of a sale, until they hear of your need, and then an agreeable idea will present itself to them of getting rid of what they consider an ungainly and awkwardly big piece of furniture, and not unnaturally they think a few pounds of hard cash would be far preferable, especially as then they could purchase a splendid brass bed, with a chain spring mattress such as Mrs. A—— or Mrs. B——possesses, and which had always been a cause of envy, malice and all uncharitableness to her neighbours.

I have explained to you what a real Chippendale, or Heppelwhite, bedstead should look like, but there is very little hope of your acquiring one, on at all reasonable terms, or, indeed, one of any kind of an earlier date than 1800. Sheraton made but few, and they now sell for fabulous sums. He was not very successful in this line, and if we may judge from his designs they were too fanciful to be acceptable to the conservative Briton.

I do not think he had much success with his " Elliptic Bed for a single lady ; " he explains to his reading public that " as fancifulness seems most peculiar to the tastes of females I have, therefore, assigned this bed for a single lady, though it will equally accommodate a single gentleman."

When you look at his design for the quaint bed, it *is* very " fanciful " and queer, and seems only to take up room at the side to no purpose.

From one cause or another, the fact remains that it is very difficult to buy a genuine four poster of an earlier date than 1800 ; but of that date and up to 1815 several still are to be found.

There is one rather simple and (in those days) inexpensive style of four poster, that is still to be found in country districts and not being usually of such majestic proportions, is better suited to flats and other cramped residences.

They were called " Field " beds, because I suppose it was possible to undo them and pack for service at war time. It seems rather quaint to us to imagine the late Lord Roberts, or the late Lord Wolseley, campaigning with such *impedimenta.*

The top is domed and formed only of thin narrow lath-like supports, which fit on to the four slender posts, and are screwed down firmly, by means of the four finials, which are usually in the form of pine apples, or little urns. The posts themselves are much more slender than those belonging to the more ponderous beds, and the hangings less ornate and fairly easy to slip on and off.

These hangings were generally made of some kind of dimity, printed linen, or calico, and usually had " knotted " fringe, which slightly resembled its degenerate descendant, the " ball " fringe which we now buy at three half-pence a yard, and which falls to pieces in the first wash, unlike its respectable ancestor which lasted several generations. Mrs. Delaney, that tireless worker of the 18th century, was always " knotting " and making whole sets of bed furniture for herself and friends, and was evidently considered a great authority on the subject.

In the middle of the century she writes to her sister, " I am verry sorry I have no knotting of the sort you want done. I cannot promise too much for you till I have finished a plain fringe I am knotting to trim a new blue and white linen bed, I have just put up ; as soon as that is done I will do some sugar plum for you."

What can " sugar plum " knotting be ? How much we should like to have an explanation of these old world terms !

Another entry is equally mysterious. " The double knotting I have sent will be too fine for you I fear. Are the curtains done in the mosaic pattern with the cloth border ? "

In 1752, Mrs. Delaney writes " just here,

Bushe made me go with her to Drumcondra, half a mile off, to see a new manufactory that is set up there of printed linens done by ' copper plates.' " This is interesting as showing that this industry was in progress as early as 1752.

To return to the camp bed, there are still a large number of these " Field " beds in America, and the one once honoured by the slumbers of Lafayette is to be seen in the Stark mansion in New Hampshire. I remember sleeping often in one of these beds in a charming old house in Dorsetshire, a typical house of the kind one often meets in novels, but seldom in real life— its date about 1700 ; its roof thatched, and latticed windows looking out with friendly eyes from under the deep projecting eaves. It had once been a farmhouse, and my friends had added (but in no way spoilt its old world character) a verandah round two sides, which was completely covered with roses, jasmine, honeysuckle and clematis, according to the season.

My room, in which was the " Field " bed, was remarkably low, only just admitting the soaring dome, a raftered ceiling and a delightful latticed window with a little pleated valance above short dimity curtains, and a seat below. The white dimity hangings with the " knotted " fringe were further adorned with a band of some pink material, and the effect was very old world and pretty.

That house and room always seemed to me

in the past, and still does so, even now, to be as
near perfection as possible. Alas! the inhabitants are almost all gone to a longer home, the
" Field " bed long since sold or gone on the
scrap heap, and even the house itself, though its
walls remain, so " improved " and generally
transmogrified that when I passed it a few years
since, I tried not to see the heartbreaking spectacle.

Of all four-posters, I think this is the pattern
you are most likely to meet with, and very charming it would look with plain white hangings, but
I fear you would have to be content with a
modern ball fringe instead of Mrs. Delaney's
" knotted " or " sugar plum " varieties.

Before leaving entirely the subject of beds, we
must glance at Day beds, which were in fact
sofas. As you will see in Fig. 5, it was not a very
luxurious piece of furniture, but was still a great
improvement upon the uncompromising settle of
earlier times.

The original form of the Jacobean Day bed
continued to exist into Georgian times, but by
degrees it assumed a more and more upholstered
form.

It was not however till very much later that
the sofa as we understand the term came into
being.   Chippendale made some—not very
comfortable, and the middle class sofa of 1790
to 1815 was often an atrocious thing. The
graceful Day bed had given way to many forms
of ugliness. Fig. 5 is, I should say, a late

Charles II. example; it does not let up and down at the head as many of them do. There are several examples in the Victoria and Albert Museum, all on the same lines, but becoming more luxurious as years passed.

It was Heppelwhite who rather unkindly suggested horse hair as a suitable covering for sofas and settees, and it is to his inspiration that we owe those successors of the Day bed covered in that treacherous material, off which one perpetually slides.

I daresay many of you know these uncomfortable pieces of furniture, generally to be found in country inns, with a fat, hard, uncompromising bolster at each end, as unyielding as a drain pipe. Sometimes the ends turn down, the back lifts out, and behold we have a fairly comfortable expanding bed. I met with such an one in a little tea shop in Chichester recently, and I should say its date was about 1805.

In these superior days does anyone read Cowper ?—he was born in 1731 and died in 1800, and he therefore saw many evolutions in furniture. His description of the sofa is worth reading :
" Those barbarous ages past, succeeded next
" The birthday of invention, weak at first,
" Dull in design and clumsy to perform.
" Joint stools were then created ; on three legs
" Upborne they stood :—three legs upholding firm
" A massy slab, in fashion square or round.

" On such a stool immortal Alfred sat,

" And swayed the sceptre of his infant realms ;

" . . . At length, a generation more refined,

" Improved the simple plan : made three legs four,

" Gave them a twisted form vermicular.

" And o'er the seat with plenteous wadding stuffed

" Induced a splendid cover, green and blue,

" Yellow and red, of tapestry richly wrought

" And woven close, or needlework sublime.

" There might ye see the peoney spread wide

" The full blown rose, the shepherd and his lass,

" Lap dog and lambkin, with black staring eyes,

" And parrots with twin cherries in their beak.

" Now came the cane from India, smooth and bright

" With nature's varnish, severed into strips.

" That interlaced each other, these supplied

" Of texture firm a lattice work, that braced

" The new machine and it became a chair.

" But restless was the chair ; the back erect

" Distressed the weary loins, that felt no ease ;

" The slippery seat betrayed the sliding part

" That pressed it, and the feet hung dangling down,

" Anxious in vain to find the distant floor.

" . . . . . . the lumber stood

" Ponderous and fixed by its own massy weight,

" But elbows still were wanting ; then

. . . . . some say,

" An alderman of Cripplegate contrived,
" And some ascribe the invention to a priest
" Burly and big and studious of his ease,
" But rude at first and not with easy slope,
" Receding wide, they pressed against the ribs
" And bruised the side, and elevated high,
" Taught the raised shoulders to invade the ears
" Long time elapsed, or e'er our rugged sires
" Complained, though incommodiously pent in
" And ill at ease behind. The ladies first
" Gave murmur, as became the softer sex.
" Ingenious fancy, never better pleased
" Than when employed to accommodate the fair,
" Heard the sweet moan with pity and devised
" The soft SETTEE ; one elbow at each end
" And in the midst an elbow, it received,
" United, yet divided, twain at once.
" So sit two kings of Brentford on one throne ;
" And so two citizens who take the air
" Close packed and smiling in a chaise and one.
" But relaxation of the languid frame,
" By soft recumbency of outstretched limbs,
" Was bliss reserved for happier days ; so slow
" The growth of what is excellent, so hard
" To attain perfection in this nether world.
" Thus, first necessity invented stools,
" Convenience next suggested elbow chairs,
" And luxury the accomplished SOFA last.

CHAPTER II

CHAIRS OF THE 17TH AND 18TH CENTURIES

CHAIRS, though small objects and convenient for the collector whose floor space is small, are not easy to find, because the self-same reasons that make them desirable to us have also made them coveted by others, and collectors of many kinds with purses of all capacities have been before us and swept all likely haunts bare and clean of the wished-for treasures. Still, perseverance will be rewarded, though much time may have to be expended, and the specimens acquired will sometimes be in a very bad state.

In " Antiques and Curios " I dwelt much upon Jacobean chairs, and those made up to the end of Queen Anne's reign, and I must ask you to look up that information, as I have not space here to repeat it, and can only glance cursorily at the different types until we come to the beginning of the Chippendale influence.

Chairs made prior to the reign of James I. are non-existent, except in public collections, in some fine old mansions, and here and there in ecclesiastical buildings.

To begin with, in those days chairs were few

46

and far between. Only the master and mistress
of the house indulged in such luxuries, the rest of
the family contenting themselves with benches
and " joyned " stools.

Then, as luxury advanced, they became a little
commoner, but even then were scarce and precious, hence the origin of the expression, " chair-
man " and " taking the chair " ; it came into use
very naturally, as the guest of greatest honour
would evidently be pressed into the seat con-
ferring distinction, and be asked " to take the
chair."

So you see, with this sparse provision originally made some three hundred and odd years ago,
it is not surprising that but few remain to us, and
that hardly any made before James I. time still
exist. In early specimens of Jacobean times the
stretcher was quite low down, the reason for
this being that as floors were often damp and
draughty these stretchers were necessary to keep
the sitter's feet from being chilled. In earlier
times the floors were covered with rushes, which
no doubt often became damp, dirty and sodden,
and the few Tudor chairs that survive, if they
have a stretcher at all, have it quite low down,
and one sees distinctly the worn marks that the
rubbing of generations of feet have caused, as they
thankfully sought the comparative comfort of
the friendly bar.

The habit of having floors covered with rushes
had long gone out in the upper classes when

James I. came to the throne, but as I am always trying to impress upon you, fashions and customs died hard, and though stretchers were no longer imperatively necessary to raise the feet from damp and dirt, there were still unkind draughts along the floor, and shivering humanity was well pleased to lift its chilblained feet on to the convenient stretcher. As years go on, and fashions slowly change, you will see it gradually alters its position and shape, but in consequence of national conservatism still lingers, though much higher up on the chair, where, no longer needed, it exists only as an ornament, and instead of having a convenient straight top for the feet, it becomes rich with ornaments, crowns, scrolls and cherubs.

Invented much earlier, but continuing (in a languid way) late into the 17th century, we have a special kind of chair with solid oak seat, and a back which, breaking away from former traditions, began tentatively to experiment with bars, upright and across; these chairs are now called Yorkshire and Derbyshire chairs. Some experts profess to be able to tell from which locality each variety hails, personally I am a little doubtful about that; patterns were discussed, lent and copied by the old craftsmen, and so became inextricably mixed. The Yorkshire type is usually supposed to be that where two or sometimes three ornamental horizontal bars have in the centre a kind of horseshoe. In both types a very marked feature is the down dropping

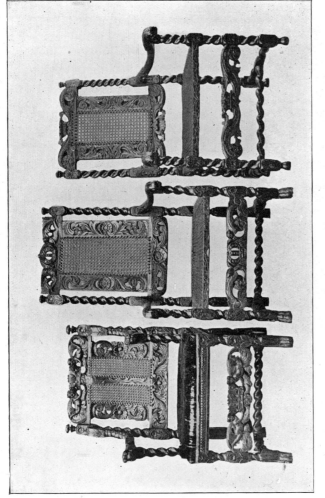

FIG. 6.—LATE 17TH CENTURY CHAIRS.
(By permission of Messrs. Gill and Reigate.)

acorns or other small pendant ornaments,
two or three hanging from each horizontal
bar. The so-called Derbyshire variety is a little
less ornate. I saw one of these chairs with the
Yorkshire horseshoe in an old lady's cottage in
Derbyshire, and because I admired it she said she
would leave it to me, but I was far away at her
death and never came into my legacy!

Now we come to a kind of chair of which many
still exist and are to be found occasionally in
provincial dealers' shops, but you must be careful,
for the species is often imitated! Naturally
these chairs, and indeed almost every sort and
kind of furniture, speaking broadly, is to be
found in the possession of first-class dealers; I
mean they are to be found with such firms as
Messrs. Gill and Reigate, Mr. Phillips, of Hitchen,
and many others, but I am now trying to help
those whose modest purses preclude them from
dealing with such houses as the above. Look
closely at the three fine specimens in Fig. 6. Unlike the other chairs I have mentioned, which
were all of oak, these are of walnut, which began
to be greatly used in England for furniture after
1650.

The chairs in Fig. 6 would probably be made
about 1670 to 1685; the special turning helps to
fix the date approximately. They are very picturesque and charming chairs, always decorative
and really (for chairs of that period) not too uncomfortable! I have friends who possess four

of the kind but without arms, and one other with arms, very much larger and higher. We also had a monster arm chair of this type, with a double caned splat, like number one in Fig. 6, only the back was nearly, if not quite, double the height of this one ; alas ! it had to be given away when we gave up our country house, and were compelled to squeeze into a " commodious residential flat with every convenience " ! The convenience not extending to sufficient floor space for this monstrous chair. It was fragile, too, suffering much from wood worms, like many of our other ancient friends, and was not safe for heavy people to sit in, so that my father sarcastically suggested that a rope should surround it and other Jacobean treasures, after the fashion of our public museums, and that a printed legend, " Please not to touch the objects on the walls, or sit in the exhibits," should be placed in conspicuous places !

By judicious arrangement and skilful piloting of stout and heavy friends to a few sturdy Dutch chairs, and one or too healthy but homely Heppelwhite's, we had avoided all catastrophies.

These chairs with the special legs are, as you see, somewhat ornate, especially the one with the double caned splat. The Tudor Rose is very much in evidence, so is the Carolean scroll and the crown, which is the distinguishing characteristic of the Restoration chair. In this example the crown is supported by small naked figures, but exactly what they are intended to symbolize is difficult to say. They are like cherubs somewhat as to their bodies, but if you look closely through a magnifying glass you will see that these plump little angels have adult faces.

I said a great deal about Restoration chairs before, so I must not linger over them now further than to remind you that by the term Restoration is meant not only chairs made in 1660, but all that, like these, bear the royal crown.

Loyalty overflowed everywhere up to the time of James II., and some very fine specimens of Restoration chairs belong to his short and disastrous reign. I have not so far met with a later specimen. Some that I have seen are more curious than beautiful, one for instance having the crown—very large, quite 6 to 8 inches across, repeated six times ; once on the centre of the back at the top, twice on each side sideways and looking very strange, and lastly, on the bottom of the splat. One could hardly imagine any-thing in worse taste.

From the accession of Charles II. and onwards till the arrival of William, furniture was be-coming more and more ornate, and though William's more austere taste would naturally have patronized a plainer style, his reign was too short to effect the radical change that was a feature of the later years of Queen Anne, and of the succeeding reign of George I. Nevertheless, although the chairs, sofas, etc., were still florid there was a change under William, which change helped and forwarded the simpler style that we call Queen Anne

I must digress a moment to remind you that the rising of the star of Grinling Gibbon on the horizon in 1671 wrought a great change in the taste of the 17th century.

How greatly we delvers into the history of the 17th century are indebted to the two great diarists, Samuel Pepys and John Evelyn ; and what is so fortunate—they each supply what the other lacks. The grave gentlemanly and erudite Evelyn tells us much more about the great events of the time, the political unrest, the self-seeking in the Cabinet, etc. . . . He gives us a most graphic account of the fire, but does not say much of the plague, and his frequent references to the King throw some interesting lights on the complex character, and manifold gifts of that interesting personality.

Pepys on the other hand, though from his public position he was well qualified to give us all kinds of interesting information on most stirring events, is so much occupied in gazing with admiration at the Duchess of Portsmouth's petticoats hanging on the line to dry, and in recounting how he and Mrs. Pepys disported themselves in various sumptuous suits—" myself and wife to church, I in my new tawny suit very fine," that he leaves us much in the dark as to important happenings. As to the great fire he

is most provoking, it is passed over with a few
words. I do not remember any allusion in his
diary to the great Grinling Gibbon, but the
cultivated Evelyn gives a full account of his
first meeting with the genius.

" This day I first acquainted his Majesty with
" that incomparable young man Gibbon, whom
" I had lately met with in an obscure place by
" meere accident as I was walking neere a poore
" solitary thatched house, in a field in our parish
" neere Sayes Court. I found him shut in ; but
" looking in at the window I perceiv'd him
" carving that large cartoon or crucifix of Tintoret,
" a copy of which I had myselfe brought from
" Venice, where the original painting remains. I
" asked if I might enter ; he open'd the door
" civilly to me, and I saw him about such a work
" as for the curiosity of handling and studious
" exactnesse I never had before seene in all my
" travells. I questioned him why he worked in
" such an obscure and lonesome place ; he told
" me it was that he might apply himselfe to his
" profession without interruption, and wondered
" not a little how I had found him out. I asked
" him if he was unwilling to be made knowne to
" some greate man, for that I believed it might
" turn to his profit ; he answered he was yet but a
" beginner, but would not be sorry to sell off
" that piece ; on demanding the price he said £100.
" In good earnest the very frame was worth
" the money, there being nothing in nature so

E

" tender and delicate as the flowers and festoons
" about it, and the worke was very strong ;
" in the piece were more than 100 figures of men,
" etc. . . . I found he was likewise musical
" and very civil, sober, and discreete in his
" discourse. There was onely an old woman in
" the house. So desiring leave to visit him some-
" times I went away. Of this young artist,
" together with my manner of finding him out,
" I acquainted the king, and begg'd that he
" would give me leave to bring him and his
" worke to White-hall, for that I would adventure
" my reputation with his majesty that he had
" never seene anything approach it, and that
" he would be exceedingly pleased and employ
" him. The King said he would himself go to
" see him—"

By 1682 the great artist was evidently in full
swing of work, for Evelyn makes a note of having
been to visit a neighbour who had " in the Hall
" contrivances of Japan skreens instead of
" wainscot ; and there is an excellent pendule
" clock inclos'd in the curious flower-work of
" Mr. Gibbons in the middle of the vestibule.
" The landskips of the skreens represent the
" manner of living and country of the Chinese.
" But above all his lady's cabinet is adorn'd on
" the fret, ceiling and chimney-piece with Mr.
" Gibbons's best carving."

You see he sometimes spells the artist's name
with an S and sometimes without, and it is not

quite certain which is correct. In a letter written by the man himself in that same year he signs his name without a final S.

"HONRED

" Sr, I wold beg the faver wen you see Sr Joseff
" Williams again you wold be pleased to speak
" to him that hee wold get mee to carve his ladis
" sons hous my Lord Kildare for I onderstand
" it will be verry considerabell or If you haen
" acquantans wich my Lord to speack to him
" his sealf and I shall for Ev're be obliaged to you
" I wold speack to Sir Josef mysealf but I know
" it would do better from you.

Sr youre most umbell Sarvant,

G. GIBBON."

From this letter one would say that Gibbon, or Gibbons, was a perfectly ignorant man, but spelling in those days was very uncertain, as we see from the letters of Lady Sussex to Sir Ralph Verney. She writes that she is in fear of the " souldiers " attacking her house, because she is reported to be a " casicoleke ! " This is most cryptic, and it is only the succeeding sentences which give us the clue that this means " catholic," for she assures us that a " gentillman " told them " i was noe papes." She goes on to say " my " protexsyon hath don me some good, one of the " men goinge to Chesome (Chesham) the lade " hold uppon his horse so i had fane to send the " protexsyon and when the saw that the let my

"man have my hors agane." . . . Then
she explains that she returns Sir Ralph some of
his property which she has had in charge lest
it should be snatched up into the hungry maw
of the army, so she sends him " twenty discs, a
" foyder (voider) and to dosen of plats."

Now this writer—with a style decidedly all her
own—was a very great lady and presumably had
the best education procurable at the time, so you
see we must not judge Gibbon's erudition too
hardly, on the evidences of his letter, and it must
not be forgotten that certainly on one side he was
Dutch by birth and so had to contend with the
difficulties of (perhaps) an imperfect knowledge
of really good English.

Before leaving Jacobean times we must glance
at chairs that appeared much earlier than the
time we are now considering and continued as
late as the end of Charles II. reign. I mean the
rather squat square backed chairs, with the legs
sometimes arranged in X shape and sometimes
square with turned formations, whilst later they
showed spiral twists and ornate carving in scrolls,
etc. . . . These with stools to match are
well seen in Knole, which the courtesy of Lord
Sackville allows us to visit. From the time of
James I. onwards we have these same chairs,
but with the passage of years the shape altered
and the backs became much higher. During the
reigns of William and Mary upholstered chairs of
this and kindred shapes were constantly made,

covered with rich velvets and brocades, as well as " Sett " work and " Turkye Werke."

The appearance of sumptuous velvets, silks and brocades was due greatly to the settling in England of the French and Flemish refugees—more especially weavers—who fled over to this country to escape the persecution following the Revocation of the edict of Nantes by Louis XIV. These weavers settled in several places, but especially in Spitalfields, and even now, if you know where to look, you may find old houses in the neighbourhood of Spital Square, where the weavers' broad windows, running all across the front of the house, still exist.

The William and Mary chairs of the caned variety do not differ greatly from those of the mid century, though there are slight differences which you will distinguish as your knowledge becomes a little more advanced.

For one example, the stretcher which in 1650 was low down and flat at the top became in 1660 or thereabouts a much ornamented affair, which gradually mounted higher and higher, but in William and Mary's time it sometimes entirely disappeared, and in its place crossed bars known as tied stretchers (because the four bars met like an X in the middle) appeared.

Also—and this variety had appeared in the last years of Charles' reign, the extreme ends of the legs had turned into kind of feet and curved outwards very slightly.

There is a good deal of difficulty in correctly placing furniture of this period, from many causes ; when Charles married Catharine of Braganza, we became connected with the East, and Holland. The taste for Dutch and Oriental methods grew with us, but the advent of William enormously increased the making of furniture in the Dutch and Flemish manner, and it is a question very difficult to decide with certainty, what furniture of this kind was actually made by Dutch and Flemish craftsmen, and what by English imitators.

Another influence at work was the Spanish style ; this had naturally permeated, more or less, the work of the Low Countries, and in the matter of furniture we see the legs of chairs and tables showing a Spanish tendency, as evinced in the cup-like excrescences, usually about half-way up.

Again, Spanish art was coloured by association with Italian workmanship, and so, like a stone thrown into a still pond, the circles of influence and environment widen and widen, and it needs much study and much weighing of *pros* and *cons* to decide exactly when, and where, a piece of furniture of about that period was made. Mr. Owen Wheeler, a most painstaking authority on furniture, is of opinion that " the construction of the Dutch and Flemish chairs was not so good as ours, that the junction of the back and seat was not so firm and that their woods were more easily attacked by wood worm."

Hampton Court is full of treasures of this period and later, chiefly of the upholstered kind, and a few visits there will teach you a great deal on many of the subjects in which it is my wish to interest you. The beds of monumental proportions, the tables, the settees, the chairs, and even the splendid mirrors, studded with ornaments of sapphire glass, give one such a good idea of the rooms of those of high degree at the end of the 17th and beginning of the 18th centuries. I am never tired of wandering through these rooms, and thinking of all those who once used them.

Next we come to the chairs of Queen Anne's time, and her successor, George I., and again I fear I must say that the collector of small means is not very likely to pick up specimens of this period.

Unfortunately our forbears of the mid 18th century despised the furniture of its earlier years, and ruthlessly made away with it in favour of Chippendale's, and later of Heppelwhite's and Sheraton's, etc.

Thus the treasures of the first quarter of the century found their way into the kitchen, and very often later on to the scrap heap.

There are of course occasional treasures to be found sometimes in old farmhouses, once more or less dependent on the great house, so that unconsidered trifles of all sorts descended to the favourite waiting maid, who perhaps contracted matrimony with a neighbouring farmer, and my lady wishing to help her, and disburden herself at the same time of old-fashioned furniture no longer considered " genteel," thus disposed of the fine old walnut furniture of Queen Anne's time.

Now, however, farmers and their wives are quite aware of the extreme value of such possessions, and by no means inclined to part with them, unless at prices which have swelled in their commercial eyes, until they ask bigger sums than those of any honest dealer ; or perhaps on the other hand, and still more unlikely to yield a harvest, they are educated people, and find the goods and chattels of a bygone time the chief glory of their drawing room.

The whole style of Queen Anne's furniture was characterised by simplicity, and its beauty depended, as a rule, upon its fine lines, graceful curves, extremely delicate veneering, and slight and restrained inlay.

The chairs broke away entirely from the narrow and upright shape and became broader and lower, and what was perhaps the greatest change of all, they developed the cabriole leg, which is one of the happiest of inventions, and for which we are no doubt indebted to Holland.

The protuberance at the knee and foot, with the corresponding concave between, gives the most charming effects of light and shade. I am entirely in thrall to the cabriole leg and think that nothing else gives the same delightful effect.

About the same time we get the cockle shell

as an ornament. It appears in different forms, and sometimes as much like a fan as a cockle shell, upon almost everything even in architecture, and one of the most pleasing devices was when the ceiling of a buffet, alcove, or the projecting top of an entrance door, represented the inside of a cockle shell.

A good deal of the beauty of furniture of this period consisted in very delicate and slight inlay : we often see on a chair the cockle shell above and a very little inlay faintly showing on the solid splat. The herring bone inlay was not suitable for chairs, so I shall speak of it in the chapter on cabinets, etc.

All the furniture of this period up to about 1730 was of walnut, and the rich honey-like tone of it, when old, is very attractive, so different to the horrid variety we see in modern " suites." Mahogany came into use somewhere about 1720 to 1725, the exact date is not known, but most decidedly it cannot have been in really general use till 1730, though no doubt a few wealthy persons had solitary pieces made of it prior to that date ; still we may say that furniture up to 1730 was mainly made of walnut, and though we associate the name of Chippendale with mahogany, it is certain that he must in the early years of his trade existence have executed many pieces of walnut.

A form of chair made in the first half of the century, which is truly comfortable, was called a drunkard's chair, but they are now very scarce, probably the hard usage they met with caused their early disappearance.

Their peculiarity was an immense width of seat, the one I know intimately is three feet four across the front and proportionately firm and substantial ; the arms are fixed rather high up, so that the toper planted in it by his friends could sleep and snore off the effects of the carouse, without much danger of falling out. I have never once seen one of these comfortable treasures for sale, but I am still on the track.

I have three very good Queen Anne chairs of honey-coloured walnut with a curious ornamentation on the fronts of the splats (solid splats, as is ever the case at this time) consisting of half inch inlays of some lighter wood, probably holly, stained yellow. These lines starting from the edge of the splat meet in the middle in the form of a V.

I always think the back of these chairs prettier than the front, the walnut is of so rich a colour ; the " patina " on these examples is very good— " Patina " is that unique polish, which, free from all such horrors as varnish, owes its lustre to repeated doses of oil and wax, and the constant and assiduously applied elbow grease of generations of notable housewives. In this old treatment, sometimes no oil was used at all, which leaves the wood somewhat lighter. It is a sad misfortune when old 17th or 18th century furniture has been cleaned and " varnished," at once the piece loses commercial value.

My Queen Anne chairs once possessed seat covers of a kind of powder blue brocade ; it was probably not the original material, very likely that was " *Petit Point* " or that kind of conventional flower embroidery in fine crewels on a white linen ground, which was the favourite work of the ladies of that time.

This kind of work is now very scarce and should you find any small pieces of it anywhere, such as are occasionally found as old and discarded cushion covers, snap them up at once, for they are rare and precious.

To return to the chairs, should you have one of this period you can easily get suitably designed linen coverings from Hampton, or Gill and Reigate, which reproduce the old patterns wonderfully well, and though, of course, it is a sham, it is a more pleasing sham than a satin or plush !

The damasks and velvets of that time and of a little earlier, and also later, were really very ugly —orange and crimson for instance, like some at Hampton Court—and with extraordinary architectural devices all over them ; such a strange idea to lean back upon a pagoda, or sit on the top of a columned fountain.

It is a good plan in studying old furniture and other accessories of the time you are considering to look carefully at the pictures of the period. From them we get sure and certain help.   For instance, we should not now know with any certainty what kind of beds were used in early times if we had not the old missals to study, with their beautiful illuminations. As an instance of this, I was very much surprised in Poitiers a few years ago to see in a sculptured entombment of the 16th century—a most naive affair—that the Apostles and helpers wore straw hats with veils, showing unmistakably that in France in the 16th century that must have been a head covering frequently seen. I certainly had no idea of it until I studied that tomb.

So it is with later times ; study the works of Vandyck, Kneller, Hogarth, Sir James Thornhill and others : it is very instructive and gives you correct ideas of the furniture, the upholstery, the draperies, the household utensils and the dress of the periods, which I consider, as I told you before, to be most essential to the study of either furniture, china, or glass of the past. One's knowledge is always one-sided and terribly restricted— no matter what the subject is—unless we also get a general knowledge of the way life went on at those dates. Among other marks of the transitional time from 1700 to the appearance of the Chippendale style, we may mention the fact that the splats in the middle of the back were solid— sometimes vase shaped, sometimes fiddle shaped, often spoon shaped, but always solid—occasionally towards the end of the reign of the first George we find them open, but speaking broadly in the first quarter of the 18th century the splats were solid, and the sides connecting the splat at the top, and joining the seat at the sides, were apt to be hoop shaped.

As we continue along the passage of time we come to the grand period when the great Chippendale was beginning to be known.

We do not know with precision at what date the second and greatest Chippendale began to work with success, nor do we know the date of his birth. Weighing one circumstance against another it seems probable that he was born in the early years of Queen Anne. We know he died in 1779 and was buried at St. Martin's, which was close to his home at 60, St. Martin's Lane, but as to the different periods of his work we know very little indeed, it is mostly conjecture.

Some rather irritable writers seem to grudge Chippendale the great posthumous fame which he has attained, and appear to consider him much over-rated as an original craftsman, averring that he invented but little that was original; that may be, but I think Mr. Robinson exactly shows where his great achievement lay. " It is not for nothing that Chippendale's name is remembered before those of his contemporaries. His book was the best of its class, even if it was not the fountain head, which inspired the rest. We have seen that when the same decorative ideas were so broadcast, it was hardly likely that from Chippendale should emanate all the good. After all, the contributions of each individual artist to the sum of advancement, is generally small. What were these new ideas ? Impalpable enough ! It is not a question of entire change of shape in furniture from that of a previous generation. That, we have seen, is a thing which seldom, or never, occurs in the evolution of furniture. If we are to sum up what Chippendale did, it amounts to this ; that he took the main shapes as he found them, somewhat plain and severe ; he left them decidedly better proportioned, lighter, more decorative, yet not less useful than they were. The ideas reduce themselves to a matter of artistic ' feeling,' a sense of proportion, which recognises, for instance, that the breadth of a chair splat is too great, or too little, for the empty spaces on each side of it. It seems a small affair this, but such affairs make all the difference between the ugly and the beautiful. For the most part, the artist is a clever thief, who takes his notions from whencesoever he can. ' *Je prends mon bien partout ou je le trouve,*' might Shakespeare and Chippendale each say, in their respective degrees. This is not to be a mere plagiarist as Manwaring is accused of plagiarising Chippendale. The cleverness alone excuses the theft ; even exalts it from the category of thefts entirely, if the plumes which the Daw borrows are found to be so skilfully dyed and arranged as to make a something which is better than the original.

Chippendale was, at his best, well equal to the task. . . . . . .

" It matters little, except to students, whence you take your idea ; it matters much what use you make of it and Chippendale at his best made better things from what he borrowed ! "

I think it may be said with certainty that this " best " was from 1730 to about 1760 ; we may consider that in that time his most splendid and distinctive work was done, for, although work coming from his hand, or pupil's, was quite as good afterwards as far as the mechanical part was concerned, he was by that time so completely under the influence of Adam's classical ideas as to have lost to a great extent his individuality.

This all-pervading classic influence of the latter half of the 18th century, which invaded architecture and all arts and crafts, passed like a wave over France and England, and personally I think it was most monotonous and tiresome.

Robert Adam, the greatest of the three brothers of that name, was an architect, not a cabinetmaker, but his idea being that external and internal decoration should correspond, he (like every one else) published books of designs for furniture, etc., and when he was commissioned to work at Harewood, Osterley, etc., he employed Chippendale to make the furniture, even the delicate inlaid work that has hitherto been generally ascribed to Sheraton.

Mr. Macquoid's tireless energy has supplied

us with the bills for furniture made by Chippendale in 1767–1770 and onwards for Nostell
Priory, the seat of Lord St. Oswald, which was
decorated by the brothers Adam.

He gives another bill of 1773 connected with
Harewood, of Chippendale and Haig's for quantities of beautiful inlaid satin-wood furniture,
gilded, inlaid and painted, so that we have proof
positive that he was accustomed to work in these
styles, and we can see at these country seats the
very pieces of furniture mentioned in his bills.

It is interesting to examine Chippendale's
sketches of examples in the celebrated book
which he calls " The Gentleman and Cabinetmaker's Director," but I really do not think
it is so informing as one would expect it to prove,
for very much of his most beautiful and valuable
work does not seem foreshadowed in this kind
of trade catalogue, as we should now call it.
One of his most favourite patterns—the ball and
claw foot—does not appear at all. The reason
for this and similar omissions may be that the
" Director " was not published until 1754, and
the ball and claw foot having been in fashion a
very long time, it is quite possible that Chippendale did not include that, and some other of his
most admired early designs, simply because he
considered them a little *passé*.

Of course, in considering this period you must
remember, as I warned you so emphatically
before, that when I speak of Chippendale I do

A WORCESTER MUG

INSCRIBED "LORD AND LADY SANDY'S HEALTH," T.G., 1759

By courtesy of Messrs. Stoner & Evans

not mean that all the specimens of which I speak are really from Chippendale's hand. I only mean that their style is perfectly in accord with his known work, and if not actually his, they are at any rate from his school, to use the same term which we apply to painters and their pupils. If Chippendale had made even half the pieces that with touching faith are attributed to him, he would, indeed, have required to live to the age of Methuselah !

Precisely the same state of things applies to Heppelwhite and Sheraton, in speaking of many articles which go by these names, and are manifestly of the time of those craftsmen, we only mean (generally) that they are made in accordance with their taste, their rules, and their proportions. It is important always to bear this fact in remembrance. There was a large number of minor furniture makers, Manwaring, Ince and Mayhew, Lock, Gillow, Shearer and others, who did beautiful work, and there can be no doubt that many pieces that emanated from these less well-known men, have passed as the productions of the three, Chippendale, Heppelwhite and Sheraton, whose names have become household words.

It is very seldom that on any article of furniture there is any mark that will indubitably prove that it came from this hand or that. Bills when they exist are invaluable in this respect. The discovery of a bill of George Heppelwhite's

F

for a set of chairs and a settee made for the ancestor of a friend of mine certainly added a good third to the price obtained for them when hard necessity and a dwindling income compelled their sale.

To return to Chippendale, there is an important matter for the furniture student to keep before his mind in relation to the ball and claw design. The treatment of this subject will often help you to guess whether the piece is genuine, or a modern imitation.

Chippendale himself, and those who either worked under him, or at any rate closely imitated him, showed a virile power in their rendering of it —the claw really gripped the ball, it did not tamely rest on it, it held it as a claw would hold. There are hundreds of chairs made—professing to be Chippendale—with these characteristic terminations to the legs, but notice what vapid affairs they are ; the eagle's claw, from the feeble way it holds, could never have executed any powerful movement, and even a mouse might almost pluck away his ball !

The earlier chairs made by Chippendale must have been made in walnut, for mahogany did not become generally used until after 1730. It was used in or about 1720 (see chapter on bureaux, etc.), but it could not have become generally in use for some years, and we may, therefore, feel certain, that his earliest work was in walnut. Of this kind you have no chance

FIG. 7.—CHIPPENDALE CHAIR.
(By permission of Messrs. Gill and Reigate.)

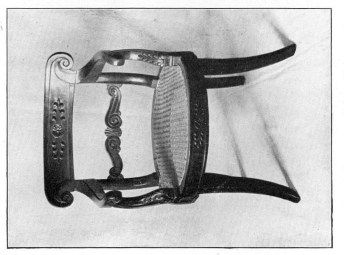

FIG. 8.—ADAM CHAIR (?).

of finding a specimen, nor are you very likely to find one with cabriole legs and ball and claw feet at all; they are much esteemed and fall to longer purses than ours.

Chairs with straight legs are rather more common. Fig. 7 is a fine example, showing a folded ribbon in the centre of the splat—this splat, with the large circle enclosing the twisted ribbon, is rather uncommon and very handsome. Chippendale himself was very partial to his ribbon back chairs, some of them are extremely elaborate, the ribbon having the appearance of being gathered or puckered up and terminating in tassels.

Some critics take exception to this ribbon design on the ground of its unsuitability to wood, but this seems to me a rather far-fetched objection. Suitability of design never seemed much to concern the old craftsmen, or surely we should not have Chippendale's eagles threatening our elbows and spines, or Heppelwhite's feathers to be crushed (in imagination) by the sacques and hoops which they accommodated, nor should we have as in Beauvais tapestry, a parrot and hedgehog upon which to sit! Fig. 7 shows the Cupid bow back at the top and some think this is a distinguishing mark of the master's own hand, but that is absurd, very likely he admired the pattern, as he did that of the ribbon, but what was there to prevent any of his workmen and imitators from copying the Cupid bow, the ribbon, the ball and claw, or anything else? Imitation is the sincerest flattery, we have always heard, and we have plenty of proof that the 18th century cabinet makers, and potters, felt no soreness or jealousy at being copied on all hands.

This universal game of "follow my leader" makes a serious difficulty in "placing" our old treasures—when Smith always imitated Jones, and Jones copied Brown as closely as possible, things become complicated.

There were, naturally, many close imitators of Chippendale, and indeed in his "Director" he gives various instructions to help these copyists, so it is not surprising that they availed themselves to the full of this assistance, and made chairs and other pieces so exactly in duplicate of the original design that it is not only difficult, but impossible to decide *who* made them. Many experts boldly profess to be able to differentiate between the work of contemporary men, but I misdoubt them greatly! I dwell a little upon this vexed question, because it touches quite as much upon the work of Heppelwhite, Sheraton and later workmen, and I want you to remember it, and not think that every wheat-ear chair must be a Heppelwhite, or every piece of later delicate inlay work must be Sheraton's.

M. S. Clouston, who is a great authority on the subject, explains the difficulties connected with it in a few lines. The passage occurs in a series of papers on minor English furniture makers of the 18th century, which were published in the "Burlington Magazine," vols. 4 and 5.

" It is too ordinary a mistake to suppose that
" any piece of furniture resembling the style of
" one of the best known exponents is actually by
" him, if it is peculiarly well executed. On the
" other hand, a piece evidently inspired by Man-
" waring, or Ince, is more likely to be authentic,
" as their work, not being so much valued in their
" own time, would not be so widely copied.
" . . . . As was natural at a time when
" small businesses flourished, instead of huge
" company promoted concerns, many of the best
" of them started shops of their own and made
" the difficulty still greater by adopting, or very
" slightly altering the designs of better known
" men. There was nothing wrong or underhand
" about such a proceeding in those days, as the
" illustrated furniture books were ostensibly
" published for this very purpose."

I should advise any student of furniture to read
carefully these articles ; they give a great deal of
useful information, in a manner suitable to those
who have no time or inclination for many tech-
nicalities, and as books on such subjects are
usually expensive, it is a comfort to know that
one can generally get the " Burlington " and
" The Connoisseur " (another useful publication
of the same kind) at most good lending libraries.

All the articles are good, but I thought that on
Manwaring especially so. His period was almost
coeval, though a little later, with Chippendale's,
and he frankly copied him as closely as possible.

Unfortunately, in his desire to strike out a new line, he became too eccentric in his designs, and spreading trees and rushing waterfalls did not add to his reputation.

One can put up with an eagle pecking at one's waist belt, but a waterfall behind one's shoulders seems going a little too far.

Manwaring, too, published a book, and the title is rather quaint, " The Cabinet and Chair-maker's Real Friend and Companion, or the whole system of chairmaking made plain and easy." I like so much the spirit of the sub title—it is like a lady's letter, in which the carping masculine critic says the whole substance is to be found in the postscript ! Again, Ince and Mayhew did a large amount of excellent work and, as Mr. Clouston says in his article on that firm, " Ince may, in fact, be looked upon as the pioneer in the transition of the Chippendale shape, to that of the Heppelwhite style, though his designs bear no resemblance to those of the later period, being simply modifications of existing forms."

It would be curious to know, if there was any possibility of arriving at such a conclusion, how many pieces of Manwaring's and Ince and May-hew's or Mayhew and Ince's—for the firm is written indifferently in both ways—are now labelled Chippendale. One may as well be hung for a sheep as a lamb, and as it is only a matter (for the most part) of ourselves naming the creator of our treasures, why be modest ? We may just as well have a Chippendale, as a Manwaring, an Ince, or a Lock, when the possession is so easily attained !

Advancing to a rather later date in the history of chairmaking we come to the brothers Adam—as I think they, and especially Robert, left his impress more on almost anything than on chairs. I will ask you to look to my short résumé of his career in the chapter on bureaux, etc.

It is extremely difficult to establish the identity of Adam chairs. The one I show you in Fig. 8 has always passed for a late example of his, and it has been in my family since its birth, which probably occurred about 1785. It is rather a curious chair, I have never seen one like it, and perhaps it was made to order ; it is perfectly round, and up to two years ago had its original caning. Unfortunately, at that time it succumbed to the constant and weighty presence of an enormous Persian cat, who would never sit anywhere else, and one morning the poor " Adam " was discovered with a large funnel shaped hole yawning in its middle. We think puss must have been caught unawares in the earthquake, because for long after it was re-caned he regarded it with suspicion, but has at last again taken possession. The wood is rather light mahogany and shows a slight carving. It is the unusual shape of the legs that make it a peculiar looking chair.

In thinking of Adam's work you must try to remember that he had no workshop, he supplied designs, but others carried them out, and we know that Chippendale, Gillows, and many other men greatly esteemed for their art, did not disdain to work for him.

If this chair really is his design, it is quite a comfort for once to have got away from the classical pose. I weary of his vases, festoons, and draperies, etc.

Next we come to the Heppelwhite period. As I mentioned in my first chapter, there is considerable obscurity surrounding George Heppelwhite's working life.

We do not know in what year he was born, or to what extent he was responsible for the book in which he collaborated with Thomas Shearer, called " The Cabinet maker's London book of Prices " published in 1788. Shearer's fame has been entirely overshadowed by Heppelwhite, but most certainly much furniture supposed to be made by the Heppelwhite firm, was designed by Shearer. Not chairs, however, Shearer shows none among his illustrations, so presumably his interests did not lie that way, whereas Heppelwhite undoubtedly felt drawn to chairs, almost more than to any other branch of his trade.

" The Cabinet maker and Upholsterer's guide " was published by A. Heppelwhite & Co., in 1788, 1789, and 1794. Heppelwhite died in 1786, but there can be little doubt that he had prepared this book and whatever part he took in Shearer's, probably some time before.

There has always been a great controversy
as to the merits, or the reverse, of painting as
decoration on wood, or " Japanning " as it was
called by its promoters. You must not confuse
it with lacquering, which was an absolutely
different thing. This " Japanning," which
reached its climax under Sheraton's hands, was
really painting with varnish colours on the wood,
and to my mind the effect is not pleasing.

A favourite form which this art took with
Heppelwhite was to paint the chair (or whatever
other piece was to be so decorated) black—the
wood in these cases being usually birch—and
decorate with slight design in gold only. Other
colours and more ambitious patterns were used
on larger articles, but as a rule he did not use
much colour on chairs and as often as not restricted himself to the pointed fern leaf in gold,
on the front of the seat and at the junction of the
legs and seat. This pointed leaf is considered
to be a proof of authenticity regarding his work
and a kind of sign manual of his.

I have a good pair of this kind, which I showed
you in my first book.

There are certain designs in chairs always
associated with his name, such as the shield
back, the wheel back, the banister back, and the
back with the Prince of Wales' feathers in the
centre. He had also oval backs, but not quite
so often as the squarish one, with the shield in
the middle.

Fig. 9 is an excellent example of what I think we may call a typical Heppelwhite, the three banisters within the shield are finely carved. Small husk ornaments hanging down from above, small flattish bosses on the two outside banisters, and an urn on the centre one. The presence of the urn shows that it is rather a late example. The legs are those, too, which Heppelwhite preferred apparently to all others, four sided, tapering to the foot which is of the spade shape.

Sometimes this form of chair was made with no carving, but small pateræ, perhaps one, perhaps three, somewhere on the back or junction of front and legs. Pateræ are flattened bosses; you will see three on Fig. 9.

A friend of mine possesses a remarkably fine set of Heppelwhite chairs with two armchairs, all in perfect condition, and showing charming wreaths of husk ornament, but, alas! a relative, during the owners' absence, pretending to do them a kindness, had all the legs made shorter and fitted with castors. It is well to draw a decent veil over the feelings of the mistress of the house.

It is only Heppelwhite's earliest furniture that had legs straight all the way down; he very soon started the tapering leg, and never after returned to straight ones.

I told you of his fondness for the wheat ear design when we were considering beds, they often appear on the open splats of his chairs.

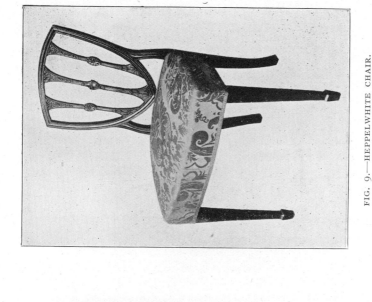

FIG. 9.—HEPPELWHITE CHAIR.
(By permission of Messrs. Gill and Reigate.)

FIG. 10.—SHERATON BERGÈRE CHAIR.
(By permission of Messrs. Gill and Reigate.)

Some find fault (and I think with some reason) of a want of proportion in his chairs. The japanned pair of which I spoke just now, show this slight defect, the back seems hardly high enough for its width and the size of the seat; there seems to be a certain clumsiness in the design that mars the effect.

My own favourites are his wheel-back chairs. I have also heard them called wheel window chairs; these must have been copied from old Brittany beds and armoires of early times. I think that design is the most taking of all; the spokes of the wheel are usually formed of long pointed leaves resembling the hart's tongue fern, which are united in the centre by a small boss.

Another pattern, which seemed to a great extent to belong to Heppelwhite, though we see it adopted by others, is the conventional honeysuckle; this is carried out a good deal on the same lines as the wheel back.

The Prince of Wales' feathers is said to have been Heppelwhite's favourite design in chairs, as the ribbon back was in Chippendale's. It is certainly often met with, sometimes carved in mahogany and often painted. In the latter style it is to me unpleasing, but I do not like " japanned " furniture in any form.

Between the chairs of Heppelwhite and Sheraton there is in some cases a marked resemblance, but there are differences to which one gradually learns to attach importance.

Sheraton lived and worked considerably later than Heppelwhite, but was undoubtedly influenced by his work. Naturally any resemblance between the work of the two can be only between the later work of Heppelwhite, and the earlier of Sheraton. It is well to take note that in Heppelwhite's time chairs began to be smaller, the broad seats and wide arms of an earlier date had given place to much smaller shapes, and when Sheraton came to work in London the chairs were still further reduced in size.

Perhaps what marks the Sheraton style more than anything else to the amateur is the introduction of satin wood.

Very many of his pretty graceful chairs are made in this wood, the less pleasing ones being painted as well. Some of his happiest examples are of satin wood, with a very slight inlay of mahogany or perhaps harewood.

One of the first differences we notice in Sheraton's chairs from those of Heppelwhite's is to be found in the shape of the back ; whereas Heppelwhite's backs are usually—of course there are exceptions—oval, round, nearly square, or shield like, Sheraton's are rectangular and the legs very generally fluted—sometimes a little carving or inlay appeared on them, but fluting is more often found.

In Fig. 10 you see a Sheraton Bergère chair, one of his later creations and strange to say plain and simple, instead of the tormented design that spoils so much of his work from 1800 onwards ; this you see is very harmonious, good, plain, in excellent taste, and would go well with almost anything. The legs are fluted, and notice how extremely well the sides are contrived ; the little pillars, similarly fluted and tapering to the top, seem to give lightness and distinction to the chair. I had a chair of this kind, whether a Sheraton or not I cannot say ; it was not so pretty, being quite plain, the caning coming to the extreme front, and lacking these elegant little pillared additions at the corners, which gave a *cachet* to the design at once.

I also possess another Sheraton chair of a plain but distinctive character, with four vertical rails at the back and the sharply curved arms which point to its being an early example. Its character is somewhat obscured by a coating of white enamel. It is of birch, and was once—in my childhood—an extremely ugly, though comfortable, chair. It was " japanned " pea green, with wreaths of minute flowers of all the colours of the rainbow across the top rail, with trails hanging half-way down each bar, also more flowers across the front of the seat and on the arms. During a visitation of measles we children occupied our enforced leisure by outlining these wreaths with a stout lead pencil, whereby we conceived we had greatly improved upon the work of the designer. I well remember, too, that punishment, swift and somewhat severe, rewarded our artistic labours.

Sheraton was fond of the lyre-shaped back, and treats it pleasingly. It was only in his later years (when, tormented by poverty, disappointment and general want of success, he frantically tried all kinds of novelties, the larger proportion of them unsuitable and strange) that we meet with chairs, and other pieces, destitute of artistic feeling. Whatever the faults of these later pieces, however, from the point of view of beauty and appropriateness, not a word can ever be said against their workmanship ; he must always have employed the best workmen, for his pieces are the perfection of craftsmanship.

In hunting for chairs of Chippendale's, Heppelwhite's, or Sheraton's, my advice is, employ a dealer, one who can be entirely relied on. I assure you they exist, though if one believed all one hears and reads, one might imagine the trade was made up of rogues, thieves and liars ! This is very far from the case, and if you mean to lay out more than a few pounds I decidedly advise you to seek their help. If you are not unreasonable and treat them well, they will reciprocate your behaviour. Tell them about the limit you are prepared to go to, and do not hurry them ; chairs of this kind do not dot the roadside, and some months may be required to find exactly what you want.

There is a type of furniture that so far has not become very popular with collectors, and therefore offers a better chance for the buyer with only

FIG. II.—FARM HOUSE CHAIR IN
HEPPELWHITE STYLE.

FIG. 12.—COTTAGE LADDER-BACK CHAIR.

a slender purse. I refer to farm house furniture, and such as was made for small tradesmen, inn-keepers and the like ; this style of furniture is comparatively cheap to buy, though rather diffi-cult to find, but well worth hunting for.

Naturally immense numbers of chairs were made in the 18th century, and even now, many attainable specimens exist.

I give you in Fig 11. and Fig. 12 good examples of two totally different types of farm house chairs. Fig. 11 is manifestly a copy of an early Heppel-white, and a very good example it is, plain, strong, and substantial—the wood oak. Most village carpenters stuck to oak, and a very sensible plan too. Long after mahogany was in full swing in large cities, oak continued in all its first glory in the country, and this was natural ; the middle and lower classes of England are intensely con-servative and do not readily give in to what they consider new fangled notions, especially if intro-duced by one they term a " foreigner," meaning thereby one who comes from the South, if they are inhabitants of the North, or even (with less distinction) a man of Norfolk, when they them-selves live in Suffolk, so it is easy to see that for some time mahogany was regarded with distrust, and oak, the tried and trusted servant of many generations, was still employed.

I think Fig. 11 is very pleasing with the pretty curve at the top of the back and the splat pierced in four places. Nothing would look better than a set of these chairs in a dining room, and would cost but a modest sum, two pounds each ought to be enough. You are not likely to find six or eight exactly alike, of course, if you did you might at once expect frauds, but diligent search will be rewarded, I think, with the discovery of those that will go well together, and not arrest the eye by a too marked divergence in style.

Fig. 12 is a very desirable possession, and you may find some trouble in picking up one or more in your rambles. The history of this one is rather quaint, it is not an old family friend and was only transplanted to its present abode six years ago. It belonged to an old lady in an alms-house in Berkshire, my cousin wished to buy it, but the old lady would not part with this beloved treasure during her life, but she struck a bargain with my relative that if she would buy it there and then, and allow her to keep it for her life, the purchaser should enter into possession at her death.

A very cheap set of dining room chairs and, to my mind, a very distinctive one, would be of the sort called " Windsor." They were and are still made in Buckinghamshire, and having been turned out in large quantities in the past, it is still not very difficult to get together six or eight alike to make a set. I do not give you an illus-tration of these, for I think they are familiar to all, the hooped back with vertical bars and a kind of small wheel in the centre is the best examples, and what no doubt greatly strengthens them, two extra bars starting from the shoulders and coming down nearly to meet at the bottom, which brings them aslant of the other back bars.

These chairs, well cleaned and kept thoroughly polished, make ideal dining room chairs, if means do not run to anything more sumptuous, and with two as carving chairs with arms would look handsome and uncommon.

CHAPTER III

BUREAUX, CABINETS AND TABLES

ALL our cabinets, chests of drawers, bookcases, chests-upon-chests, escritoires, bureaux, tall boys, commodes, etc., have all been evolved from the chest, or coffer, of mediæval times.

It is difficult now in these days of luxury to remember that once everything was put into chests only, when these chests not only represented all the storing room for clothes and personal possessions, but were also the only travelling conveniences. The chest represented everything now comprised in cabin trunks, dress baskets, saratoga boxes, suit cases, dressing bags, hat boxes, etc.

I must admit, however, that there are proofs that " hold-alls " existed as early as the 15th century, and very likely considerably earlier. In Bruges, Memling's set of beautiful jewel-like pictures, glowing on the *chasse* of St. Ursula, was finished in 1489, and in two of its little compartments we see St. Ursula and her 11,000 virgins preparing to land, clasping somewhat feverishly in their hands substantial hold-alls. Again, a most curious and interesting picture in the

Dominican Church of St. Paul in Antwerp shows the same thing. It is by the elder Teniers, who was born in 1582 and died in 1649. It represents the Seven Acts of Mercy, and in it one can study a wonderfully realistic collection of cripples of all kinds.

The picture is arranged like a doll's house, there is no front wall to the principal building, and we look into the actual rooms, where everything is going on in great publicity ; succouring the homeless is depicted by ragged unfortunates who are waiting in forlorn misery crouched on the stones in the road, and one is resting on an undeniable hold-all of the sausage-like shape still favoured by our German neighbours, though in the passage of years they have changed the leather sausage of Teniers' time for one of worsted work of many colours, or a Holland variety with ornate decorations, executed in blue or scarlet braid.

They are conveniences not to be despised, and like many inventions of that practical nation, both comfortable and useful ; but it is curious to note that the idea in the main is so old, and that the 20th century has altered it so little.

The chest—upon which I must not dwell now, for I spoke at length upon it in " Antiques and Curios "—was the treasure house of the whole family, it was the wardrobe, the plate chest and the bank, and was fitted with a good lock, sometimes with several.

Locks and keys and other small fittings of iron were greatly valued in the 16th and 17th centuries, and we constantly meet with notices of them in old inventories, the fact that a " truncke " or a " chist " had a lock and key would be carefully stated.

By the middle of the 17th century " trunckes " and " portmantles " were in use, and evidently greatly prized. Miss Bradley, in " The English housewife of the 17th and 18th centuries," has unearthed a delightful note of a confiding country parson, who, in a rash moment, lent his " portmantle." " I bought in London a portmantle costing 5s. 6d., and a male pellion 1s., and a locke key to the portmantle 6d. This ' portmantle ' and all that belonged to it I lent to my cousin Lewen, which he never returned." Miss Bradley concludes, " We can imagine the childish joy of the simple gentleman in the ' portmantle ' with a lock, a rare luxury. Words apparently failed him with regard to the conduct of cousin Lewen."

Locks were so precious, that even those on doors were taken on and off as occasion required, and we find from Claydon papers that this was done as late as 1650, when an enlightened member of the family discovered that this constant removing and returning of locks greatly injured the doors and decided that in future they should be permanently fixed.

To return to chests, the first advance in luxury

was to add a drawer at the bottom. This was doubtless considered a great improvement, an almost startling innovation. The next change was to divide the chest with doors in front instead of keeping that front immovable, and also having the drawer at the bottom.

From these humble beginnings we got the cupboards of all kinds and shapes, the court, the livery, the corner, the buffet, the press and the armoire, and later the bureau, the cabinet and the book case.

At the same time and along another line, the chest of drawers, nest of drawers, chest-upon-chest, tall boy and wardrobes of all kinds were being evolved.

He must have been a bold and daring spirit who first conceived the idea of sweeping away the upper part of the chest and making two or three drawers of the whole original piece of furniture.

Before passing on to the subject of this chapter I must mention two articles that were early evolved from the chest. First, the dresser, without a back—a simple long narrow table, with drawers and legs, few or many, according to the length. There was no back, and it is a much simpler piece of furniture than the so-called Welsh dressers, so much sought after now. The kind I am speaking of is rare. I know one in the city, I will not say where it is, but if I had an inch of room to spare I should endeavour to transfer it to my house. It is in a tea shop. I have many friends in the way of furniture in these comfortable retreats, one in Buckinghamshire shelters a miniature gate-leg table that I greatly desire, another conceals two Sheraton chairs. I am not so much moved by envy here, because—though I hardly presume to whisper such a sacrilegious sentiment—I do not care much for Sheraton. But I love the dresser, it is very shallow and so long that there are four drawers with original brass handles and eight legs.

The bacon settle, too, has grown from the chest, that was a simple enough evolution, a back added which was deep enough to contain the flitches of bacon. It usually, but not invariably, opened at the back, and arms added at the sides, made it a fairly comfortable seat by the farm house fireside. A friend of mine has a particularly fine example (opening in front), but the local photographer made such a mess of the photograph that I am unable to show it to you.

Soon after the advent of chests of drawers we get the bureau. Bureau is French for office, and probably this special piece of furniture got the name from the various contrivances within the flap—usually a slanting one—to tabulate, and often to conceal, important papers and other valuables.

At the same time that bureaux began to make their appearance " nests of drawers " are first heard of. These are very scarce, especially if they are early specimens. You will see a good specimen in Fig. 52 upon which the tea china is shown, but it is much later, being a Queen Anne piece. They must have been rather fragile things and if much moved about were pretty sure to be broken.

These old pieces—Bureaux especially—have often secret drawers or holes for the concealment of valuables. The little Queen Anne " nest " has two such arrangements in the concave portions each side of the centre, where there are hidden four little cunningly concealed boxes let into the sides like coffins in a vault.

Bureaux were also called " escritoires," and we hear of them inventoried as " scrutors." In France the slanting flap to the bureau was not quite so popular as with us, at least not till a very much later date, and the *secrétaire* was more frequently made with a straight cupboard-like flap. The *Bureau de Roi*, so well known from pictures, and the bureau of the same period made for Stanislas Leczinski, King of Poland, both show a roll top, like our present office desks.

Both Riesener and Boulle made *secrétaires* with the flat front turning down when open, and humbler men made many hundreds of the same kind. To me they are not very pleasing, and have a tomb-like aspect.

It was a common thing to find secret hiding places in these old bureaux, and the usual way of discovering them (unless by chance) is to examine closely, with a view to finding if the external size is accounted for by visible drawers, or partitions, if it is not, you will almost certainly find some false bottom to a drawer, or perhaps some space *behind* a drawer, fitted with a box, or you will discover that a bit of carving, a scrap of moulding, or some ornamental pillar moves and leaves a convenient space.

It was in this way we found the little coffins in my Queen Anne piece. I gave an illustration of it in " Antiques and Curios," but the one here at Fig. 52 is too much obscured by the china to tell you much. On each side of the centre there is a concave panel, just to the right and left and above the tea and coffee cups, and this seemed in no way accounted for, and so looking everywhere we pulled out the centre drawer, it looks like two, but is in reality only one, and then we discovered the little catacombs. We did not find any treasures, however, as people do so agreeably in novels.

I possess a very curious and valuable bureau, full of secret hiding places, but I told you about it in a former book and must not be tedious, its interest lies in the impossibility of opening it at all unless you are in the secret of its very singular mechanism. One meets with bureaux in oak, walnut, mahogany and satin wood.

Mr. Robinson is of opinion that bureaux did not come into being until walnut was the wood most in use. Certainly we have no definite date of which we can say, in this year bureaux were first made, and the oak ones sometimes met with

FIG. 13.—BUREAU.
(By permission of Messrs. Gill and Reigate.)

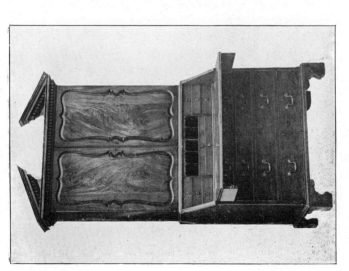

FIG. 14.—BUREAU CABINET.
(By permission of Messrs. Gill and Reigate.)

may very possibly, and even probably, have been made in the country, where carpenters—many of them did not at all claim to be cabinet makers—clung to their old and tried friend, oak, and were not to be turned lightly aside to walnut and mahogany.

I have known two oak ones, in close home friendship—one very handsome, in which the drawer and flap were banded in cherry wood. I do not know its history with any certainty before 1730. The other quite plain, was remarkably small, its history could be traced back to 1750, but beyond that was lost in the mists of obscurity. Both these oak examples were of the dwarf variety, like Fig. 13. Bureau was indeed really a name reserved for this type of piece, and when it is surmounted by another part, it should be called a bureau bookcase or bureau cabinet. Fig. 13 is of mahogany, and is not very old, belonging only to the last quarter of the 18th century; it is of a plain serviceable type and will doubtless be in as good condition a hundred years later as it is to-day.

I like the little dolls' cupboard in the middle, which seems such a transparently obvious place in which to put anything that needs a lock.

Fig. 14 is a more ambitious piece with a cupboard above, in which either china or books might be kept, it is of rich San Domingo mahogany, and the cupboard doors show beautiful figure in the wood.

You see there is but little ornamentation, the wood in itself is enough. The open space left in the pediment was to show off some fine Oriental jar or vase. This example is, I should think, somewhat earlier than the last.

Bureaux of the Queen Anne period were of walnut and when of the " Burr " variety are extremely pleasing. Those having delicate bands of herring bone inlay are the most valuable.

In the herring bone pattern two narrow strips of walnut were so chosen, that when cut, the " figure " should run diagonally across them. These, when put side by side, showed the " figure " lines meeting in the centre, in the shape of a V. Books were not plentiful in those days, and so the cupboard parts above, whether with solid doors or with glass ones, were usually filled with china, or perhaps other curios, probably from India.

Akin to these bureaux and cabinets were cupboards of all kinds. Corner ones did not come in till the reign of Queen Anne, and have continued almost uninterruptedly to the present time. They were made to stand either on the floor, or to be fixed to the wall, and were made of oak or walnut and much later of mahogany. The glass door variety came in late, not, I think, until the last quarter of the 18th century.

We find these frequently in old cottages, and it is in them that the owners keep their few treasures of glass, china, and earthenware, so often broken, alas ! The peasant has no idea of having anything of that kind mended, and an application of seccotine, or a bit of stamp-paper, is considered to meet the exigencies of the situation.

The older kind with wooden doors, of which I possess one, are usually put together somewhat roughly, and the hinges should be (if the piece is genuine) of iron.   The shelves within are hollowed out each side of the centre.

About this period of walnut and early mahogany, a cockle shell was a very common ornament, it effloresced upon everything and was certainly very decorative.   It appeared in many varieties, and was often quite as much—especially when inlaid—like a fan, or the rays of the sun, as a cockle shell.

The cabinets of Chippendale, Adam and Heppelwhite are very desirable, and do not often come into the market suitable for the minor collector, but it is well that you should educate your eye by studying them.

Between Chippendale's style and Heppelwhite's there is a great resemblance, but if there are legs to the piece, then we usually find a marked difference, for Heppelwhite very early showed his characteristic of tapering legs, with square or spade feet.   You will remember in the charming bed which I showed you, and which is evidently an early one, the lower part of the legs do not taper and the feet are perfectly square, but in the upper part of the foot posts he begins to show his tendency to the tapering form, though it is turned upwards, instead of downwards. Heppelwhite, coming between the two eras of Chippendale and Sheraton, may be said to have partaken somewhat of the style of both. It is certainly very difficult to differentiate between Chippendale work and early Heppelwhite.

Another difficulty is that both men were influenced by Adam. To Adam more than to anyone else we owe the marked classical taste of the late 18th century. Robert, the best known and cleverest of the three brothers, had a natural leaning towards this style of art, and he early determined, if possible, to steep himself in the traditions of classic art. In 1755 and 1756, he made a long artistic tour, visiting France and Italy, but neither of these countries gave him just what he wanted, which was to see a house of the old Romans and absorb into his brain their ideas on domestic architecture and adapt them to the requirements of the 18th century.

He attained his object in 1757, when, accompanied by the French architect, Clérisseau, he gave himself up to the study, at Spalatro in Dalmatia, of the remains of Diocletian's palace.

In 1762, four years after his return to England, he was made architect to the king, so that he must have mounted the ladder of success very rapidly.

After he returned from Spalatro, everything that Adam and his brothers did partook of a classical character, and his influence was so great that he infected all other architects and artist craftsmen with his own ideas ; henceforward classical wreaths, pillars, urns, vases, draperies and mythological subjects, appeared upon everything.

It is necessary you should understand this idiosyncrasy of the second half of the 18th century, for it was at the root of much that would otherwise be mysterious.

It is also well to recollect that Robert Adam was an architect, not a cabinet maker, so that pieces of furniture that go by his name were indeed designed by him, but he employed other craftsmen of the first rank, especially Chippendale, to carry out his ideas.

Fig. 15 and 16 are both Sheraton pieces, though they do not bear much resemblance to each other.

At the risk of being a little tedious, I must digress here to tell you something of Sheraton's own history, for it seems to me that without some slight knowledge of his very curious personality we cannot properly understand the strange versatility which led him to try everything, and to wander into all sorts of strange ways. He was a Baptist minister, and a publisher, as well as a designer, and, in spite of exquisite designs and perfect workmanship, with artistic ideas almost amounting to genius, he yet dragged out a disappointed existence of extreme poverty, unknown and unappreciated.

Now his pieces sell for sums running into four

figures, and in his lifetime he could not afford enough cups and saucers to go round—the irony of it.

We know really little about Thomas Sheraton's early life, except that he was born at Stockton-on-Tees, in or about 1751. Apparently in youth he had belonged to the Church of England, but subsequently, at what date is not known, he became a fanatical Baptist. In 1790 he came to London, lived for some time in Davies Street, then in Wardour Street, and finally for some time in Broad Street, Golden Square, where he had a house and untidy shop and where he eventually died, worn out with overwork, financial anxieties, and it is greatly to be feared, at times want of actual nourishment, and the necessaries of life.

It is quite by accident that we get a painful light on poor Sheraton's home life. It comes from an interesting memoir of Adam Black—subsequently the head of the great publishing firm—written by Alexander Nicholson. He is describing the great difficulties Mr. Black encountered when he first came to London. Apparently it was as difficult then, as now, for the unemployed to find work.

" He (Adam Black) was willing to do any honest work by which he could make a living, and inquired in all directions, but in vain. At last he heard of a man called Sheraton publishing a book called ' *The Cabinet maker's Encyclopædia*,' who might give him something to do. He called on

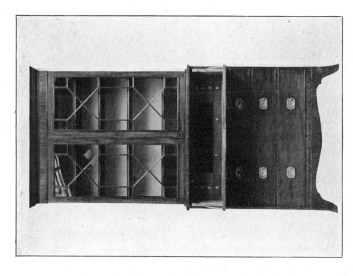

FIG. 15.—BUREAU BOOKCASE—SHERATON PERIOD.
(By permission of Messrs. Gill and Reigate.)

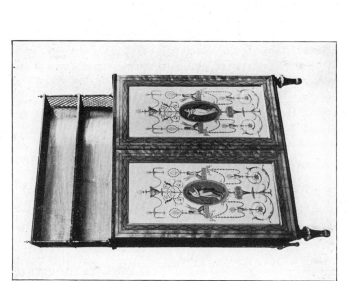

FIG. 16.—PAINTED SHERATON CABINET.
(By permission of Messrs. Gill and Reigate.)

him, and found the worthy encyclopædist and his surroundings painfully humble, but as he wanted an assistant, A.B. agreed to help him in whatever way he could, either in writing articles, or in a less intellectual capacity.   Here is his description of the man, and his place : ' He lived in an obscure street, his house, half shop, half dwelling-house, and looked himself like a worn out Methodist minister with threadbare black coat.   I took tea with them one afternoon.   There were a cup and saucer for the host, and another for his wife, and a little porringer for their daughter.   The wife's cup and saucer were given to me, and she had to put up with another little porringer.   My host seemed a good man, with some talent.   He had been a cabinet maker, was now author and publisher, teacher of drawing and, I believe, occasional preacher.   I was with him for about a week, writing a few articles, and trying to put his shop in order, for which I was remunerated with half a guinea.   Miserable as the pay was, I was half ashamed to take it from the poor man.   He is a man of talents, and, I believe, of genuine piety. He understands the cabinet business—I believe was bred to it.   He has been, and perhaps at present is, a preacher.   He is a scholar, writes well, draws in my opinion masterly, is an author, bookseller, stationer and teacher.   We may be ready to ask how comes it to pass that a man with such abilities, and resources, is in such a state ?   I believe his abilities and resources are his ruin, in this respect, for by attempting to do everything he does nothing.' ''

Poor Sheraton, he was one of the vast army of those who have too many irons in the fire. Like all the cabinet makers of the century he published trade catalogues. The best of these was '' The Cabinet maker and Upholsterer's Drawing book.'' This came out in 1791, and one gains some insight to the poor fellow's embittered feelings, as will be seen, when in his preface he alluded to a book brought out prior to Chippendale's, and he says, '' It gives no instruction for drawing in any form, but we may venture to say that those who drew the designs, wanted a good share of teaching themselves.''

When he comes to speak of Chippendale's '' Director '' he is affably condescending. '' As for the designs themselves, they are now wholly antiquated and laid aside, though possessed of great merit, according to the times in which they were executed ! '' He has some scathing remarks on Ince and Mayhew's book ; then he comes to Heppelwhite's '' Cabinetmaker's and Upholsterer's Guide.'' Here words fail him to express the mean opinion he has of the production. In alluding to it he says, '' In which are found no directions for drawing in any form, nor any pretension to it. The whole merit of the performance rests on the designs, with a short description to each prefixed. Some of these designs are not without merit, though it is evident that the perspective is, in some instances erroneous . . . . . . but if we compare some of the designs, particularly the chairs, with the newest taste, we shall find that this work has already caught the decline, and perhaps in a little time will suddenly die in the disorder."

After all these spiteful remarks about his predecessors, the concluding lines of his preface read very funnily ; " Notwithstanding the ill nature of some, who hate to speak well of anything but their own productions, I only wish that a comparison be made with any other book hitherto published for the use of cabinet makers and upholsterers, and then it will sufficiently speak for itself."

The best furniture produced by Sheraton was his earliest, probably a good deal of which was made at Stockton-on-Tees. It was entirely free from the absolutely fantastic ideas which entirely spoilt his later work. We associate him chiefly with the use of satin wood and certainly he used a great deal of that beautiful wood, but also he made large numbers of articles in mahogany. Fig. 15 seems to be in his earliest and simplest manner. It is of mahogany, a small beading round the drawers, but no inlay, the figure of the wood being the only decoration except a tiny line of carving at the top. Observe the handles, they are typical early Sheraton ones. A great deal has to be learnt about handles, they teach us much as to the age of the furniture they adorn, if they are genuine. There are, however, many

H

difficulties that beset the beginner. It is more
than likely that the handles are *not* the originals.
You must learn exactly what shaped handles go
with different periods of furniture. Always examine carefully to see if there are marks, and
holes (filled up) where former handles have been,
and what the back of the drawer looks like ; that
will almost invariably show signs of former
handles, if the existing ones are not the originals.
Sometimes the curious fact is proved that the
handles on a piece of furniture are older than the
chest or cabinet itself. I have an example of
this, the chest is mahogany, date about 1790,
a good enough piece, solid and substantial, but
quite plain except for a tiny line of holly stained
black round the drawers.

It has always been in the nursery, a position
not conducive to long life in handles. These
should have resembled what you see in Fig. 15,
which is typical of the Sheraton period, but it
was rather a fragile kind of handle and ill-
calculated to resist rough usage, which I am
sure it received in my great-grandmother's time,
for there were thirteen children.

Probably, therefore, they fell off, one by one,
and were replaced by the existing set, which no
doubt being extra handsome, had been saved
from some other defunct piece of furniture.

They are large, heavily-moulded lions' heads
holding massive rings in their mouths, the very
opposite style to Sheraton's delicate and almost

flimsy handles and plates. I imagine that their extreme beauty saved their lives, and they were stored away for future use.

To the professional " faker " bright new handles do not appeal, he knows they give him away at once, and he has many ingenious devices, some simple, some complicated, to give to the brand new Birmingham handles and plates, the necessary look of old age. Acids are largely used, and to insure the requisite softly rounded edges, they are put into a cylinder—a large number together and the instrument is made to revolve until by constant friction among them- selves, sharp edges are disposed of, and some- thing approaching the softness of old age is attained.

After treatment in this manner the contents come out very passable " antiques." This is very clever, and in no way wrong unless with an intention to deceive. There are not nearly enough old handles to " go round," and honest dealers employ these means to make imitations quite legitimately, only they tell you, that old as they look, are only clever deceptions.

I have a set of Louis XV. " handles " arranged in this way, but I was frankly told about them ; they were not passed off on me as genuine antiques.

Now we come to Fig. 16, a very ornate example of Sheraton's work. It is a really beautiful specimen of its kind and worth a large

sum, but I do not like painting on furniture, it
seems to me a kind of " painting of the lily."
The whole thing is over-decorated.   The cabinet
is of satin wood, and the doors on which are the
oval paintings are white enamel.   The paintings
are typical of Angelica Kauffmann, or Pergolisi.
It is doubtful whether Angelica Kauffmann was
in England at all, during the period when Sheraton
was designing this kind of furniture.   She had
done an immense deal of work for the Adams,
but in 1782, after her marriage to Zucchi, she
went to Rome, where she lived for the rest of her
life.   It seems probable that the paintings on
furniture, often attributed to her—especially
on Sheraton pieces—are really the work of
Cipriani and sometimes of Pergolisi, perhaps.
As far as workmanship goes, Fig. 16 is a gem ;
look at the delicacy of the shelves and the
graceful gilt brass lattice sides.

Some time ago I saw sold at Christie's for a vast
sum, a pair of side tables, or as they are sometimes
called " occasional " tables, such a frightful
name ! Why could we not think of some such
nice and suitable term for the same thing as the
French have done, they call them *Tables Am-
bulantes* ; occasional tables is a silly term, and
always reminds one of an auctioneer's catalogue.
Well, these " occasional " tables were of satin
wood, and all round the edges, a band about six
inches wide was decorated with the eyes of
peacocks' feathers, it was lovely work, inasmuch

as it was so skilful, but not at all pretty to my mind, and very garish. Wedgwood plaques were also sometimes introduced and this variety is, if possible, worse ; the rather hard blue of the Wedgwood screams at the honey tone of the satin wood. The French *ebénistes* pursued the same plan, but I fancy with slightly more success, but the effect is not pleasing. You can study this style of furniture well in the Jones collection at the Victoria and Albert Museum.

In Fig. 17, you see a fine cabinet of Italian workmanship, the main part of the piece is ebony, and the ornamentation such as the elongated bosses on the drawers, etc., is of tortoiseshell, covered at the back with brilliant vermilion which shows through the tortoiseshell. This piece probably was made about mid way in the 17th century. It was in Italy and Spain, also the Low Countries, that these cabinets were produced.

One peculiarity in pieces of this kind, is the centre. The small doors where you see the key hole, opens and discloses a tiny pillared and arched hall, with domed ceiling, lined throughout with mirror glass and quite in the style of a doll's house. Sir Ralph Verney, whom his friends pestered to bring them things, had to find a cabinet of this kind, " My Lady Lisle desires an Ebony Cabanet and for Dores or none, she leaves it to me. . . . I cannot meet with an Ebony Cabanet, that's good, I can have choice of tortus shell, garnished out with very thin silver or guilt brass, which I like much better." No doubt this must have resembled Fig. 17. There is another variety of this kind of work which is much more beautiful, namely where gold is put at the back of the shell instead of scarlet.

Fig. 18 is not very old. It was made for my great grandfather somewhere between 1790 and 1800. It is of rosewood and was constructed especially to contain the very curious and valuable Dutch glass picture in the centre. I do not very well understand that form of art, but I am told that this is of great merit. The background is of some opaque bottle green, and the bowl which contains the flowers seems to be a kind of blue green enamel with decorations in ormolu. I should say that the picture is far older than the cabinet, indeed I always heard that it was so. It looks to me to be work of the early 17th century. The bright line at the edge of the oval is gold, but it is on the under side, and only seen through. The photograph makes it appear too light ; in the thing itself, the effect is quite subdued.

I must apologize for my old friend, the central dish on the top. I did not see that he had dropped a morsel of his anatomy. The continual vibration of motors has upset his feeble constitution, and he has shed a mended piece.

This cabinet has a point of interest that was to me quite unexpected. It has a secret spring in the part above the top shelf, which on pressure

FIG. 17.—ITALIAN CABINET INLAID WITH
TORTOISESHELL

FIG. 18.—CABINET—1790-1800—WITH
TWO HIDING-PLACES.

releases the panel holding the picture, this discloses a shallow cupboard with three shelves. All that I knew, but what was my astonishment to find a cavity in the top about six inches deep and 14 long. It is in the middle under the big plate and copper coffee pot, and the extra depth is accounted for when you open the panel. Though it had been in our house over a hundred years no one had ever discovered this hiding place until I did so myself, some years ago. The wooden lid to it is so beautifully fitted that it can only be fished up by inserting a pen knife. I must now pass on to tables, or I shall leave myself no space.

As I explained to you in my former book, tables at one time were merely planks put upon trestles and were removed after a meal and the diners sat upon similar planks of a smaller kind. The first improvement was to make what they called a " standing " table, which was of immense weight and solidity, standing on four or six legs, which legs were united by stretchers. There was not much ornamentation about them, generally a band only of incised carving just under the top. The next development was the same with handsomely carved enormously bulbous legs. This fashion lasted long and we see examples made in the 17th century.

We have also the " drawing " table, which has lasted with variations to our own day. We still have the " drawing " table almost exactly as it was at the end of the 16th century. These tables, whether drawing or not, very generally had a " carpett of Turkey werke," the carpet being, not what we understand by the term, but really a table cloth.

" Turkye werke " began at this time to be much in request for making cushions to soften the unyielding oaken chairs and benches.

Mr. Litchfield in his " Illustrated History of Furniture " gives us some inventories of that time, and we hear a great deal about " Turkye werke " and " quysshens."

" Inventory of the contents of the parler of St. Jone's within the cittie of Chester (1589). A drawinge table of joyned work with a frame valued at xi shillings."

" Two formes covered with Turkye work."

" Sixe joyned stooles covr'd with nedle werke xvs."

" One longe carpett of Turkey werke."

" A shortte carpett of the same werke."

" Sixe quysshens of Turkye."

" Sixe quysshens of tapestrie."

At the beginning of the 17th century, the hitherto prevailing fashion of all the household dining together, began to be abandoned, and the " with drawing " room and the " summer par- lour " had to be furnished with articles of a less massive construction, and so we begin to have smaller tables.

At first they resembled their forerunners, but

FIG. 19.—GATE-LEG TABLE.

FIG. 20.—JACOBEAN SIDE TABLE.

were smaller, and then appeared the gate-legged variety, which though heavy—it was, of course, made of oak—was still capable of being moved about. I must not linger on gate legs—you will see a pretty example of a rather small one in Fig. 19. I judge it to be of the time of James II. or William and Mary, on account of the feet slightly turning outwards, which was a feature of that period. I possess two others, one very large, at which seven people can sit without crowding. It is much older than Fig. 19, and I guess it to be one of the first made. It is very heavy and of a splendid glassy polish, which only centuries of wear and rubbing can achieve. My other little gate leg is of Queen Anne's time, or perhaps William and Mary's. The legs tuck away as usual, but it has only one leaf instead of the usual two, and the solitary one turns over, instead of under. These tables are made in all sizes, and late in the 17th century they had specially turned legs, a form of turning often called " barley sugar " turning.

A few of these tables are made of immense dimensions—Mr. Robinson mentions one that is 19 feet long. I have myself seen one at St. Giles-in-the-fields, which must be not less than fifteen feet long, perhaps more, my measurements being somewhat roughly taken with an umbrella.

Fig. 20 is a table of the mid 17th century, with the legs showing some recollection of the bulbous or melon type. The fashion still holds of having the legs connected by stretchers to lift the feet from the cold floor. Look at the handles, they are quite wrong, those kind of handles were not made till a hundred years later, so the original ones must have disappeared, and these have been put on not earlier that 1760 or 1770, probably much later.

In the 17th century large tables were still the rule, and really small ones had hardly appeared ; they were called forth by the advent of tea and coffee. By Queen Anne's time (she herself was a great tea drinker) the prevalence of tea drinking, and tea parties, necessitated the appearance of various small tables, of different sizes and kinds, and these being found to be extremely convenient, tables for other purposes soon made their appearance, such as those for writing, with a place for the knees in the middle, and two or three drawers on each side. Serpentine writing tables did not come in till later.

With the first years of the 18th century card tables, made expressly for the purpose, appeared. Up to that time, though there was plenty of card playing, the gamesters were content with ordinary " gatelegged," or something of the same kind. It is only after Queen Anne's accession that we have the card table made expressly, and then it was always of walnut.

In Fig. 21, you see the form that with many minor changes lasted from the early years of the 18th century until the Sheraton period.

We are now approaching the time when mahogany made its appearance.

It had been brought to England much earlier by Sir Walter Raleigh, but neither accident nor circumstance brought it into use till 1720, or thereabouts, the exact date being uncertain.

Tradition points to the following chain of small events, as leading up to the development of the commercial value of mahogany for furniture.

It is well to remember the little story because it fixes in our minds the approximate date of the general use of this new wood.

It seems a certain Mrs. Gibbon wanted a candle box—we do not use such things now, but in those days rush lights and candles were the only illuminating power ; they were made at at home, and in large numbers, and careful storing was all important ; unless secured in boxes of solid wood, rats and mice soon devoured the housewife's store, and so it was beyond all things necessary to have a box that would—at any rate for a long time—defy the teeth of these industrious rodents.

Mrs. Gibbon therefore determined, like the good manager she no doubt was, to have a thoroughly substantial candle box made, and her husband remembered that his brother had brought him some planks of a singularly hard wood from the West Indies.

They had been stored in an outhouse as of no

immediate importance, but now at last they
were to turn in usefully.

The carpenter was secured, and the work
begun, but behold ! the wood turned the edges
of all the tools and the carpenter was inclined
to strike work, but evidently the doctor was a
man who knew his own mind, and insisted upon
the re-grinding of tools and the resumption of
labour. Eventually the box was finished, and
must I should think have been rat-proof. How
interesting it would be to see that box now ; no
doubt it no longer exists.

When finished, it was considered so rich
looking and unusual, that pieces of the wood were
anxiously sought by friends, and this, as far as we
know, started first the enthusiasm for mahogany
in England.

From this little story you will see that furniture
made of this wood cannot be " hundreds of years
old " as fondly alleged by possessors of elderly
mahogany pieces.

It was certainly in use by 1725, but probably
did not come to be much known until quite ten
years later. Very much of Chippendale's early
work was executed in walnut.

Thus you see the card tables of the first quarter
of the 18th century were of walnut. At this
period gambling was carried on to a serious extent,
and card playing, even in its most innocent form, was
almost universal, therefore large numbers of card
tables in some form or another are in existence.

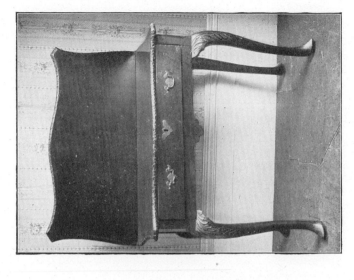

FIG. 21.—MAHOGANY CARD TABLE.

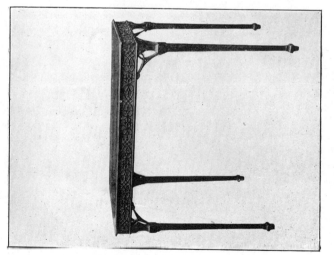

FIG. 22.—CHIPPENDALE TABLE.

(By permission of Messrs. Gill and Reigate.)

Throughout the 18th century the card tables were more or less of the form seen in Fig. 21, at least until very late indeed. Generally, but by no means always, they were covered with cloth, and when not so arranged, which is the case with Fig. 21, presumably a cloth was thrown over the top to prevent the cards sliding.

The usual form as to the legs was cabriole, with slight ornament on the knee, such as a cockle shell, or acanthus leaf, and round the edge a little very simple carving, such as you see in my illustration.

There were various ways of supporting the flap; sometimes, the two back legs pulled out as you would draw out a concertina, sometimes a fifth leg between the two back ones, acted in the same manner, and very often, as in Fig 21, one of the back legs was made to swing out, and so supported the leaf.

In the best examples, there are four slightly sunk spaces at the corners, which accommodated the candles, and occasionally, when these conveniences are absent, a small slide pulls out in two sides to receive the candle in the same way as the slide acts for the teapot in Fig. 53. Also on each side, are found in the same specimens that show the sunken candle stands, smaller oval receptacles also sunken, for money, or counters.

The more ornate kinds show elaborate carving on the knees—cabochons, lions' heads and fine masks, the feet being of all varieties, hoof, snake, club, and ball and claw, etc. The edges of the slab, too, show in good pieces a little carving, such as is seen in Fig. 21.

Later on, when the less graceful straight legs came in fashion, they were often decorated with a very slight string-like carving down the front.

Tables of this kind (if without depressions for candles and counters) were found very convenient because of the small space they occupied when not in use, and the system was adopted, with slight modifications, to make a dining table of enlarging and contracting dimensions ; two of these tables made a fairly large dining one, or, three or four, a very spacious size ; when they were employed in this way clips were used underneath, so as to make the construction absolutely solid.

This kind of arrangement was found handy, for such a long table was not often needed. Two tables made sufficient accommodation for ordinary use, and the other two were always convenient for cards, or other requirements.

I have a French friend who possesses a quaint pair of card tables, made by the *ebéniste* to the infamous Egalité, they have also the bill and date in 1792. They are curious, but not pretty, the wood chestnut. When shut, the upper flap shows an inlaid chess, or draught board, when open, faded and much moth-eaten green cloth,

but no depressions for candles or counters. I
mused as I looked at them, as to *who* in that grim
time had sat around the delicate little inlaid
trifles ? Egalité himself, perhaps, darkly brooding
on the Judas-like treachery which he meditated,
and which eventually carried him the length of
voting for his royal cousin's death, that cousin
who, poor man, whatever his faults of government might be, was ever a true and faithful friend.

In those dark days no one could trust his neighbour, and as the revellers dealt their cards on
these little tables, how many must have been
wondering whose turn would come next to mount
the fatal tumbril, and close their eyes for ever to
ambition, love and life, under the swift guillotine.

It has always been said that women are more
revengeful than men, and certainly I rejoice
greatly to think that Egalité quickly paid the
penalty for his treachery.

In all card tables there was some kind of drawer
in which to store the cards, sometimes more than
one, and I have an old table, not at all pretty and
only about a hundred years old, which folds in
half as usual, has no drawer, but a fairly large
receptacle underneath for the cards, which receptacle is opened by twisting the entire top of the
table half-way round.

Of card tables of the Sheraton period, curiously
enough, there do not seem to be so many about
as of an earlier date. They were very frequently
round and oval, but doubling in half like the

earlier ones. If you can light upon a simple one of mahogany very slightly inlaid with a lighter wood, it is a nice thing to possess, for its capabilities of extension and compression are very valuable in these days of flats and apartments. They are to be found at moderate price, and unlike the early walnut ones are not attacked by worms.

A satin wood example is, of course, a great treasure, but these little gems do not often cross our modest road. I know one—at a dressmaker's—I look, I long, I languish, but I know it is not for me.

To pass to other tables, a considerable number were made by Chippendale, Ince and Mayhew, Heppelwhite and their imitators, in the style of Fig. 22.

This is what we should call a sitting room centre table. You see it has good fret-work under the top, but the legs are not very graceful to my mind, and I dislike the silly little braces at the top of the legs, which Chippendale in his later work was so fond of.

Small writing tables, screen tables and work tables, did not appear much till after Chippendale's time. Sheraton made many of these delicate trifles, and was especially fond of combining two or three purposes in one piece of furniture.

We have in our family a quaint little piece which, I suppose, would be called a screen table, though the table part is a negligible quantity, it is

OLD CHELSEA PORCELAIN PORRINGER AND COVER

GOLD ANCHOR MARK

From the James Ward Usher Collection

about 18 inches wide, with two upright supports of mahogany, between them is placed a piece of clear glass, which fits into a frame, and slides up and down to any height convenient. Across the front is a little shelf which lets up and down with brackets, and underneath is a padded foot rest covered in scarlet leather.

The shelf is just wide enough to write at, so you can occupy yourself with writing or needle work, warm your toes, and take care of your complexion all at the same time.

Brought into the family at the same date, probably part of a bride's or bridegroom's outfit, is a rather large lady's work table, made of light mahogany and banded with rosewood, which has a pleasing effect, it is rectangular in shape with two flaps, and is altogether somewhat of the shape that about 1800 came into fashion and was called a " sofa " table, because it was a convenient shape at which to read or write when seated on a sofa. It is supported, as is the plan with this kind of table, on two pillars, one at each end, these supports terminating each one in two curved legs, and in the early specimens these ended in handsome brass lion's paws.

Work tables did not come into general use till the end of the 18th century, though I think it probable that some of the large boxes, which are usually called Bible boxes, might, when mounted upon a stand, have often served the purpose of a lady's work table. This is, of course, only con-

I

jecture and to be taken only for what it is worth, but they would have been so convenient to contain the stores of worsteds that were used in the wonderful Jacobean embroidery that we now gaze on with such respect, and wonder.

However that may be, it is certain that the work table, as we know it, did not have much vogue till about 1785, and though very popular in the 19th century, seems now once more to have dropped into oblivion.

This is not an age of needlework, a very small box, or basket, is now considered ample provision for the housewife of the 20th century. Everything is made by machinery and in vast batches. No doubt we save time by these means, but do we gain much after all, and how uninteresting it is when everybody's *lingerie* and table linen is pretty much alike ?   I should like to know what Matilda and the industrious ladies who worked the Bayeux tapestry would think of our idle fingers, and I should greatly like to introduce them to a sewing machine. Sheraton was strong on work tables, and we see them from his inspiration, in every shape, the round ones are particularly dainty and are the rarest of all.

On these pretty little pieces there is often a small shelf on which was fastened the silver or brass bird that held the end of the piece of work as it proceeded, instead of compelling the worker to the vulgar expedient of pinning the work to the table.

What can have become of all these sewing birds, they must have been made in large numbers, and yet I have only seen two in all my life, one of brass and one of mauve Derbyshire spar mounted in silver. Many pretty trifles of a bygone age, which at one time were so numerous, seem to have disappeared mysteriously ; for instance, what has become of all the handsome ormolu bell-pulls that used to exist in all well-appointed houses, attached to pieces of wool work embroidery, some three to five yards long, according to the height of the room ?

We may ask, too, and many of us do so, where are all the pins gone to ? Some prosaic, but well informed person, affords us the explanation that they are found in the main sewer, in huge coagulated lumps ! This kind of knowledge, however, does not help us to a solution of the mystery with regard to bell pulls, sewing birds, tatting shuttles, silk winders, etc., just the hundreds of little things that speak to us so eloquently of the industries of the past.

I have a small and delicate little work table that must have come, I think, from the inspiration of Adam in his first years of work, it has no bag or pouch, that was an invention of later date, Sheraton revelled in it. My Adam table if, indeed, it is one, is very slender and delicate, the lid lifts up and fixes itself behind the body of the piece so as to need no artificial support. As far as my experience and observation goes it was only the very early tables of this kind that had lids like this. The later ones had drawers only. Mine shows when open a cavity for work without any compartments, but underneath is a drawer of similar size.

I possess another table of this kind, but of a much later date, made by Gillow, a firm still in existence and now amalgamated with Warings.

I have not said much of the minor furniture makers, for lack of space forbids it ; it is, however, well to know and remember that the Gillow firm has existed and worked for more than two hundred years. The reason probably that it has remained to a certain degree obscure, though well-known to genuine lovers of good furniture, is that they, unlike other makers, never published books, which were, of course, in reality, advertisements.

But what is keenly interesting to know is that the firm has a set of " cost " books which have sketches of some of the pieces executed, and what makes them, too, extraordinarily useful to the student, is, that not having been written for the public as advertisements, but solely for their own use, we see the actual articles made, and the prices paid for them.

Robert Gillow, the original founder of the firm, was living at the end of the 17th century in Lancaster, where he worked as a joiner. He seems to have been a man of extraordinary force of character and full of pushful eccentricities, and, combined with these qualities, was a care as to detail, and honest and conscientious work; these characteristics having been inherited by his descendants, have made their furniture justly prized.

It seems that the original Gillow, when he settled in London—which move he mentions in his diary as " The Adventure to London "—first settled near the Custom House, probably on purpose to be near a wharf, for he had previously taken to shipping furniture from his Lancashire home to London. After that he settled in Oxford Street.

It was his son Richard, a Catholic, and educated at Douai, who became the most famous of the firm, but all the same it must be remembered that it was the enterprise and commercial instinct, combined with the hard work, and sterling honesty of the father, who started the business, and left it in a prosperous condition to his better known son.

The little table I possess made by this firm is too young to class itself as an antique in any way, for it was born as late as 1825, when it was ordered as a wedding present; a silver plate under the sloping writing board explaining that fact to us. The wood is root of walnut, at least I imagine it to be so, though it is as yellow as satin wood; the top covered with red leather slides forward, so that the writer's knees do not come in contact with the drawers. This writing part also rises to any slope desired, and the exquisite finish of the parts underneath is an object lesson, in these days of scamped machine work ; the two work drawers are lined with rose coloured silk, so is the pouch bag, which slides out under the two drawers.

The lower drawer possesses a tray, which lifts up and down by two silver rings, which rings, ingeniously disappear as the tray sinks into its place. I cannot say it is a pretty piece of furniture, but it is so beautifully made, that it is a positive pleasure to open and shut the drawers and to play with the little silver rings.

It is too modern to be of value, but in studying furniture, one needs to watch its gradual evolution even in the ugly early 19th century.

Besides this table, I have a splendid chair of unusual dimensions made by the same firm, and in the same year.

It is of mahogany and thickly padded, being covered with scarlet leather. It extends in such a manner as to make a most luxurious bed, and all the mechanism works as smoothly as the day it left the maker's hands.

By pressing under the padded arms, the back sinks back to a horizontal position, a large foot rest comes out, and by adjustment, joins the seat in front, so making a bed seven feet long and $3\frac{1}{2}$ feet wide.

I remember that all we children convalesced on this wonderful couch-like chair, and we considered it a great distinction to be allowed to lie there, almost worth being ill for, and we looked with kindly condescension at the less distinguished healthy members of the circle.

I have not left myself much room to speak of the many other tables that began to be in use in the 18th century, and I must be drawing this chapter to a close, but I should like to remind you of a convenient kind that even now is occasionally to be met with ; I mean the dumbwaiter—this consists of two or three circular tables—tapering to the top on a centre pole, sometimes the tables revolve, sometimes are fixed ; in either case it is a very useful piece of furniture for a flat dining room, combining in itself the uses of a sideboard and a butler's tray. N.B.—I think the butler's tray is an invention of the evil one, it takes up an immensity of space, and has an agreeable way of doubling up as to its legs, which spells disaster.

These dumb-waiters are now usually to be found in country inns, and sometimes find their way into provincial auctions. They are certainly worth having, and worth six or eight pounds if in good condition.

" Pie crust " and " dish top " tables are also desirable possessions, being small and folding up into but little space against the wall.

I think the terms " dish top " and " pie crust " really come to us from America, where they display great ingenuity in fitting suitable names to all kinds of furniture.

The " pie crust " had an ornamental moulding round the edge, very often scolloped out, and these scollops, as we see from pictures, were meant to accommodate the small cups and saucers that were fashionable at that time.

The " dish top " had also a moulding, but it was quite plain, and had the appearance of being turned over like a hem, and there were no scollops.

It seems probable that these tables first made their appearance about 1740 or 1750 ; some of them have the centre pillar well carved, and the knees of the three legs springing from it have acanthus carving and cabochons. A small kind of brass bolt and pin secures the slab in proper position and this being removed, the table falls flat and stands comfortably against the wall.

PART II

HOW TO COLLECT OLD POTTERY AND GLASS

To collect old china, pottery and glass is in some respects more difficult and in some others easier than getting together a small collection of furniture.

It is in this way easier, the articles are small and more portable and easily accommodated than chairs, tables, bureaux, etc., but, and this is a large but for the modest collector, everyone knows the great value of old china and pottery, and so pieces do not hang long on hand in the shops. It is only of late years that the public has woken up to the idea that earthenware is of value, thirty years ago it was despised by all but the real connoisseurs. I always go on the principle that my readers know nothing, and wish to learn the first rudiments concerning whatever subject we are considering, for that is the way I like to be taught myself, nothing is more provoking to me than to read in some learned book, "as you all know," when I do not know at all, and got the book on purpose to learn.

So to begin at the beginning, porcelain, unless it is exceptionally thick, is more or less transparent, but earthenware is always opaque.   Keep this fact always before your mind.

There is very little marking of pottery.   The early slip ware was sometimes signed, but usually there is no mark until we come to Wedgwood, who very generally marked his productions simply WEDGWOOD impressed or " Wedgwood and Bentley" during the lifetime of his valued partner, Thomas Bentley.

A good many of Ralph Wood's figures are signed too, but speaking broadly there are but few marks to help you and you must learn to do without them ;   study your subject well, and accustom your eye and touch to do without them.

I only aspire to give you an easy start on the road, with a little very simple knowledge, and thus give you a taste for deeper things.   My books are intended as an " apéritif," as the French call their before-dinner drinks, which are meant to stimulate a sluggish appetite.   So I, too, hope that my little efforts will tempt you later to attack with appetite such books as I indicate at the end of this chapter.

One piece of advice I am most anxious you should absorb, and that is make friends of all small dealers, and such men as buy up the poor possessions of those who are compelled to move house suddenly, or who, in some financial crisis, are obliged to part, one after another, with their cherished household gods.

This special kind of mean and shabby secondhand shop is not quite so likely to yield finds in the way of pottery, and glass, as furniture, but they are not to be neglected, usually if we have a stroke of luck it is just when and where we least expect it.

I often think, in looking at those slummy little shops, what sad tragedies of broken lives, and brave struggles against misfortune, they conceal; the bitter struggle to keep the head above water, and at last, the collapse under overwhelming odds, and the visit to the dealer " round the corner," always waiting like a spider in his web for the distressed fly of circumstances, there to sell with many a heart pang, mother's clock, grandfather's old chair, or those decanters " that used to belong to Great-Aunt Simpson."

I always remember, for it made a most painful impression on me, a scene at the death of an old dependant of my father's. Owing to the stupidity of her landlady (their colossal non-intelligence is something beyond belief), the old lady's sudden death had not been at once reported to us, and though immediately we received the news, my father sent me to her, she had been dead two days, and the same intelligent landlady had entirely failed to make the undertaker understand that his bill would be paid, so, before promising the funeral, he sent a man in to see what her possessions were worth.

I arrived in the nick of time, and I shall not easily forget the scene that greeted my eyes.

Her clothes were spread on the chairs, and table, and on the bed, actually beside the dead woman were a copper kettle and a tiny silver saucepan. I was young and impulsive then, and over the scene that followed it is as well to keep a discreet silence. At any rate I had the bitter satisfaction of turning the man out with contumely, and employing a different undertaker.

I have often thought of that scene as I look at the flotsam and jetsam from lives that have " gone under," at these smaller shops.

But to return—always make friends with dealers, whether small or great, I have always done this myself, for though not a collector (having already far too many treasures in my flat), I have done a good deal in the way of helping others.

I establish friendly relations first, that is not difficult with a little tact ; after you have succeeded thus far, buy some trifle once or twice and you will be allowed the run of the shop ; interest the owner in your tastes and try to find out what are his. Leave a stamped and addressed envelope with him, and get his promise to let you know if anything of the kind you like comes in his way.

I have always found dealers quite human, and surprisingly like other people, not by any means the conscienceless sharks they are often described ; they like a bargain, of course, but so do we ; is not that the very reason we are in their shops?

In transactions concerning valuable articles, and with well known dealers, you must always ask for a warranty—the failure to comply with this request would at once make me pause.

With small secondhand dealers, however, who are those with whom, probably, you will have most to do, there would be no question of a warranty ; they very often do not know anything of their wares of this kind, and cannot go beyond the statement, that such and such a thing is " wonderful old."

You may very often find nice little bits of pottery, an old Toby jug, or a Staffordshire cottage or figure, animal or human, in small provincial towns, not in villages, the villages have been drained dry by the dealers.

I recommend small provincial towns as a good hunting ground, because of late years the rush to London has caused the sudden, or gradual (as the case may be) disappearance of the natives from the neighbourhood, to realize as, they fondly hope, golden harvests in the streets of London.

This causes in many cases the sale of everything, so as to avoid the expense of moving goods, and also to insure the receipt of a few pounds of ready money.

Curiously enough tea services are very seldom met with at small shops : it seems that whatever else the owner will part with, these at any rate are kept sacred ; they have been so often a wedding present either to themselves, or their forbears, and so, come storm, come sun, those they will retain.

Do not begin to buy until you have acquired at any rate a little knowledge. One of my pleasant and really very enthralling occupations is to give opinions as to the age and " social standing " of various curios. Sometimes very valuable things are sent to me, and sometimes great rubbish. A year or two ago a lady sent me the cracked lid of a pomatum pot, about 40 or 50 years old, very common and bad in style, evidently belonging to a toilet set, such as one sees now only in lodging houses. She sent it, she said, for my opinion, but with the courage of absolute ignorance she added, " I consider it to be of Henri-deux ware."

Very likely, and no blame to you, you do not know what Henri-deux ware is, any more than she did. Well ! the delightful point of the story is, that Henri-deux ware, as its name implies, was made early in the 16th century. It was a most exquisite and delicate craft, and has always been somewhat of a mystery ; even *where* it was made is not really known, there are various suppositions, but no proof. There are only 65 pieces known to exist, and each one is well known to all connoisseurs. I must not linger to tell you about it now except to say that any one possessing even a very small piece, could sell it for such a sum that they could eat the bread of idleness for the rest of their days. So I leave you to imagine what answer I gave the owner of the cracked pomatum pot.

If you manage to get together a few pieces of pottery, be very careful of it, for once broken it is difficult to mend. Some kinds break like biscuit, and shatter all to pieces.

In olden days it was considered of no account, was not taken care of and thus it is rather difficult to find now.

With regard to old glass, even now it is not very popular with amateur collectors ; a few years ago, good cut glass was easily found of reliable quality, but lately, especially since Mr. Hartshorne's monumental work was issued, collectors have sprung up on all sides and dealers are keen over old glass, and to such an extent has trade increased that " fakers " are improving their shining hours by most clever and ingenious reproductions, especially of those beautiful drinking glasses that have ruby and sapphire threads, running up their stems.

I have never ventured to buy one of these, they are too doubtful ; the real ones were rare always, so suspicion fills one's mind when they are discovered on all sides.

Waterford glass is, perhaps, more esteemed than any other—see the chapter on cut glass. With luck, you may pick up a small piece here and there, a sugar bowl of the kind that used to live in a tea caddy, between the two divisions for black and green tea, a celery glass, which, long despised, has come down to being used as a flower vase, small spirit bottles, one of twins perhaps, also disregarded because the companion is gone, and occasionally an odd sauce bottle may be discovered. What I like best of all are the cream ewers, they seem to have been made in hundreds, both in England and Ireland, and still many exist to gladden our eyes. If your taste lies in the direction of cut glass, persuade your dealer always to let you know if any comes his way, he will soon take an interest in you, and try to help forward your collection, and his own pocket at the same time. Sometimes, though not often, good decanters are seen, odd ones, generally despised, because of the disappearance of the twin, they are always worth buying, and often patient search will discover the twin, or one so nearly alike, that they will pass very well for a pair.

BIBLIOGRAPHY

*English Earthenware . . . *A. H. Church*
The Life of Josiah Wedgwood *Llewellyn Jewitt*
The Life of Josiah Wedgwood *E. Meteyard*
The Art of the Old English
    Potter . . . . *M. L. Solon*
English Earthenware and
    Stoneware . . . *William Burton*
*Chats on English Earthenware . . . . *Arthur Hayden*

Staffordshire Pots and Potters
                    G. W. and F. A. Rhead
Old English Pottery   .   .   *Frank Freeth*
The Wood Family of Burslem   *Frank Falkner*
Old Leeds Pottery *Joseph R. and Frank Kidson*
Two Centuries of Ceramic Art
    in Bristol   .   .   .   *H. Owen*
The "Burlington" Magazine
The "Connoisseur" Magazine
*English Table Glass   .   .   *Percy Bate*
Old English Glasses   .   .   *Albert Hartshorne*
Glass   .   .   .   .   *Edward Dillon*
*Early English Glass   .   *Daisy Wilmer*
Two Centuries of Ceramic Art
    in Bristol   .   .   *Hugh Owen*
Old Derby Porcelain and its
    Artist Workmen   .   .   *Frank Hurlbutt*
Old Spode   .   .   .   *Thomas G. Cannon*
Old Glass and How to Collect
    it   .   .   .   .   *J. Sydney Lewis*

K

CHAPTER IV

ENGLISH EARTHENWARE

I PASS over all the earliest stages of pottery making as being quite outside the scope of this book; for those who are meaning to study the subject thoroughly, there are plenty of splendid books, but if I went into the consideration of the early beginnings of the craft, I should need to fill a large book, rather than one section of a small volume.

At page 132 you will find a list of useful books, with a cross against the cheaper ones. One which I have read with the greatest interest and profit, and which I am sure would be useful, even to beginners, is "Staffordshire Pots and Potters" by the brothers Rhead. I think it so instructive, and at the same time so interesting, that I have quoted several times from it, by kind permission of Mr. G. W. Rhead.

In the preface, in a few well-chosen lines, he points out the reason of the curiosity and interest that has always been felt in the Potteries, and the various arts and crafts carried on there.

"The district," he says, "known as the "Potteries, with its contradictory characteristics,

" its beauty and ugliness, its enterprise and
" lethargy, its humour and stolidity, quaintness,
" squalor, and prosperity—is teeming with in-
" teresting matter, not alone to those connected
" with the ceramic arts, but to the ordinary
" citizen.   This is amply confirmed by the interest
" evinced, by the fragmentary (and often un-
" authoritative) records of incidents connected
" with potters and potting."—N.B.—This is
rather crushing, the cap seemed to descend in a
good fit on my head at once.   I feel sure he
would consider my humble efforts " fragmentary "
but I think and hope, not unauthoritative !

" The craft itself," he continues, " is peculiarly
" fascinating, from the element of mystery
" which has been inseparably connected with
" the potter's art of all times.   Its complexity,
" its variety and the numbers of processes,
" necessitating a considerable knowledge of
" chemistry, of physics, and of art—both plastic
" and pictorial—make it far more comprehensive
" than any other craft or industry.   Moreover,
" accident, chance and investigation are always
" leading to fresh discoveries, chemical and
" technical, and the attempt to preserve such
" secrets have often provoked devices for their
" discovery, of a dramatic and romantic nature !
" The authors may perhaps claim to be peculiarly
" well fitted for the task they have set them-
' selves, as they are natives of the district they
" endeavour to describe, and have been closely

connected with potters and potting all their
"lives. They are natives in the fullest sense,
"their forbears having dwelt in North Stafford-
"shire for at least four centuries."

Mr. Rhead has also in his family a grand
collection of pottery of all kinds, and he writes in
that pleasant manner which shows the author's
own interest in his subject.

To proceed—I pass over the inevitable Roman
period in potting, and leave the student to make
that his own—it is a very necessary study to the
understanding of the craft, but want of space
forbids including it here.

It is most strange to find everywhere traces—
no matter in what direction we go—of the
Romans ; they were like a veritable swarm of
locusts, no place escaped their presence—personally it rather provokes me, I always want to
get behind them, and I never can succeed in my
endeavour.

I regard with abhorrence local museums of this
country, and on the Continent, full of chips and
morsels of pottery, having no beauty either of
colour or shape, labelled *Roman period*. Connoisseurs, and those who fain would be considered such, go into quite hysterical raptures
over a broken fragment some four inches square ;
it may, when entire, have been beautiful and
decorative, but it certainly is not so now.

I am aware that the learned ones would mark
me down as a Philistine and regard me super-

ciliously as one beneath contempt, but I have the courage of my opinions, and say that though it is necessary to study the Roman period thoroughly if you intend to get a proper grasp of the subject of pottery, it is, nevertheless, to my commonplace mind, rather a weariness to the flesh.

There is a small but excellent collection of Roman pottery and glass in the British Museum, better arranged and more interesting than is usual in such places.

It is true, however, that we owe the Romans incalculable thanks for their teaching and influence, and without them we should never have had the countless varieties of pottery that now delight our eyes. I admit all that gratefully, but I remember, and retain bitter grudges, against the boring people on the Continent, who, on many grievous occasions, have insisted upon my going into ecstasies over Roman temples, arenas, etc. Ah! and over Etruscan remains often of infinite-simal proportions, and doubtful authenticity.

I am sure some of my readers must at one time or another have suffered from the " instructive " man. He flourishes largely in Italy, and is almost invariably an Englishman. When I encounter the man with a mission to instruct, I fly from him as from a pestilence. He usually has a respect-able following, many listen to him from the com-mercial feeling that they are getting something for nothing, and a still larger number are drawn within his net, by virtue of a kind of magnetic attraction, and a laudable feeling that they do not wish to appear rude.   But I *can* appear rude, and I run from him without compunction ; once mounted on his hobby, especially if it is the Roman period, or Etruscan remains, he rides—you know where !   You may perish with cold, be swamped with rain, be languishing for your tea, that monster cares not, he goes on like the brook " for ever."

Of the Saxon pottery we know very little, and it is only by the 12th and 13th centuries that we find the influence of the Normans telling on the industry, in consequence of the monastic settlements they had established.   They introduced refinements hitherto unknown, and so created a market for different goods.

In earliest times, all the family sat round one rude pot or basin, and helped themselves unabashed with their fingers from this common receptacle, but the first Normans introduced the luxury of separate bowls, and so, by slow degrees, the need created the supply.

Pottery of the Norman period is naturally very scarce.   There is in the Victoria and Albert Museum a truly charming jug, green glazed, in the form of a knight on horseback.   The horse is of a very strange anatomy, the legs seemed to prove a great difficulty, the effect is somewhat that of a seal, but even the bridle is carefully represented.   Mr. Rhead thinks it is as early as

the time of our Henry II. We find that after the
dissolution of the monasteries, the potters, no
longer under the protection, and to some extent,
perhaps, the control of the monks, began to come
more to the front, made a much greater variety
of articles, and sold them, how, when and where
they pleased.

It must have been a great difficulty in those
days, as it continued to be even up to the establishment of the Trent and Mersey canal, in 1870,
to convey the pottery to any mercantile centre,
indeed it seems to have been sold almost entirely
by pedlars at that time.

Mr. Falkner, in " The Wood family of Burslem," gives an illustration of a pottery pedlar
carrying a crate of his wares on his back. It
seems a very rough affair, and could only have
contained very little merchandise ; the poor pedlar
had to tramp many weary miles over the atrocious
roads of Staffordshire to earn very small sums.

Later on, and up to the opening of the canal,
the wholesale trade was carried on by the employ-
ment of pack horses, who often fell exhausted and
died, as they struggled mile after mile over roads
so deep in ruts that wheeled traffic was out of the
question. It was in Elizabeth's time that various
causes led to the establishment of potters in a
large group, in that district we now call the Potteries.

The first group established was at Tunstall and
Longton, no doubt because these places were near

the highways to London, Liverpool, etc., they were also near to a coal supply—coal digging was just beginning to be a recognised industry. The remoteness of the districts in Staffordshire where pottery was chiefly made, is, no doubt, fortunately responsible for the distinctive character of the articles made.

These simple potters saw few outsiders, whereas at Fulham and Lambeth, the makers came under the influence of Continental workers.

The bellarmines, or grey beard jugs, were made in large quantities, but there seems nothing to connect them with Staffordshire, they probably all came from Fulham, which, from its position, was much more open to the influence of foreigners.

Of the Tudor period, earthenware showed no great variety, buff colour was the commonest, and there was an orange red, and a bright green. These three tints still constitute the main scheme of colour in the larger number of Continental pieces.

Of the Stuart period, we get some very quaint and illuminating pieces of information from Plott's " History of Staffordshire," 1686. He has a good deal to say of the early making of slip ware, and the mottled glaze, which must probably have given Whieldon his first ideas for splashed, agate and tortoise-shell ware.

It seems that in Burslem and the surrounding district one of the principal trades was in butter pots, used presumably in the same way as in the present day, for the preservation of a winter store of salt butter.

At this period the earthenware became, in some instances, but by no means always, more artistic in form, and there are some Pilgrim's bottles and candlesticks that are really pretty. These bottles were made with ears, through which a strap passed, so that the vessel could be slung over the back, and, to facilitate matters, they were of a flattened shape.

The idea still exists in parts of Italy. I bought a very picturesque one from Chioggia, not far from Venice. It is, however, round, because not being needed for a pilgrim who tramped the roads, the flattened shape is not necessary, it being usually hung on the mast by the fishermen who chiefly use them.

Most people know the heavy grey stoneware splashed with blue, to which we apply the term *grès de Flandres*. In old days, as in the present, much was " made in Germany," though probably the larger quantity really did come from Flanders. This particular ware was also made at Fulham, but only to a limited extent.

The greater number of pieces of this kind which seem beyond doubt to be English, are not earlier than about 1660 and 1665, and some a good deal later, but there exist one or two fine specimens, mounted in silver, of an earlier date.

SLIP WARE. Of the early slip ware of the 17th century we have many examples in our public collections. Dwellers in London have the opportunity at the British Museum of studying a small but most representative collection of earthenware, and china, and the fact that it is small is, to my mind, an advantage. The student does not become confused by seeing such a mass before him, but can give time to each small section, until he has mastered it.

Of this early period jugs are plentiful, they were the common drinking vessels of the time, with from two to eight or ten handles, and were so made, in order that they might easily pass round a table, after the manner of a loving cup.

The smaller ones incline in form to a mug, and the bigger are often rather curious, and varied in shape, and including those unpleasant varieties called puzzle jugs, especially designed in the rough humour of the age, to get a laugh at the drinker; the same elegant form of practical joke was shown in the use of the glass yard—see chapter on cut glass. In the Salisbury Museum (a very good one for a provincial town) there is a jug with four handles, and a charming inscription, evidently it was made for a christening present. It is a warm madder brown and round it is written

Here is the gest of the Barley Korne
Glad ham I the cild is borne.

I. G.
1692.

I never knew the meaning of " taking him down a peg " until I studied jugs, but now it is clear to me. The expression comes from the old custom among topers of seeing who could drink the most, and to assist this unrighteous habit, small lumps, or " pegs " of clay were placed at intervals, inside the vessel, and he who could drink at one draught to a further " peg " than his rival, was spoken of as " taking him down a peg."

The process of making slip ware, which attained a great popularity in the 17th century, is curious ; the pattern on the vessel was produced thus—sometimes first roughly drawn on the article and sometimes not, but left to the native talent of the artist, then the light coloured " slip " was placed in a little vessel, almost identical with the invalids' feeding cup of to-day, the spout of which enabled the lighter clay to come through in a small stream, big or little, according to the pattern required, and when a stop in the design was needed an abrupt end was put to the supply by the artist putting his thumb over a hole in the top.

In due course the slip was painted on, and some painted pieces were produced at the earlier period, though the method was not the usual one.

The feeding cup method was almost identical with that employed in the present day to ornament birthday, wedding and christening cakes and the legends " Many happy returns of the day," " Good luck to you," and " Welcome, little stranger," are produced in exactly the same manner as the old wares of the 16th and 17th centuries were ornamented, only the medium is different !

Mr. Burton, in " A History and Description of English Earthenware," gives a good short description of what we may look for in the old slip ware. " Every collector is familiar with the large " deep dishes having wide borders, decorated with " elaborate trellis patterns in white slip, the centre " being filled with uncouth renderings of Royal " personages, cavaliers and ladies, heraldic beasts, " or broadly treated floral devices, and the quaintly " decorated cups, jugs, posset pots and toy cradles, " generally bearing inscriptions in raised slip letters, " which can be traced to various primitive potters " of this region. The majority of these pieces, " especially the dishes, bear in broad slip letters " names generally supposed to be those of their " makers, and from the frequency with which the " name Toft appears, the appellation ' Toft ware ' " has been rather foolishly applied to the whole " group of slip decorated pottery . . . . ."

I have a great weakness for pottery with inscriptions and verses, and slip ware is peculiarly rich in them. The British Museum has quite a large collection of these, the spelling generally presenting many varieties. One rather large jug has these words encircling it, " When this you see remember me. Obeay God's wourd." Another, evidently a gift from a sweetheart, runs thus, " Ann Draper, This cup I made for you, and so no more. I.W., 1707." This is delightfully succinct, the swain evidently felt that no one could have turned the matter better, and further words were superfluous.

Another slip inscription on a dish is replete with good advice, " Keep within cumpas, and you shall be sure To avoid many troubles which others indure."

Then comes a dish of later date, 1726, with an elaborate conventional pattern of leaves, and at the top, a bird of archaic appearance, firmly grasped with four large stumpy fingers, whilst two other birds sit defiantly on twigs of the design. Above the captive bird is S.M., and underneath, enclosed in a circle " One bird : in The : hand is worth Two : in the bush." There must be some little romance hidden here, if we only had the clue to it.

One of the handsomest pieces in the British Museum collection is a large Wrotham jug, embellished with medallions and lozenges of various shapes, this was a very favourite decoration, wet pieces of clay were put on of the desired shape and stamped with all kinds of designs, such as the Tudor rose and coats of arms.

Wrotham is in Kent, but the ware from that place and from Staffordshire resemble each other so closely that it is difficult to say which is which, unless some name is inscribed on the pieces.

In Fig. 23 I show you a Thomas Toft dish representing a mermaid with a finely developed tail. This piece is in the Victoria and Albert Museum, and has the potter's name, as you see, at the bottom, a trellis pattern round the edge and that characteristic ornamentation between the figure and the rim-like flattened oval heads, which Mr. Rhead likens to sausages, and a very good similitude it is. His description of Toft's mannerisms is so excellent, and so descriptive, that I give it you in full.

"We know well the faces, which are alike, the "eyes and nose like a pair of scissors, often done "with one continuous line; we know the curious "hands and feet and the favourite *motif* between "the border and the principal subject, shaped some-"thing like a string of sausages. . . . . Although "Toft's personages have all the same face (an ex-"tremely quaint face, however) they are generally "recognisable as the persons for whom they are "intended. It may be by means of the wig, the "lace, the crown, the trunk hose, or all in combina-"tion—no matter—the *tout ensemble* amusingly "suggests the subject. His mermaid in the South "Kensington Museum has the same face as King "Charles and Queen Anne, and a most extraordin-"ary tail. To quote the famous ' bull,' ' She has "plenty av back bone, an knows how to bring ut "to the front,' for there is a distinct vertebral arti-"culation from the neck to the centre of the torso. "But she is a mermaid all the same, and, more than "that, a good piece of decoration. Toft's figures

FIG. 23.—SLIP DISH—THE MERMAID.

FIG. 24.—SLIP DISH—LADY AND GENTLEMAN.

" are not imitations, but abstractions ; not copies,
" but symbols, in the sense that heraldic achieve-
" ments are symbols rather than portraits of the
' objects they symbolize."

I think, if you study well the specimens in the
British Museum and in the Victoria and Albert
Museum you will recognize the value of this
description.

Whether Ralph Toft was a brother or son of
Thomas is not known, nor is it certainly decided
whether they had a little place of their own, or
only worked for others.

Mr. Rhead, who has such exceptional opportunities of knowing much that is hidden from
others, says that his family owns property at
Tinkers Clough, the place closely associated with
Toft's name, and that his opinion is, that Toft had
small works close by ; also Mr. Solon speaks of a
dish with " Thomas Toft, Tinkers Clough—I
made it 166—" scratched on the back.

How the present generation blesses the Tofts
for signing their work ; if everyone had done that,
there would have been no need for experts.

The Tofts were certainly the best known pro-
ducers of slip ware—but naturally (to say nothing of the fine Wrotham examples) all the existing and succeeding potters imitated them, and
here we begin to get into difficulties. Some fine
dishes and jugs, etc., carry names, but not being
well-known, like the Tofts, we do not really know
whether the name is that of the maker, or the

purchaser. Ralph Simpson, of Burslem, is well-known, but there are other Simpsons whose names appear.

A potter called Glass, too, is well-known and he seems to have made a speciality of cradles—ordered evidently as Christening presents, just as we give silver mugs, forks and spoons now-a-days.

It is worth nothing that the primitive method of decorating pottery with slip has never really fallen into disuse, seeing that we have still the brown baking dishes splashed, and decorated, though very roughly, with yellow twirly-gigs, and sometimes they are rudely notched round the edges, which must be the degenerate survival of the beautiful gophered handles and rims of the old Tygs.

These baking dishes, divided in compartments, are used in artisans' families for the cooking of the Sunday dinner, and we meet them *en route* for the baker's with meat and Yorkshire pudding in one division, and potatoes in another. They are usually offered for sale in poor and populous neighbourhoods on cheap-jack's stalls.

In Fig. 24 you see a very handsome and quaint dish, made presumably by William Talor, but exactly in the Toft manner. This lady and gentleman are evidently not royal, for there are no crowns ; the gentleman seems to carry a single sausage in his right hand and to hold the lady's elbow with his left, but look at his legs and feet, they hardly seem adequate to supporting his

FIG. 25.—TYG, PUZZLE JUG AND CANDLESTICK.

FIG. 26.—ENGLISH DELFT PLATE, SACK BOTTLE AND PLATTER.

weight. The lady carries a bag in her left hand, which, as space is limited, flies upside down without difficulty, her waist is of the wasp-like order, and her hair most luxuriant. There are several other well-known dishes, William and Mary, William alone and Queen Anne, are favourite subjects and " the pelican in her piety " is a familiar one—this last is a wonderfully graphic piece, all the greedy little pelicans are feasting on their mother's blood in the most voracious manner, and there is great vitality in their eyes and grasp of claws. There are no sausages, but quite a new idea in the *Fleur-de-Lys* behind the pelican's neck.

In Fig. 25 you see two other examples of the slip ware and a puzzle jug of the early part of the 18th century. The design of this last is curious, representing the Serpent and Dove. It is always said that there is one position with these jugs in which you can drink from it with impunity and not suffer a deluge, but I cannot discover it !

The jug is a good example, dated as you see 1663, with various ornamentations of the Tudor rose, scrolls and conventional flowers. You will notice, if you turn to the chapter on glass, and look at the beautiful Chastleton covered cup, that the form of the handles is exactly similar, though the glass ones are beautifully quilled or gophered, whichever term you like to apply to their pretty decoration. There is some question as to the age of the charming Chastleton example, and it is possible—in agreement with some family

L

traditions—that it is older than the early part of Charles II. reign, but I think everything seems to point to that time as the date of its creation.

The candlestick is of about the same age as the jug, and is in perfect condition. I could linger long on this subject, it is full of fascination, but we must pass on.

FULHAM WARE. At about the same time as the Dutch brothers Elers were working at Burslem (of whom I shall speak presently) and for about twenty years previously, John Dwight was potting at Fulham and making his ware " vulgarly called Cologne ware," a kind of stoneware that we call *grès-de-Flandres*. Exact information of the history of Dwight's career is still to seek, we know, however, that he was a gentleman by birth and education, an M.A. of Christchurch, Oxford, and seems to have acted as secretary to various dignitaries of the church, before starting his business, and one wonders when and how he came to have time to acquire the exact knowledge he possessed of his craft.

The year when he set up works at Fulham is not known, but we do know that in 1671 he obtained a patent for the making of " transparent earthenware," so that it is clear he must have been working some time before that. This refers to an attempt of his, attended certainly with some measure of success, to make porcelain, in imitation of that which came from the East, but we must not stay to glance at this matter except to show that he was a clever man and full of resource.

He must have been a singular man, one does not believe all the strange stories told of him, but allowing for exaggeration, he must have been what we call a " crank."

He is supposed to have buried all his moulds and tools long before his death, partly in disgust at what he considered the small appreciation he had met with in his art, and partly because he wished to prevent anyone from copying his designs.

His output in the rough grey and blue Cologne ware was great, he made all sorts of jugs, mugs, bowls and bottles of this kind, but perhaps he is best known by his busts, especially the masterly one of Prince Rupert, a most vigorous and vital piece of work. It is really a mystery at what period in his busy life he could have found time to acquire the knowledge and skill shown in what came from his works.

There is in the British Museum a most charming little bust supposed to be that of Mrs. Pepys. I do not know on what this supposition rests, but having just waded—with immense enjoyment though—through six volumes of the gay ruffler's diary, I feel I know poor Mrs. Pepys fairly well and regard her bust as that of an old friend.

Poor woman, she died before she was thirty, worn out and heart broken, we cannot but suppose, by her clever husband's infidelities and callous indifference to her comfort. Dwight's bust

with Delft, had gradually grown from observing
the kind of pottery coming from Spain and Italy,
which was possessed of a white surface in many
cases that enhanced the colours placed upon it,
far better than the old brown and yellow pottery
of an earlier time, but equally surely, the distinguishing factor that at last produced Delft ware,
as it is best known, was the sight of " the blue
and white " porcelain brought from the east,
almost all of which passed through Holland.

Naturally, the Dutch, when they began to
imitate this, had no knowledge of the constituents
of porcelain, or the processes by which it was produced, nevertheless, in their dogged way, they
set about making as near an imitation as they
could.

They proceeded thus, the body of the piece
was made of the usual yellowish brown clay ;
this was fired to make it hard, and it was then
glazed with a thick whitish enamel, it was then
fired a second time to harden this glaze.

The main difference between the Dutch and
Lambeth Delft, is, that the English dark brown
clay did not absorb so well the opaque glaze,
because it was harder and less porous, with the
result that the reddish colour was inclined to
show through.   Dutch Delft is rare, valuable and
extremely decorative, and the same may be said
of the Lambeth variety.

An immense deal was brought over to England
from Holland, with which country at that time

there was a close connection, as shown by the Dutch fair held every year at Yarmouth.

Naturally, the next move was to try to set up an English " Delft " industry, and this must have been done before 1672, as we see by Charles' proclamation.

The locality was decidedly the Thames side, though we do not know the exact spot.

There is some reason to suppose that the first Lambeth Delft was made by Dutchmen, and that it only gradually became a settled English industry. We know there were factories at Bristol and Liverpool and all along the Thames side from Lambeth eastwards, but the precise spots escape us.

In the British Museum are some good examples, side by side with the Dutch. I like especially the one of William III. on a huge dish, bestriding a horse which has the long feathered fetlocks of the English cart horse. The monarch wears a prodigious wig, surmounted by an unstable crown, which will certainly fly off in the exertion of the leap which his majesty is executing—the aerial perspective being such that he appears to be flying over trees and fields.

In Fig. 26 you see on the right an octagonal plate, with unflattering portraits of William and Mary. Next to this is a wine flask, these can still be occasionally picked up, their shape is very pretty, and they usually have " claret " or " sack " printed on one side and often the date ; this one shows a coat of arms.

On the left is an example of the " merry man "
plates—this was a very favourite series, and we
meet with them over and over again. Sometimes they are round, sometimes octagonal in
shape, the latter are by far the more pleasing.
You can see two sets in the British Museum.
The set consists of six plates, with a line upon
each plate, thus :

" What is a merry man ?
" Let him do what he can.
" To entertain his guests,
" With wine and merry jests.
" But if his wife do frown
" All merriment goes down."

There are still many of these plates about, and
also the wine flasks, but I do not think you are
at all likely to meet with the large dishes and
platters.

There is an idea, but without real proof, that
Delft was made in Staffordshire also, and Shaw
says that the art of making it was introduced
there by Heath, of Lane Delph, in 1710. Certainly the name seems rather suggestive. We do
know, however, that in the early 18th century
both Bristol and Liverpool potters were making it.

Enormous numbers of drug pots must have
been made, to judge from the very considerable
number still to be found, but it seems probable,
from some distinctive touches, that many of
these really came from Italy, and we know that

Italian potters were particularly addicted to the making of them.

Snuff jars are also found occasionally, and very decorative and attractive they are. What has been said of Lambeth Delft will apply equally well to that made at Liverpool. The works there were in existence as late as 1760, when, seemingly, the manufacture was given up in favour of the cream coloured ware, so successfully made in Staffordshire.

SALT GLAZED WARE. With regard to the first appearance of salt glazed ware, both on the Continent and in England, the evidence is very conflicting. Experts hold widely different opinions, and it is beside the scope of this book to enter into the controversy.

Before the discovery of salt glazing, the glaze was produced by lead, or by some glassy substance.

It is necessary that you should know roughly how this ware was produced. The following passage is clear and simple, and occurs in Mr. Church's " English Earthenwares," a most valuable book, simple enough for a beginner to understand and, crowning charm of all, it is inexpensive, though fully illustrated.

" Of the English ceramic products which we " have so far been considering, the glaze, when it " occurs, has been produced either by lead or by a " glassy substance, generally by the former, ap- " plied in the form of powdered galena, the chief

" ore of lead, a compound of that metal with
" sulphur . . . but with the introduction of
" common salt as a glazing material, an entirely
" new step in ceramic progress was taken. This
" glaze we shall see could only be produced at a
" high temperature, and, in consequence, the ware
" to which it was applied must be of a kind to
" resist a great degree of heat without fusion, or
" even softening—in a word the *ware must be
" refractory*. Such a body, properly burnt, be-
" comes a stoneware, and is partially vitrified,
" showing in fact, when microscopically examined,
" a texture like that of true hard porcelain.
" Stoneware was not always glazed, nor, if glazed,
" always with salt . . . . still, the mention of
" stoneware always recalls the process of salt
" glazing."

With regard to the discovery of salt glazing
in England, which has made such an immense
difference in our earthenware, as I said before,
there are several theories, but none of them are
susceptible of positive proof.

For many years the brothers Elers, from Holland, were considered to be the introducers, and
it seems that Wedgwood was of that opinion,
but later research has a tendency to disprove this
assertion. Some have thought that instead of
introducing it into England, the Elers learnt
it themselves of Dwight, of Fulham, but on this
subject there is still no light. In Atkins' " History
of Manchester," published many years ago,

we read at page 526, " It was in the memory of
" some with whom a friend of ours was well ac-
" quainted that the inhabitants of Burslem flocked
" with astonishment to see the immense volumes
" of smoke which rose from the Dutchmen's ovens
" on casting in the salt, a circumstance which suf-
" ficiently shows the novelty of this practice in
" Staffordshire potteries." This is, of course, true,
but it is still quite possible that the Elers learnt
the process from Dwight, who made a kind of
salt glazed ware, which process Mr. Solon suggests
he probably learnt from Continental workers. It
is only a supposition that the Elers, on landing
in England, made the acquaintance of Dwight,
but very many circumstances seem to suggest it.

Dwight was a most enterprising man, and often
employed foreign workmen, and it is very possible
that salt glazing was known at Fulham long
before it was used in Staffordshire ; news travelled
slowly then, and potting secrets were jealously
guarded. It is difficult to separate truth from
fiction in speaking of the Elers ; it does not
require any great acumen to see that the settlement of foreigners in their midst was regarded
by the old native potters with extreme jealousy,
and everything done at the secluded works at
Bradwell Wood was observed with critical eyes,
that sometimes saw more than actually occurred.

The mere fact that these strangers showed an
evident desire for secrecy at once prejudiced their
neighbours against them, and started all kinds of

wild stories that probably had little foundation in fact. Therefore, we must accept traditions concerning the Elers with some grains of salt.

They came to England in or about 1689, either with, or immediately after, William of Orange, and their advent undoubtedly gave a great impetus to the pottery industry. They were men of good family and combined energy, taste and probity.

They settled near Burslem, at Bradwell Wood, a very secluded spot, but well furnished with suitable clay. Here they could carry on (as they thought) their potting operations with absolute secrecy.

Their ware, as far as our knowledge goes, was of a peculiarly fine kind of red clay, but they did not sign their work, and it is now difficult to say which pieces were actually made by the Elers, and which by their imitators.

Besides this red ware, they made a good deal of a much lighter kind, which is by no means so attractive. There was a sad national loss of Elers ware in the disastrous fire at the Alexandra Palace.

We see in all collections beautiful examples of the smooth, deep red ware, with finely turned lines round the shoulders and bases, but whether they were all actually the work of the Dutch brothers is open to doubt. They might well have been made by Astbury or some other of their many imitators.

They did not work in England after 1710, at least, not in Staffordshire. There is, however, an idea—though without proof—that John Elers, after leaving Staffordshire, was associated with the glass works at Chelsea, started by the Duke of Buckingham, and that some years later he had a china and glass shop in Dublin. If the Elers brothers really did introduce salt glazing into Staffordshire it seems certain they employed the process very little themselves.

They worked but a short time among us, but they left a strong impress on the potting craft, and certainly it was from them that Astbury got his ideas.

Having considered the evidence for the Elers having taught us salt glazing, I like to turn to the picturesque story of the pork and the boiling brine! At least let us keep pure and undefiled a few of our youthful traditions. In these latter times, unkind historical research (not always correct though all the same) has done so much to shake our comfortable convictions, so firm and crude in youth, that everything, especially virtue and vice, were divided into black and white ; of that we were sure, but now behold, as we grow into middle life we are astonished to find that there are so many shades of grey !

We are now taught that Lucretia Borgia was a model of the domestic virtues, that Cromwell and William III. were noble souls, whose actions were never sullied by a thought of personal aggrandizement, and who were actuated solely and entirely by the exalted motive of benefiting the down-trodden sufferers of England.

All the same, I cling to the pork curing story, though Mr. Solon will have none of it. On the other hand Mr. Rhead, who knows his Stafford-shire so well, and every move of the potting industry, comforts me as to the old tradition, for he says, " there is nothing really unlikely in the story."

This is the story, given with some minor variations by many chroniclers. It seems that a farm servant (even identified by some writers as working for a Mr. Joseph Yates) about the same time as the arrival of the Elers, was one day pre-paring a strong brine for the pickling of pork in an earthenware pot over the fire. In the absence of the maid, the brine boiled over from the red-hot pot ; it was left to cool, and the discovery was made, that the earthenware was coated with a hard, bright glaze, " which washing and scraping failed to touch." Such is the story, and probably now we shall never know the real truth of the first appearance in Staffordshire of salt glazing. Whatever its origin, it was soon adopted by all the potters, and every kind of article was made with the process.

There is ample opportunity for study of speci-mens in the British Museum. First came a white ware, of a somewhat imperfect kind, having often a dull greyish tone in it. The first improvement was to have ornaments in relief, some of which are stamped with seals, and some made in moulds. Then what is known as scratched blue appeared, the pattern being incised with some instrument like a skewer, and the colour dusted into the little channels produced.

Thirdly came enamelling in colours, a very beautiful and brilliant style—a few pieces of this vivid kind wonderfully brightens a dark corner.

Then comes " graffito," where the whole piece is dipped in colour either lighter or darker (usually lighter) and the pattern scratched or cut through it to the ground below, and lastly, printing either in black, puce or sometimes red, and later on in almost all colours.

There are varieties of all these methods, and in some specimens the processes are mixed. The vast improvements in salt glazing resulting at last in charming pieces that bear a strong resemblance to Oriental porcelain which was at that time imported in such large quantities, is greatly due to Astbury, though he gained his knowledge by a dishonest fraud, in which he was joined by a man named Twyford.

Both these men were potters—and conceived the idea, apparently not in unison—of taking service with the Elers, and pretending to be idiots, or at any rate slow of understanding, so that they might be unsuspected and free to learn all they could of any new methods which came under their notice, whilst working at Bradwell.

It seems improbable that the Elers brothers would have employed idiots, but presumably they were supposed to be a little " soft "—far, indeed, from the truth.

At any rate, in some such way, these two men learnt all there was to know. Every night on returning home Astbury made careful notes of what he had seen and done. All this newly-acquired knowledge he soon turned to account, but it is to his son, Thomas, to whom no stigma of deceit attaches, to whom we are indebted for such a variety of designs, and ideas, and to him, and to Whieldon, must be accorded the credit of the rapid improvement in the decorative ware of Staffordshire.

The pieces, however, that I love best of all, and which are, alas, too few and precious to be found straying about ready to fall into the hungry grasp of the collector, are the early uncouth but life-like figures, such as the two so-called Pew groups, Fig. 27 and Fig. 28.

Fig. 27 is in the early imperfect white, about seven inches across. It is in the British Museum, where it can be enjoyed by all. A lady sits in the centre, with a hood and hoop, a wasp-like waist and tightly braced bodice, an attendant swain on each side crowned by a beautiful wig carefully curled on each side, and arranged over the brow as if with gophering irons, the lady holds her hands in a kind of pious coyness, she has two

FIG. 27.—PEW GROUP.

FIG. 28. PEW GROUP IN THE COLLECTION OF DR. SIDEBOTHAM, OF
BOWDON, CHESHIRE.

spots of brown on her cheeks, which, if you " pretend " very much like the marchioness, you may
imagine to be the tint of the damask rose. The
gentlemen, however, are unkindly left with the
sallow complexions given them by nature, un-
corrected by art, and the three pairs of eyes stare
stonily at the spectator.   It is a favourite piece of
mine, and I never visit the gallery without renew-
ing my acquaintance with the three patient
sufferers in the Pew—those were the days of
" Now, dear brethren, we arrive at the seven-
teenth division of my discourse." The other
group, Fig. 28, which is from the collection of Dr.
Sidebotham, and which by his kindness and that
of Mr. Frank Falkner I am enabled to show you,
is in some respects still more quaint and entertaining than the other. It is full of character and
vitality, but the work is rougher than in Fig. 27.
Mr. Rhead speaks thus of it : " This piece presents several variations on either the British
Museum's or Mr. Solon's specimens—the addition
of the bottle, doubtless to contain sustenance
during the sermon, and the three Brobdingnagian
masks on the back of the seat, together with the
general character of the whole. We have meditated deeply upon this ' Pew group,' and we have
come to the conclusion that it is *not* by the same
hand as the other two specimens, but rather by,
we will not say an imitator, but one who has seen
and wished to emulate the merits of the others.
We are of opinion that similar ones by this same

M

artist must exist, that the artist has trodden the same path before. The thing is altogether too skilful in certain ways. The lady's arms, and the gentleman's too, for that matter, are arrived at by means of a simple roll of clay, pinched at the ends to form the hands, but they are, nevertheless, singularly expressive. The three Brobdingnagians at the back are probably intended as a piece of humour, or are they celestial spirits (wingless because the artist doubted his own powers in this particular) intended to counteract in some mysterious way those which presumably are contained in the bottle, the artist placing little faith in the eloquence of the preacher ? However this may be the piece is a veritable masterpiece in its way, and represents the extreme high water mark of the humourously grotesque."

I think myself that though these special groups are called " Pew " groups, it is probable they are not so really, and that the wooden high-backed enclosure, in which the figures are seated, are just secular settles ; they are not in reality at all the shape of the old " horse box " pews of the 18th century, and the bottle and comic masks in Dr. Sidebotham's example do not certainly point to a church.

I have seen a third group which must have been made by the same hand as this last one, for the lady's striped skirt and quilted *revers* are identical ; the arms are of exactly the same worm-like construction, whilst the noses have the same

heavenward tendency. The gentleman is blow-
ing with great vigour upon bagpipes, apparently
to charm the lady, and this again does not seem
to point to the interior of a church.

After the early stages the salt glaze ware became much whiter, it was, however, somewhat
slow in arriving at that stage, not, indeed, till
about 1718 or 1720, when Astbury was thought
to have brought white clays from Dorsetshire
and Devonshire, and mixed them with that of
Staffordshire.

There are in the British Museum many examples
of the white ware, partly moulded and partly
stamped. There are teapots of all sorts, one or
two very quaint, with camels and houses combined. The odd idea of a cottage as a teapot,
with a camel's neck as spout, is most singular.
The cottage is quite complete, even to a chimney,
which forms the knob of the lid, but I like still
better the one representing a camel entire, with a
kind of howdah on his back. Here the mixed
idea as to decoration is most queer, the camel
shows a dreadfully hungry-looking set of well-
developed ribs and his howdah is strapped on
with practical thongs and buckles, but what can
we say of the curious floral designs that meander
all over his meagre body, and the head which resembles a snake's, and has no distant cousinship
even with that of a camel.

Those dear old potters had the courage of their
opinions, and if a thing to their minds was good,

suitable or not, it appeared on their pots and pans, and they mixed up religion and witchcraft, mythology and 18th century domestic scenes, classical figures and realistic flowers without a qualm. If a pattern was good, and fitted well into the space needing decoration, in it went, no matter what incongruous ideas it rubbed shoulders with.

The raised patterns were effected with moulds and these were often constructed of several separate pieces, causing seams and divisions, which apparent disadvantage the potters turned into the reverse by making them into panels with different designs, which perhaps, account for mythology and domestic life shouldering each other upon the same piece.

Much later we have the really decorative and beautiful enamelled examples of which I give you two specimens in Fig. 29, the one in the centre with the inscription " Success to Mr. John Calverly, of Leeds," is very brilliant, there is a great deal of bright turquoise blue about it, quite of the Sèvres tint ; the lip is of a soft pink, diapered in black, and on one side a gentleman is playing the flute, you can just see his legs, his music stand and the end of his flute, or rather it is a kind of miniature trumpet. The mug to the left is equally showy ; the bust of Frederick the Great is on a turquoise background, with a border of pink. The other mug is a humbler specimen and was probably made to celebrate a

FIG. 29.—SALT GLAZE JUG AND MUGS.

FIG. 30.—WHIELDON, ELEPHANT AND TEAPOT.
FIGURE OF SPRING BY NEALE AND CO.

wedding. Benjamin and Elizabeth Taylor look
out at us complacently, and between their heads
is inscribed, " If it be fild oftens, it will make us
merry. 1780."

Astbury's name is so intimately connected with
the best manufacture of salt-glazed ware that we
hear constantly of Astbury ware as if it were a
special kind of its own.   In one way this is true,
certainly, inasmuch as Thomas Astbury was the
man who worked up his wares to such a pitch
of perfection with the enamelled colours.   He
just improved and perfected what others had
begun.

John Astbury, the father of Thomas, after
having—as I have already explained—in con-
junction with Twyford, mastered by a trick the
potting secrets of the Elers brothers, set up for
himself, and worked on much the same lines as
they did.   He died about 1743, and his son,
Thomas, succeeded to his business in which he
worked for many years, always improving and
enlarging his father's scheme of colour, till he
gradually produced pieces of real beauty, and
delicacy, painted with enamel colours, and bearing
a considerable likeness to the porcelain of the
East, though always naturally failing to get the
white translucent ground work.

The early Astbury pieces of a rich reddish
chocolate may be the work of either of the father
or son, there is nothing that can tell us definitely.
The well-known piece called the Portobello bowl

was made to celebrate the capture of Portobello by Admiral Vernon in 1739, and as both potters were then working, it is uncertain who was the maker.

The Astbury grenadier, also in the British Museum, near to its family friend the bowl, is probably an early piece, and very likely made by Astbury *père*, but all the enamelled wares are the undoubted work of his son.

They also made black ware of the Elers type, and some that was marbled. Like all the potters of that time they tried their hand at everything.

If you are so fortunate as to possess a piece of the old salt glaze ware, or to have the chance of picking up such a piece, remember that it often exhibits a kind of pitting, the surface resembling somewhat the skin of an orange.

The best period was up to 1780. It was made long after that, but decline had set in, and we no longer see anything original.

WHIELDON'S WARES. "Thomas Whieldon was certainly the head and mainspring of a large school, we have imitations largely influenced by him, though retaining special characteristics of their own. Even such a giant in the art of potting as Josiah Wedgwood owed much to Whieldon ; he worked with him, and there saw the agate and tortoiseshell ware, that eventually he made on his own account at Etruria."

The above sentence is from Mr. Hayden's " Chats on Earthenware," and it summarises well the position of Whieldon in the potting world.

So many potters who subsequently became
men of repute, at one time or another worked
with Whieldon. Besides Josiah Wedgwood, may
be mentioned Spode, Heath, and Aaron Wood.

The tortoiseshell and agate wares are perhaps
those with which we chiefly associate Whieldon's
name, and very attractive they are, though lacking the brilliancy of Astbury's enamelled pieces.
So, too, the cauliflower, pineapple and melon
ware. Of these the cauliflower is the favourite,
and in these days, if a specimen comes on the
market, it commands a ready sale and a large
price. It is very ingenious and clever, but it
seems rather out of place to be pouring tea out of
a vegetable, just as in the salt glaze we have been
considering it is a trifle incongruous to be doing
the same from the interior of a camel, or out
of the side of a house. But these queer ideas
constitute half the charm of the old earthenware, and without them it would be a dull
affair.

As far as artistic beauty goes I think the tortoiseshell carries off the palm, other potters made
it, but none quite so successfully as Whieldon,
his colours were rich, somewhat subdued and
lacking the crudity shown in some other specimens, especially taking are the eight-sided plates
in this and the agate ware.

One cause, probably, of Whieldon's success was
his possession of the modest but invaluable gift
of discerning at once the talents of others, for,

as we know, he had as apprentices, and partners, much of the surrounding native talent.

Whieldon's account books, for which we are indebted to Mr. Llewellyn, are full of interest to the student of the 18th century. They throw a searchlight upon the social status of master and man, and upon the rate of wages at that time.

First come some entries as to Josiah Spode, which I quoted before, but I think you will forgive a repetition, as it is so very curious to read them, when we remember to what heights of talent and success Spode rose so quickly.

1749.

April 9.   Hired Siah Spoade to give him from
                this time to Martelmas next 2s. 3d.,
                or 2s. 6d. if he deserves it.

2d. year   0   2   9
3d. year   0   3   3
Pd. full earnest   0   1   0

Apparently this munificent payment was appreciated, he certainly must have " deserved " it, for the next entry three years later is,

1752.   Hired Josiah Spoad for next Martelmas.

Per week   0   7   0
I am to give him earn   0   5   0
Pd. in Part   0   1   0
Pd do   0   4   0

Two years later, as he continued deserving, we find him in quite a wealthy state, for he has £19 a year and £1 11s. 6d. earnest. I suppose this was a kind of retaining fee.

Another somewhat astonishing thing we learn from these accounts is that payment was made in kind—old clothes helping out the regular wages.

Here are a few entries proving this.

1749.

Feb. 14.   Then hired Thomas Dutton   o   6   6
               Pd 1 pr Stockins ......   o   3   6
               Pd do in 7yds Cloth ....   o   8   9

Feb. 28.   Then hired Robt. Gardner
               per week ....   o   6   6

I am to make his earnest about 5s. more in something.

1751.

April 6.   Hired Wm. Kent, per week   o   7   6
               To give in earnest ......   o   12   0
               Pd in part ....   o   1   6
               To give a new shirt at 16d. per yard.

You see it was all arranged on strictly commercial principles, the value of the material is accurately stated.

Then comes a vaguer bargain.

Dec. 26.   Then hired Cupit pr week   o   2   3
               Pd earnest ....   o   0   6

I am to give him a old pr stockins or something.

1753.

June 21. Hired Wm Marsh for 3 years. He is to have 10s. 6d. earnest each year and 7s. per week. I am to give a old coat or something abt 5s. value.

After some other particulars Whieldon adds, "nothing further unless I chuse to give him a old coat—he is to work for me at any time when I want."

These particulars, I think, cannot but be of general interest, when, as now, we have the whole country convulsed and trade brought to a standstill because unskilled labourers in many cases think £3 and even more per week, insufficient remuneration for their talents.

The exact date of starting Whieldon's works is not known, but it must have been before 1740 at Fenton Lowe, neat Stoke.

From 1754 to 1759 Wedgwood was a junior partner with Whieldon, and as he had invented a fine green glaze, as we see it now on old-fashioned dessert plates, he, no doubt, also helped in some improvements in the mottled agate, and tortoiseshell varieties, for which Whieldon was so famous.

It does not appear that, with the exception of the emerald glaze, Wedgwood originated anything special during this partnership, but he, no doubt, developed and improved what had been already started. There must have been a great simplicity in Whieldon's old-fashioned method of doing business, for, prosperous as he was, he did not disdain to travel himself with samples to the tradesmen with whom he did business.

His trade was large in various small articles, such as knife handles, pickle trays, tea caddies,

snuff boxes, cosmetic pots, etc. Mr. Rhead
divides Whieldon's principal productions under
five heads as follows :

Black glazed tea, coffee and chocolate pots.
" Image toys " and chimney ornaments.
Solid agate.
Marbled, mottled and tortoiseshell wares.
Cauliflower, pineapple, maize, etc.

His explanation of the making of " solid
agate" is so graphic and easy to understand that I
quote his exact words for the benefit of those who
are unable to get the book itself. They occur
at page 193.

" The ' solid agate ' was made by beating out
" thin layers of clay of different colours and plac-
" ing them on top of each other.   The whole mass
" was then doubled over, or rolled up, according
" to the effect the potter desired.   It was then cut
" crosswise with a wire, and the effect in section
" was similar to a slice of ' roly-poly ' pudding
" made by a pastry cook. If broad veining was
" required, the clay was used in the state described
" above, the irregular curves being given by the
" convolutions of the clay in thrown ware.   But
" if finer veining was needed, or if the ware had
" to be 'pressed' in moulds, the mass of clay was
" doubled over and cut by the wire several times.
" The more doublings the finer the pattern, and
" variations in the style of marbling were ob-
" tained by cutting the mass obliquely."

He also speaks of the perforated double teapots

which were a great feature of the Whieldon works, but I have never been fortunate enough to see one. No doubt he got his ideas from the Chinese, who were fond of this device—the real teapot was enclosed in an outside one which was deeply perforated.

The great success that he had with his tortoise-shell and agate seems due in a measure to his clever handling of colour ; he had always enough and not too much, just a thought here, a touch there, but never a crude effect.

I like best of all of his productions his octagonal plates, and a collection of these in a room papered with the right tone of yellow would be very taking. Alas, these plates are rare, and even with great good luck we are not likely to meet with more than two or three. In Fig. 30 you see two specimens of Whieldon ware, a cream elephant splashed with dark brown, extremely well modelled and a teapot of the cauliflower variety, in which the green of the leaves is wonderfully brilliant. In the chapter on Staffordshire figures you will see in Fig. 35 a cornucopia with two goats of Whieldon's make, dated " about 1760 " on its label, it is a very pleasing group, well modelled and natural. It is instructive to note the difference in the tone of the paste between pieces of this period and those of some twenty to thirty years later, when the groundwork had become very much whiter.

WEDGWOOD. I devoted a good deal of space

in my last book to the ever interesting subject of
Wedgwood and his numerous wares, so that this
time I must be somewhat brief. I am indebted
to Mr. Cecil Wedgwood for kindly supplying me
with the illustrations for this section. The rise
and progress of the industry which owned Josiah
Wedgwood as master, was unusually rapid for
those days, culminating in the triumphant business carried on at Etruria, where it still exists in
a flourishing state.

Josiah was born in 1730, when George II. was
king. His parents were comfortably off, though
not apparently in great affluence. When he was
nine years old his father died, and the boy was
put to work with his brother, though not as it
seems exactly regularly apprenticed, which did
not occur till he was fourteen. Prior to this,
when he was about eleven or twelve, he had small
pox virulently, so badly indeed that he was an
invalid for some time, and eventually causing the
loss of his leg.

This calamity really proved a blessing in dis-
guise, for during his long convalescence, perforce
tired of his sofa and chair, he had time for continuing his education, and acquiring information,
which, with the shadowy ideas prevalent in those
days of the necessity, at least, of the groundwork
of a solid education, would in other circumstances
never have been possible to him.

His acquirements were far before those of his
time, as one can see by comparing his letters with

those of his contemporaries, who passed for fairly well educated men.

It was when he was about fourteen that he was regularly apprenticed to his brother Thomas. The terms of the indenture would surprise the youth of the present day by its far-reaching strictness. I copy a few sentences from it, published in Mr. Jewitt's " Life of Wedgwood."

" During which said term the said apprentice
" do his said master's will and faithfully shall
" serve, his secrets keep, his lawfull commands
" everywhere gladly do. Hurt to his said master
" he shall not do, or wilfully suffer to be done by
" others, but the same to his power shall let, or
" forthwith give notice thereof to his said master,
" the goods of his said master he shall not imbezil
" or waste, nor them Lend, without his consent to
" any, at cards, Dice, or any other unlawful
" games he shall not play ; Taverns or Ale Houses
" he shall not haunt, or frequent ; Fornication
" he shall not commit, Matrimony he shall not
" contract ; from the service of his said master
" he shall not at any time depart or absente
' himselfe without his said master's leave, etc."

What would the Trades Union men of the present day think of such a contract as this ?

Josiah had only been apprenticed a year when the country was convulsed by the rising of 1745, so that in his too short life of 65 years, he had witnessed some stirring scenes.

In spite of the strictness of his indentures, we

may feel sure that he was (after the fashion of boys of all time) among the onlookers, when the unfortunate stragglers from the Highland army were hunted down like noxious vermin. We may also feel sure that Josiah, who never willingly hurt anyone by word or deed, was horrified at the cruelties displayed, though, as we should all do in similar circumstances, he could not keep away from the horrid sight !

No one can manage a business well who does not understand it, in its minutest details. As a boy he began at the bottom rung of the ladder, and soon became a skilful " thrower," this art had to be learnt very young, if it was to be done in perfection. He was only nine years old when he began " throwing " and his skill in this art has been dwelt upon by all who knew him ; in consequence of the painful affection of his knee after the small pox, the potter's wheel became impossible to him ; all the same his hand and his eye retained its cunning, and to his last day in business it was impossible to deceive him, as to the perfection of any piece " thrown."

After he left his brother's works he joined a Mr. Harrison in business near Stoke-on-Trent, but this connection did not last long, and we next find him a junior partner with Thomas Whieldon. If you will refer to what I said about Whieldon, you will see how much that partnership, though it did not last long, was to their mutual advantage.

During his time there Wedgwood worked naturally at all the different wares Whieldon was turning out, the agate, the tortoiseshell, and the mottled wares among others ; he also made large numbers of knife handles, which at that time were very popular.

It was during this period that he perfected the lustrous emerald green glaze that we still see and admire, and that was so largely used in the cauliflower ware.

There was a time, and not long ago either, when green dessert dishes, often in the form of vine leaves, and filled with oranges and rosy cheeked apples, were considered only fit for the tables of the vulgar ; but now that research has proved the great Josiah Wedgwood to have been the originator of them, they have suddenly become most precious and beautiful, and every-one is ambitious to possess green dessert dishes for the common or garden orange and apple !

Alas ! what snobs we are ! If it is beautiful now, so was it beautiful before, but because ceramic knowledge—especially of monetary values—has penetrated to regions where before it was unknown, we suddenly see beauty where once only " commonness " was observed.

Seemingly the partnership between Whieldon and Wedgwood was dissolved in 1758, though perfectly amicably, and in the following year the latter set up for himself and soon began to be very successful. He came of a long line of

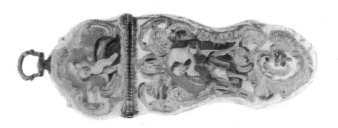

BATTERSEA ENAMEL

In the possession of Messrs. Stoner & Evans.

potting ancestors, and even as early as 1691 a John Wedgwood signed his name and the date, on a jug now in the Victoria and Albert Museum.

This John was the great uncle of Josiah, and Miss Meteyard, the indefatigable chronicler of the Wedgwoods, speaks of an earlier ancestor who lived near Leek in the 15th century.

When, in 1759, Wedgwood started on his own account, it was at Ivy House, Burslem, belonging to his cousins. These premises soon became too small for his rapidly growing business, and he annexed the Bell works, or, as they are sometimes called, the Brick House works; you will find them thus indifferently alluded to.

It was here that he made his great success with the celebrated cream ware, and having secured the Royal patronage, it henceforth became "Queen's ware." I think we may say with certainty, it was that branch of the business that brought him the great financial success he attained.

Other people made cream ware, as we know, but there was a delicate finish about that of Wedgwood that surpassed all others.

In my family is a dessert service of this kind still fairly perfect, with a pattern in Pompeiian scarlet and black; one characteristic, marking this cream ware from others, is its extreme lightness, and I find on trial that I can carry with ease twelve plates and eight dishes.

It is clear that in business acumen and financial

N

enterprise Wedgwood was far in advance of the potters of his time. He travelled constantly, a most unusual proceeding in those days, and in every locality he sought out new ideas, and observed how others were conducting business.

A proof of his astute and far-seeing policy was his associating himself with Brindley, the engineer, in his enterprise for cutting the Trent and Mersey Canal. There were, of course, in-numerable difficulties and rival interests and schemes to be fought.

Wedgwood, with his usual clear-headedness, saw that James Brindley's scheme was the best, and he threw all his interest and energy into supporting him. Mr. Jewitt quotes part of one of Brindley's letters, showing how energetically Wedgwood was supporting him. The spelling is quaint, Brindley was evidently a better engineer than scribe!

"On Tusdey Sr Georg sent Nuton in to
"Manchestr to make what intrest he could
"for Sir Georg and to gather ye old Navogtors
"togather to meet Sir Georg at Stoperd to make
"head aganst his grace. I sawe Dr. Seswige
"who sese hee wants to see you aboat pamant
"of His Land in Cheshire. On Wednesday
"ther was not much transpired, but was so dark
"I could carse do aneything."

"On Thursday, Wadgwood of Burslam came
"to Dunham and sant for mee and wee dined
"with Lord Gree and Sir Hare Mainwering and

" others. Sir Hare cud not ceep His Tamer.
" Mr. Wedgwood came to seliset Lord Gree in
" faver of the Staffordshire canal and stade at
" Mrs. Latoune all night and I whith him and
" on fryday sat out to wate on Mr. Edgerton to
" selesit Him.   Hee sase Sparrow and others
" are indavering to gat ye Land owners consants
" from Hare Castle to Agden."

The spelling is quite cryptic ; who, I wonder,
was Sir Hare who " cud not ceep His Tamer " ?
Does it mean he could not keep his temper ?

Wedgwood supported this extensive scheme
with all his influence, and also with considerable
financial assistance. An act of Parliament was
obtained, and the canal became a reality, and
the greatest comfort and blessing to the whole
of that part of England ; the first sod was cut—
most appropriately—by Wedgwood in 1766.

Up to this time the pottery had found its
way to the chief towns on pack horses, a long
string of these poor over-burdened animals
trudged wearily along, and not infrequently fell
under their heavy loads never to rise again.

In 1768 Wedgwood took into partnership
Thomas Bentley, of Liverpool, and in the following year he bought a plot of ground near Burslem,
which became the famous Etruria.

Thomas Bentley shortly became the manager
of the London branch of the business, and more
especially directed his attention to the ornamental
side of the output.

The business relations, as well as a close
friendship, continued between the two men until
Bentley's death in 1780. He is buried in
Chiswick Church, not far from Hogarth.

His death was a serious blow in many ways
to Wedgwood, for, not only did he miss one to
whom he was united by the closest ties of long
friendship, but he also greatly missed Bentley's
keen and yet honourable business instincts.

After his death, the large London stock was
necessarily sold, and the sale at Christie's
occupied twelve days.

Wedgwood never ceased striving to perfect
his cream ware ; he made many beautiful
perforated pieces in the style of the Leeds work,
and also many of the open work twig dessert
baskets. There were all sorts of varieties ; sometimes it was ornamented with bas reliefs, sometimes
painted, sometimes transfer printed, sometimes
a mixture of two styles appeared on one piece.

The cream or " Queen's " ware seemed to be
especially the child of his love, and though he
laboured incessantly for the improvement
of the Jasper ware, the commercial side of his
character caused him to realize to the full the
monetary value of the " Queen's " ware.

Most people have heard of the remarkable
service of cream ware made for Catherine of
Russia, and owing to the kindness of Messrs.
Wedgwood, I am able to show you in Fig 31 five
of the plates.

FIG. 31.—PLATES FROM THE SET MADE FOR THE EMPRESS CATHERINE.
(By permission of Messrs. Wedgwood.)

Tradition says there were 1,200 pieces in the service, and the expense of making it was so enormous that though the price paid for it was £3,000, Wedgwood confessed that the sum only covered the expense of production, and left nothing for profit. This remarkable service showed on every piece a different landscape, or country seat, no duplicates were allowed, and the number of these views shows us at once how many artists must have been employed, and how expensive the work was.

These views are executed in a purplish brown; the border green and mauve, and you will see that each piece has a frog on it, because the Empress purposed using it at her Palace of La Grenouillère.

Mrs. Delaney, who never failed to see everything that was to be seen, and fortunately for us, almost always recorded her impressions in her delightful correspondence, describes the service, but does not mention the frog, which is curious, as, unless she knew the reason, it would have seemed surprising to picture this reptile—so alarming to some people—on a dinner service.

" I am just returned from viewing the Wedg-
" wood ware that is to be sent to the Empress
" of Russia. It consists, I believe, of as many
" pieces as there are days in the year, if not
" hours. They are displayed at a house in Greek
" Street, Soho, called Portland House. There are
" three rooms below and two above filled with

" it, laid out on tables ; everything that can be
" wanted to serve a dinner. The ground, the
" common ware, pale brimstone, the drawings
" in purple, the borders a wreath of leaves, the
" middle of each piece of a particular view of all
" the remarkable places in the king's dominions
" neatly executed. I suppose it will come to a
" princely price ; it is well for the manufacturer,
" which I am glad of as his ingenuity and in-
" dustry deserve encouragement."

Mrs. Delany's letters have preserved to us
many interesting particulars of the 18th century
and when she was not working at her acres of
delicate embroidery, she seemed to be perpetually on the " go " and writing letters.

It is rather amusing now, with our knowledge
of what prices genuine pieces coming from the
direct personal influence of the great Josiah will
fetch, to read Mrs. Delany's condescending affa-
bility, as to the benefit to his pocket, and the pro-
priety of rewarding his industry and ingenuity.

This remarkable service can hardly be considered one of his great successes, because it was
not made after his own refined taste, but in
accordance with hard and fast instructions.

To pass on now to Jasper ware, with which
Wedgwood's name is primarily connected.
Jasper ware, according to the idea of the man in
the street, is always blue with a pattern in white
on it. Generally his ideas go no further, and
he is quite unaware that this Jasper ware was

made with a ground work of other colours than blue.

There are mauves and pinks of various shades, olive greens, yellow and black.

The dark full blue I like least of all, especially as it is the tone in which coarse imitations of this beautiful pottery are made. Hideous biscuit boxes, jugs, flower pots and tea pots, with the roughest possible scenes in white on them, are to be found everywhere, each one more frightful and crude than the last. It is an abomination that such a beautiful art should be so mal-treated. It is not because they are modern, for the real Wedgwood, modern as it is, is refined, delicate and a thing of beauty. I possess a comparatively modern piece, about 60 years old, and it is a charming thing, a jug in pinkish mauve, with a chocolate handle.

There is in the old work a lovely pale blue with an inclination to lavender that I admire greatly. I showed you in " Antiques and Curios," a fine vase of this tint, with a design of adorable little cupids playing blind man's buff ; this was an original conception of Flaxman's.

This pale blue is rather uncommon, I have not seen many examples of it.

It was in 1775 that Wedgwood brought his Jasper ware to perfection, and at once the classic feeling that showed itself everywhere at the close of the 18th century, was apparent in his new development.

He was, as we have seen, far in advance of his time in education, and in cultivated tastes, partly no doubt on account of his long illness, which made him seek the companionship of books, and partly in his association with Bentley, who was a good classic and general scholar.

All this tended to make Wedgwood an apt exponent of the wave of classical taste, that for many reasons, was, at that time, spreading over Europe.

The Jasper discovery came not unnaturally after his successes with the red, the buff, and the black basalts.

The red ware no doubt originated with the Elers, and Mr. Burton thinks that the buff and the black did so also.

Jasper ware is of two kinds, " solid " and " dipped." In the first the colouring matter entirely permeated and was incorporated with the clay, and " dipped " as its name implies, was the white body, simply dipped in the colouring matter, and thus only affecting the surface.

The " solid " Jasper was always blue, and it seems that as soon as the process of dipping was thoroughly understood and brought to perfection, the solid Jasper was not often made. The manner of making was thus, I quote Mr. Burton for his explanations are so easy to understand.

" On the coloured ground of solid Jasper, or

" of Jasper dip, ornamented reliefs in the shape
" of foliage, conventional scrolls, figures, medal-
" lions, or portraits, were applied, usually in
" white, but occasionally in coloured Jasper.
(N.B.—I have never seen an example of this).
" The method by which these bas reliefs were
" applied was the old method of " sprigging."
" Into a mould of Plaster of Paris, or " pitcher "
" bearing the subject in intaglio, the moist Jasper
" clay was squeezed by the thumb of the work-
" man, until it filled every line and dot of the
" intaglio ; superfluous clay was then scraped off
" with a modelling tool, or a sharp knife, level
" with the face of the mould, and, after a few
" minutes drying, the clay impress was removed,
" by skilfully lifting it with a modelling tool. It
" was then applied to the piece by simply
" wetting the surface with a little clean water
" and pressing the relief upon the wetted surface,
" so as to adapt it to the shape, and to secure
" adhesion to the coloured ground."

In studying the work of Wedgwood, I should
like you to read all that Mr. Burton has to say. It
is an expensive book, but one procurable at good
circulating libraries. He only devotes 30 pages
to the subject, but his information is so excellent
and condensed, that it is an efficient help to the
beginner, and also he has many beautiful
coloured illustrations, which are more useful to
the student, than plain black and white ones.

He gives an interesting reason for the pleasing

kind of especially dark blue ground, occasionally met with ; he says in speaking of the seven colours employed as ground work—namely two shades of blue, two of green, one more olive than the other, a bluish pink, a yellow and black. " The yellow colour is the rarest ; the lilac is " the most variable in tint, as one may expect " from the nature of its colouring matter ; while " the dark blue is generally most beautiful when " it has been spoilt somewhat in the firing " by the introduction of reducing gases, a defect " commonly known among the workmen as " ' sulphuring.' Under these circumstances, it " develops a remarkably fine indigo tone, greatly " superior to that which it more commonly " possesses." The favourite and most valuable pieces are in the tri-coloured scheme, that is, with a ground work of one colour, a border of another, and the bas reliefs in white. I have a cameo of this kind which is of considerable value, the subject is a nymph sacrificing. The ground work is a pinkish mauve, with a border of olive green, embellished with a wreath of oak leaves. This cameo, which I wear as a pendant, so excited the interest of a dealer whom I encountered in an omnibus, that I had the greatest difficulty in persuading him that no money would buy it.

In my former book, I gave a full account of the Barberini vase and Wedgwood's copies of it. It was one of his greatest achievements.

FIG. 32.—WEDGWOOD PORTRAIT CAMEOS.

FIG. 33.—THE EMPRESS CATHERINE AND JOHN ELERS.
(By permission of Messrs. Wedgwood.)

Personally I do not like it, wonderful as it is, the original being of glass is translucent, and the effect is very different from that of white upon a perfectly opaque groundwork.

Besides Flaxman, it is known that over forty designers and modellers helped Wedgwood in his creations. Flaxman's name seems to dwarf the others, which is unfair, and yet amongst those others were Sir Joshua Reynolds, Roubiliac, Stothard, Tassie, and several well known Italian names.

Wedgwood never spared expense to make everything that left his works as perfect as industry, energy, and taste could achieve.

It is difficult to select the most suitable examples for illustrations, and I want you to have some idea of the portrait medallions from which Wedgwood rightly gained so much fame. I consider these among his most beautiful and most distinctive works.

In Fig. 32 we have portraits of well known men ; I like especially Nelson and Pitt, the latter looking quite boyish. In Fig. 33 are two very interesting specimens, Catherine of Russia, the owner of the celebrated dinner service, and John Philip Elers. This last is particularly taking, and considering how much mystery and more or less of romance hangs round the man of whom we know so little, it seems like meeting a friend face to face to see his picture, which we may feel pretty sure was a good likeness.

The various charming trifles in the way of cameos for rings, brooches, pendants, chatelaines, and also small plaques for dainty furniture, look their best when mounted in cut steel. Wedgwood's great success brought in his train endless imitators, and a large book might be written on the subject.

LEEDS POTTERY. It seems superfluous to say that the Romans were the first potters there—of course they were—they had a real nose for "clay." All round the district suitable clay was found, and those old fellows never left anything unutilized.

The brothers Kidson, to whose beautiful book, "Old Leeds Pottery," any writer on, or collector of Leeds ware must be grateful, think that probably between that remote period and that of the "Humble, Green and Co." time, some kind of simple ware was made there, and that its existence led to the establishment, in the 18th century, of the above firm. Their book is beautifully illustrated, which is always such a help, especially to the beginner.

They give a full account of the old factory buildings, some of which it appears still exist. The windmill, however, was pulled down about sixteen years ago. The authors tell us of a notice concerning a catastrophe which befell this same windmill. I quote it, for these little touches seem to make us live in the time of the old works, and help us to differentiate between the different

factories. It seems they were a little too anxious
to make money quickly, and so worked Sundays
as well as week days. The notice occurred in the
" Annals of Leeds," probably from a newspaper
of the day. " On Sunday, July 31st, 1774, the
" sails of the windmill belonging to the Leeds
" pottery fell down with a tremendous crash,
" which being looked upon as a judgement for the
" desecrating of the Sabbath, the proprietors
" resolved that the mill should never be allowed
" to be worked afterwards on the Lord's
" day."

The first establishment of the works, as usual,
seems uncertain, and Mr. Kidson says that even
in the days of its greatest glory, from the time of
Hartley joining the firm, the records are extremely
meagre, and so no continuous and full history
of it can be written. What the earliest ware was
like in the Humble and Green time we do not
know with certainty, though probably much like
the usual type of Staffordshire pottery at the
same date.

Its real time of beauty dates from somewhere
about 1781 or 1782 to 1820, when Hartley died,
after which the business soon fell to pieces.

We now begin to get on to a time when pottery
and china was sometimes, though far from always,
marked. Of the old marks of this factory
LEEDS POTTERY repeated and crossing each
other—HARTLEY, GREENS, & CO.,and LEEDS
*POTTERY, sometimes in a semi-circle and

sometimes in a straight line, may be looked for, also occasionally only L.P.

The later marks are not worth recording, because no one wants to collect modern earthenware.

The Leeds factory has a special interest because it was a formidable rival to the Staffordshire cream ware, which was made, more or less, by every potter in that district.

In or about 1783 the firm began to make cream ware like Wedgwood's, which at that time was taking the world by storm ; they also made black basalt, but this appears to me (I possess a small jug of it) to be far less smooth and satiny than that produced by the great Josiah. In 1783 the first pattern book was published, this was due probably to the enterprise of Hartley. These pattern books, with printed lists of the things made, and explanations, are very scarce and valuable. Mr. Kidson prints one for our instruction— they seem to contain every imaginable article.

There are in all china and earthenware factories, ramifications and connections that make " confusion worse confounded," and in this case we have commercial transactions with the Swinton and the Don works—Swinton eventually became Rockingham—and in 1737 one or more of the Leeds partners seemed to be doing business with them.

Very likely this was an astute move to prevent rivalry in the making of the cream ware.

Their connection with, or part ownership of

the Don works makes a great confusion, as they, too, were near to Swinton. I must say, if you begin the study of china and pottery in adult life, instead of growing up with it, as it were, it must seem well-nigh hopeless, and to make such a large and puzzling subject fairly clear to beginners, as I am trying to do now, seems sometimes to bring one to the brink of despair.

I must pause a little here, to say a few words on the Rockingham works, at that time called the Swinton factory. Partnership with Leeds was severed in 1806, and the Rockingham firm became that of Brameld and Co.

At this place was, and still is, made the brown tea and coffee pots that we all know so well. No doubt a silver teapot is the ideal thing and makes the best tea, but if you have not that, a brown Rockingham pot is the best substitute.

Later on the Brameld firm made delicate china, but as we are now dealing only with earthenware we must pass on.

After the death of Hartley, in 1820, the old Leeds firm gradually, but surely, declined, and the beautiful cream ware, pierced and plain, was no longer made.

Undeniably the taste of the mid 19th century was bad, and very little was made that would have competed successfully with that of the 18th century, either in pottery, china or glass.

Now with regard to the appearance of the old cream ware, which, though by no means the only production of the factory, is certainly the most important.

The colour is rather a full cream, and the glaze very translucent, some of the pieces show a very slight, almost imperceptible tinge of green, especially underneath, as if it had something to do with the setting of the glaze.

I have only one piece, which I greatly prize. It has a pierced pattern of the kind called " rice grain," such as you see in the centre of the toy chair in Fig. 34. It was given to my mother about 1860, by a very old lady from Leeds, who inherited it from her mother, it must, therefore, have had its birth in the best time of the factory.

It is a plate, and in the interstices of the angles in the pierced border there are unmistakable signs of the greenish glaze. These signs, however, are so very slight, that unless you expected them, they would be certainly overlooked. The pierced examples are the most valued, and the most characteristic. You will see two pieces of this kind in Fig. 34, one is a chair, which, I suppose, was a chimney ornament, and the other is a dessert dish. This last is very pretty with a fluted or corrugated centre, a pierced border and a variety of the cockle shell at the four points. The best known and most esteemed patterns are those consisting of varieties of the well-known " rice grain " form, which I can best describe as being a good deal like *Broderie Anglaise.*

Other factories besides Leeds used this piercing

FIG. 34.—LEEDS PIERCED CREAM WARE.

FIG. 35.—TOBY JUG AND GROUP OF GOATS.

and punching, and Wedgwood was fond of it,
especially in the basket work form, but I think
the *Broderie Anglaise* pattern was peculiar to
Leeds.

Of this pierced Leeds ware there are some really
splendid examples as centrepieces, some of them,
too, as well as being pierced, show a bas relief
pattern, combining the two styles with very
happy effect.   I prefer the open work style to any
other, because it is more distinctive and especially
when it has the " rice grain " border.

How nice these sumptuous pieces must have
looked in the old days, when, after dinner the
cloth was removed and the dark shining mahogany reflected the piled up fruit in the elaborate
erection in the middle, often showing charming
little hanging baskets for flowers, or for sweetmeats.

There would be no effect on the white table-
cloth, but on the mahogany, which reflected all
the lights and colours, it must have been very
striking, especially when the decanters and wine
glasses of cut glass made a ring all round the table.
You must not run into the easy error of attribut-
ing all pierced cream work to Leeds ; it was
being made everywhere in potting districts, and
the strongest similarity exists perhaps between
Wedgwood and Leeds.

In weight they are both extraordinarily light,
and the tone of the cream is in strong resemblance,
but an important difference lies in the glaze.

O

Wedgwood glazed thinly and Leeds thickly, with the result that Wedgwood table ware (of the useful kind, such as plates and meat dishes) rather easily showed signs of wear.

I have a solitary and much prized Wedgwood dish, with the feather pattern in blue and gold. It has been now in constant use for at least a hundred and thirty years, and shows a multitude of scratches which have almost made away with the glaze in the middle. This dish was rescued as I related in " Antiques and Curios," from a jumble sale.

With regard to the shapes of the more important Leeds pieces, they resemble most other attempts of the same kind at the same date. Rock work, shells (escallop shells were very favourite designs), hanging baskets, birds, flowers, fruits, and sometimes a cornucopia, or a figure, crowned the erection.

Some of these centre pieces were very large, even attaining the height of four feet, a veritable fortress in the middle of the dining table. I have never, myself, seen anything quite so sumptuous in size as this ; these large centrepieces seem distinctly of Leeds—other potters do not appear to have attempted them on so opulent a scale.

Other large examples belonging to the factory were cisterns, something like a filter of the present day, and chestnut baskets, almost globular and richly pierced ; these are still occasionally to be found.

Until I read Mr. Kidson's book I never could understand why they were called " chestnut " baskets, why not sweetmeat or cherry baskets, but now I understand : he says that each basket once had a ladle, and armed with it the consumer dived after the hot nuts.

The " twig " baskets—Wedgwood made the same—are very light and pretty, they have all the appearance of being constructed of twigs, and frequently have a slight line of colour round the top. Considering their extreme fragility, it is wonderful how many have survived to the present day.

The fruit dishes (as well as the pierced edges) often show a quadrooned or fluted body.

With regard to tea table ware, cups and saucers are scarce, but tea and coffee pots are more numerous. Look out for twisted handles, they were often made so at Leeds ; it is a style always giving a very graceful appearance, and from that factory they are generally fixed to the body of the piece with a flower or leaf.

These handles, however, cannot be considered distinctive, for we see them from many other potteries, but on the whole Leeds handles are more often twisted than not.

The Leeds factory did a large trade with the Continent, so it is not surprising that collectors with large means—like Lady Charlotte Schreiber —should scour the countries, especially of Germany, Denmark and Holland, for treasures.

A very large number of pieces have foreign inscriptions on them, evidently made to order.

It is amusing to read Lady Charlotte's diaries; it seems that she and her husband spent their entire lives in collecting; they were hardly ever at home, no sooner had they returned from a collecting tour in Denmark and Holland, than they heard of some rare thing in Russia; immediately the tents were struck and off they were on the trail. Some amusing incidents are recorded: They were *personæ gratiæ* in diplomatic circles, and more than once, when it became suddenly known that they were near, their attendance at some important dinner or ball was urgently solicited.

This was awkward, but was still a negotiable difficulty, but worse was to come, for twice they were invited by Royalty at half an hour's notice, and as a Royal invitation is equivalent to a command, great difficulties occurred, seeing that Lady Schreiber on one of these occasions had been separated from her luggage, which, she says, even had it been at hand, would have been of the most meagre description!

It is quite sad to see the difference in the journal after Mr. Schreiber's death; the records before had been so gay and happy, full of vitality and interest in everything, but with his death, all her spring of life was gone; she could collect no more; the associations were too painful, and her only sad consolation was to bestow their

splendid collection—gathered in happier years—
on the nation as a fitting memorial to the dear
companion of the past.

I have not left myself much room to speak of
the other wares made at Leeds, but they, after
all, resembled that made at other factories, and
were not of so much consequence as the pierced
cream ware.

Of these kinds, the transfer printing was among
the most largely used. I have described this
process before in my other book, and must ask
you to refer to it.

A few figures were made, and tortoiseshell
and agate varieties and lustre, but all these things
are in no way distinctive of Leeds.

In Fig. 34 you will see a teapot has intruded
itself by mistake, it has nothing to do with Leeds.
It is a strange little pot in the British Museum,
labelled as made by Greatbach, the date, judging
from the dresses, would be about 1750. I fancy
it must represent a fortune teller, for the lady at
the back is looking very sourly on a paper which
has the legend "no husband for you!" The
lady in front also has a paper, which, as far as I
can decipher it, says, " A husband for £20." On
the table in front of the man are piles of money.
Apparently matrimonial agencies were known
even in those days.

STAFFORDSHIRE FIGURES. Almost all
the potters in Staffordshire and other districts
made earthenware figures, few or many, according

to their particular fancy. Of the very early ones, of a rude and archaic description, but few exist, now and again one sees a strange animal or bird, such as the puzzle jug in Fig. 25. I have a large money box, resembling this early work, though its date is only 1829. It was no doubt imitated from one of the primitive old ones.

It is to the Whieldon and Wood period that we must turn for the best and most interesting examples.

The finest figures of all are those of Ralph Wood, the elder, his son, and his nephew, Enoch, at least that is my feeling, and I believe it is the general opinion.

Ralph Wood, the elder, and Aaron his brother, both modellers, were the sons of a miller in, or near, Burslem. Of Aaron, though he was a most clever and artistic workman, we hear but little, though it is very probable that he inspired many of the figures attributed to others of the family. He was the father of Enoch Wood, who made the celebrated Wesley bust in 1781, when he (Enoch) was only twenty-two. He lived to be an old man and died in 1840.

Ralph Wood, the uncle of Enoch, and the first member of the family about whose work we know something, died, it is thought, about 1772. His son, Ralph, only survived him twenty-five years, dying in 1797.

The ramifications of the Wood family, with

their repetitions of names, are a little difficult to follow, but you must try to keep something of these dates in your head, because it will help you in trying, however imperfectly, to assign different pieces to their possible, or probable, makers. Besides the three Woods, one finds figures of Voyez', of Whieldon's, of Wedgwood's, of Walton's, of Neale's, and of many others, but I shall only speak of the best known, so as to be as little confusing as possible.

With regard to the different kinds of figures, there are several, but, of course, the most interesting are those that are entirely original, no matter how crude, such as the early " pew groups," see frontispiece, and later " the Vicar and Moses," and a few also of the early Toby jugs.

In this category we may include Voyez figures ; he worked for Wedgwood at one time, but seemed to be rather " a loose fish," and Wedgwood got rid of him. In a letter published in Mr. Frank Falkner's book—a delightful volume to which I am greatly indebted—entitled " The Wood Family," we find that the cause of the rupture was that Wedgwood, going into the workshop found his erratic modeller, as the writer expresses it, " somewhat in liquor," engaged in modelling the figure of a girl in a very inadequate costume. The well conducted Josiah was furious, the more so that the girl was related to someone in his service, and swift dismissal and punishment followed, for this was the culmination of many acts of insubordination, and Voyez got three months' imprisonment, and the cat. After the establishment on a firm basis of the porcelain works at Bow and Chelsea, etc., we have the group of figures which aimed at being close imitations of the porcelain originals. Many of these are extremely interesting, they are numerous, and we find plenty of crude reproductions, of the Hawthorne and Arbour groups of Chelsea, and Chelsea Derby. Lastly, and somewhat later, we have figures and groups of men, women, birds, animals, cottages, churches, money boxes and castles, these were made expressly for the decoration of peasant interiors, and even to this day are still made. The Toby jugs, called indifferently " Toby Fillpots " or " Philpots," are a class quite apart, and many people like making a collection of them alone.

Such an immense number were made that even now it is not very difficult to pick up genuine specimens, though the best are certainly appropriated. The Tobys, as you all know, were generally seated figures of a stout and dwarfish formation, clasping in their hands a jug of ale, sometimes the hat lifts off, or I should rather say lifts out, revealing a cup within. I do not see exactly the use of this, as the drinkers of that day generally imbibed from the jug itself and would have thought poorly indeed of such a thimbleful as could be contained in this cup, which at most would only hold a gill.

I have seen three of these, two of which were genuinely old, as we could trace their pedigree— concerning the third I have my doubts.

The general conception of these figures is much the same, the cocked hat, the white stockings and buckled shoes, very generally a scarlet coat turned up with blue, or vice versa, and always clasped on the fat knees, a jug.   In Fig. 35 you see one in the British Museum of the most common stamp, it is attributed to Ralph Wood, and the date is considered to be about 1780.   As you see, there is a good deal of character in the face.

Sometimes the original idea is carried out a little differently, such as in the Falstaff jug in the Stoner collection, and the sailor also in the same set.   The Falstaff jug does not please me, though it is considered a remarkably fine specimen, and is over fourteen inches high, it appears to me lacking in character.   I greatly prefer one in Mr. Falkner's collection, it seems to me to be much better conceived, with more go and vitality ; when the faces are namby pamby all pleasure in them is gone.

If you are not too particular you may still get together a nice little collection of these jugs ; most that you will find will be probably of early 19th century time, but with this drawback understood, it may be done.

Like other Staffordshire figures I do not think they look well singly, and if possible, a whole shelf should be devoted to them.

Walton's figures—he lived some time after the Woods—belong to the first years of the 19th century, and have not the quaint simplicity of earlier pieces. The original work had vanished and, though still pleasing, and often very well modelled, they partook more of the nature of copies from porcelain examples.

In Fig. 36 you will see in the centre the well-known " Old Age " by Ralph Wood, the subject was repeated again and again and is well known to all. This especial one is in the British Museum. The artist has succeeded well in portraying the somewhat painful idea of human helplessness.

To the left is a bagpiper and to the right Apollo with his Lyre, both by Ralph Wood ; the piper being a little the older of the two, labelled about 1750, whilst Apollo is ten years younger, as becomes him.

Ralph the elder was the maker of many celebrated figures and groups—the best known is that of the " Vicar and Moses." I do not give you an illustration of it because being so very familiar I think it is better to show you something not quite so often seen. Pretty well everyone knows the somnolent vicar in the pulpit, and the unctuous clerk below.

This group was made over and over again, and as time went on, each production proved less and less satisfactory, and further removed from the first simple and delightful piece of colouring.

There are two different ways in which the

FIG. 36.—BAG-PIPER, OLD AGE, AND APOLLO.

FIG. 37.—PARSON AND CLERK.

potters decorated their figures. The first process, and that generally adopted by the elder Ralph Wood, was that of colouring the glazes themselves and painting them on. This gave a somewhat subdued but charmingly artistic effect, and is well shown in this group of the " Vicar and Moses " in the Victoria and Albert Museum. You cannot do better than study it carefully.

The main colour is the warm purplish brown, which is caused by manganese, which we see so frequently in the Whieldon clouded and tortoise-shell ware, the lining of the vicar's half of the structure is subdued green and the rest is an uncertain grey, there is nothing garish or arresting to the eye in any single tint, all is harmonious. The second process, very generally, though not always adopted by the second Ralph Wood, is that of painting in enamel colours and glazing a second time, and you can understand that the effect is much more brilliant, cruder and certainly less pleasing.

The " Parson and Clerk " group, see Fig. 37, ·some think was suggested by Aaron Wood, and some that it is the work of the younger Ralph ; the colouring is different from that of the " Vicar and Moses," being in the enamel process.

Anyone interested in the subject of Staffordshire figures and tentatively hoping to make a modest collection should make a point of studying carefully Mr. Frank Falkner's, " The Wood family of Burslem." He is the great authority on the subject, and himself possesses remarkably fine specimens. In his book he has 54 plates, and many of them have 12 separate examples in each.

My limit being small, I can only give but few, and of all pottery studies I think that of the figures is the one especially that cannot very well be pursued without seeing many specimens.

The group of goats and cornucopia, Fig. 35, is a Whieldon piece, well modelled, and very subdued, and yet effective in colour.

The statuette of spring in Fig. 30, between the Whieldon elephant and teapot, is dated 1780, and signed Neale & Co. I do not like it so much as the earlier ones.

With regard to collecting, I do not think that one or two isolated examples look well in a collection, and it is an artistic sin to mix them with china. They are not beautiful, or even pretty, but they are generally fine pieces of colour, quaint and original, and placed some 15 to 20 on a shelf by themselves are very effective. The brilliant Tobys always give a nice touch of colour to a dull corner. If your collection is still smaller in number, they will look well with agate or tortoiseshell pieces of the Whieldon school.

On no account put them with other highly coloured things, such as the full rich blue Staffordshire plates—each kills the other.

Of all the varieties in the pottery groups and

FIG. 38.—STAFFORDSHIRE FIGURES.
(By permission of Messrs. Gill and Reigate.)

FIG. 39.—STAFFORDSHIRE FIGURES.
(By permission of Messrs. Gill and Reigate.)

figures, I think I like best of all the animals. The squirrels are particularly taking, the cows wonderfully spotted as to their bodies and preternaturally curly as to their tails—the cats with extraordinarily developed ears, spaniels much spotted and very glassy eyed, bears with all their teeth seemingly growing outside, the artist evidently being fearful that the terror of their appearance would be discounted if every tooth was not visible, horses, striped and spotted, and with a development of mane and tail that would be a fortune to a circus.

Messrs. Gill and Reigate often have one of their windows full of Staffordshire figures of all kinds, from which collections they have kindly given me some illustrations.

Fig. 38, chiefly represents animals ; on the top row, a bear somewhat resembling a far from amiable polar bear at the Zoo, a sheep and a dog. The second row has a pair of bird's-nesters, and a cow and boy in the middle, and on the bottom tier we have the favourite subject of St. George and the Dragon (the Dragon is receiving the spear with an air of amiable thankfulness) and two cows with milkers, the one on the right forms a cream jug, the cream being poured into the back where you can see a little lid.

In Fig. 39, you see more ambitious attempts "Tragedy" and "Comedy," "Winter and Spring," etc., and on the bottom row the three

best pieces, the " Farewell," and " The Return,"
and one of the much-loved cottages.

If you are going in for a small collection, I
think I should advise the line of animals, they
are usually smaller, and such immense numbers
were made that even now, though dealers and the
collectors have scraped the country as with a
small tooth comb, they are still to be found—but
beware—they are easily counterfeited, and I am
told, though I have no proof of the truth of the
statement, that certain gifted ones make good
imitations, bury them for six months or more
to acquire a worn and mellow appearance at
points where the glaze has not touched, then dig
up their buried frauds, and enter into a dishonest
compact with the " innocent " villager for him
to display these " antiques " on the family
mantelshelf, for the ensnaring of the unwary.

The supposed owner with pretended reluctance
to part with her honoured great grandmother's
Toby jug, pair of spaniels, or crockery cottage, is
at last persuaded to hand over the coveted
article for 7s. or 10s. 6d., in consideration of the
hardness of the times, and her virtuous desire to
part with anything " rather than be a burden on
Polly or Dan'l " !

Of that sum she fingers perhaps 1s. or 1s. 6d.,
and the rest goes into the hungry maw of the
ingenious " faker," who puts his tongue in his
cheek, as he considers the comfortable gullibility
of the collecting public.

Perhaps you remember the sentence in the false Roger Tichborne's diary, which in spite of its astuteness was the cause of his undoing. " Some has money and no brains, and some has brains and no money, and them as has money and no brains, is made for them as has brains and no money ! "

I do not vouch for the truth of the statement touching buried figures, it seems to me a game hardly worth the candle, but I warn you and leave you to your fate.

Some while ago I was living in the Midlands, there were still many genuine treasures of this kind to be picked up, but the last 25 or 30 years has made a great difference.

The variety most in evidence were woolly lambs, stags spotted like leopards, and above all, spaniels of the King Charles type, very yellow and curly ; often they had collars and sometimes ribbons on their necks, usually one sat at each end of the mantelshelf and stared into space, balanced by a nice pair of brass candlesticks ; the centre was frequently occupied by a castellated mansion in crockery, or a humble cottage, and great was the joy of the children if on birthdays, or other feasts, a candle was placed inside, and the light was seen shining through the windows.

The cottager of the past did not disfigure his room with the tawdry bits of unsuitable ornamentation that we see now, and which is the outcome of so-called education.

The children attend art classes, and the result is blue glass vases with sprawling flowers depicted on them, odious little smelling paraffin lamps, adorned with silk shades and cotton lace, all the flower pots tied up in coloured muslin petticoats, or crinkled paper flutings, and worst of all a plethora of disastrous photographs in frames of the most venomous description; Mother herself is sure to be there, attired in her best Sunday gown, made according to the current fashion, as suitable for a girl of 20, and if she is unusually stout, I am sure it will be cut square and " filled in " with cream lace, a fearful snare to the over plump, and she will have elbow sleeves, terminating in under ones of the same fatal lace, from which her honest, kind, and useful hands protrude, purple in hue, naked and unashamed.

I have often wondered, with that work of art before him, how any swain is found courageous enough to court the daughter who is " so like mother," fortunately in that class imagination is not active.

How nice it must have been when the peasant, the farmer, and, indeed, people of all classes dressed in accordance with their position. Nowadays, young and old, rich and poor, all dress alike, and as to suitability there is no such thing. I am often inclined to wish sumptuary laws could be brought in again.

It is wonderful the number of figures of all

kinds that Mr. Falkner considers may be attributed to the Woods, besides those that I have mentioned. There is " Hudibras on horseback," the " Haymakers," endless Toby jugs, the " Bird cage group," some ambitious figures (not so good) of " Minerva," " Venus," " Neptune," and " Jupiter." Portrait figures such as Franklin's shepherds, and shepherdesses, " Cupids on Lions," squirrels, elephants, rams, stags, the " seasons," and more important busts such as the Wesley one. In fact what have they not made.

Enoch Wood, the son of Aaron, was an enlightened man, he was born in 1759, and died in 1840, so that he lived through a very strenuous period of history, and saw the introduction of many strange novelties.

In many respects his was the most interesting personality of the Wood family. He was not only himself a fine modeller and potter, but he had that useful quality, so valuable for his descendants and the public generally, of being extremely interested in his own art, and that of his fellow potters, and he formed (what was most unusual in those days) the splendid collection of native work, that we enjoy to-day in our national collections.

Enoch Wood came under the influence of Wedgwood at the Brick House works, before he was apprenticed to Palmer, of Hanley Green, and when he was twenty-four he set up for himself.

P

We know from his celebrated bust of Wesley what a clever portrait modeller he was, but of works such as these I say no more, because they are of a totally different character to the figures we have now been considering.

In 1790, James Caldwell became a partner with Enoch Wood, though he seems to have been what we now call a sleeping partner. It was to this period we owe his Falstaff figure, which was certainly imitated from the Chelsea Falstaff, and there is a similar one of Chelsea Derby design.

In spite of many heroic efforts at condensation and " boiling down," this chapter on earthenware has expanded itself further than I intended, and yet I have only taken for consideration the most prominent factories ; there are many other kinds of pottery still to be studied, the Liverpool, the lustres of all kinds, Turner, Adam, etc., and the various homely Continental sorts.

I hope I have stirred up your thirst for knowledge, and that you will now venture upon the further study of the subject in the many books of which I give you a list.

CHAPTER V

OLD ENGLISH AND IRISH CUT GLASS, ETC.

IT is only in quite late years that table glass has been numbered among the desired treasures of collectors. Until thirty years ago, it was in no way difficult to find bargains in old glass of the early 18th century, and charming old drinking glasses of all kinds, even with air-twisted stems, and those with opaque twists were to be picked up, as the saying is, for a song. Not so now, collectors have awakened to the knowledge that early glass is of the greatest interest and value ; this fact is proved by the talented exertions of the fakers, who have directed their genius to the making of " antique " air-twisted and opaque twisted stems to the wine glasses which pretend to be of the early 18th century, especially those much prized ruby and blue threaded ones, also manufacturing some drawn glasses with a tear in them and—excellent speculation—Jacobite club glasses. The demand ever produces mysteriously the supply. So far cut glass, which we are chiefly considering in this chapter, seems to have somewhat escaped the atentions of the imitator, perhaps because the modern cut glass is so very

beautiful and follows so closely the patterns of
the old, that the ground is, as it were, cut from
beneath the faker's feet.

It was not until towards the end of the 18th
century that cut glass—that is to say, glass cut
in facets, was produced in the beautiful manner
belonging to that period. It was a great discovery when it was realized what dispersive
power on rays of light lay in flint or lead glass,
and how exquisite were the prismatic effects
produced.

Until the discovery of the making of flint glass
this facetting would not have been possible.

Without being too technical I should like to
give you a very brief and general idea of the different periods of glass making in England ; it can
only be a few superficial lines, for it is a wide subject, and would occupy alone a very large volume.

If the subject interests you, Mr. Hartshorne
and Mr. Edward Dillon have written splendid
books on this art. Hartshorne's " Old English
Drinking Glasses " is devoted almost exclusively
to that line, but also gives all kinds of illuminating information. Mr. Dillon's " Glass," in the
Connoisseur's Library, will also afford you interesting reading. As yet there is not much
literature on the subject, but one or two cheap
books, and excellent if cheap, have been written,
and I give you the names in the Bibliography.

Of the earliest days of glass making in England
we have singularly little information. It seems,

however, from the few sources of knowledge—
mostly speculative—that we have, that when the
Romans held sway here, the art was carried on in
many different parts of the land, for in all the
places of their settlement, remains and fragments
have been found, but apparently after their
departure the craft languished and died. The
next notice we have of it is in some deeds concerning Chiddingfold, in the early 13th century,
when a grant is given to a " Vitrearius " and
again the " ovenhusveld " is given as among the
boundaries.

Chiddingfold, on the borders of Surrey and
Sussex, was in the 13th century probably the
home of glass making, and there were several
other small places, more or less in the same
neighbourhood—Loxwood, Fernfold, Kirdfold
and Wisboro Green.

The probable cause of the concentration
of the industry was the bracken and undergrowth in this—at that date—well-wooded
locality. This glass was called in France *Verre
à fougère*, because it was necessary to have
large quantities of woody matter among its constituents.

There is now hardly a trace of the once flourishing glass industry that followed the line of the
above villages, which at that time were nothing
more than hamlets.

The following passage occurs in Mr. Dillon's
book, which I should advise all students to read,

as it affords all the essential information that the collector needs.

"Fragments of green glass have been found
" on the site of a glass house at Chiddingfold. In
" the museum at Lewes are two bulbous flasks
" with long necks of this green Weald glass.

"There was another centre of the glass indus-
" try in East Sussex, in the country to the north
" of Hastings. In a mediæval document concern-
" ing Beckley in this district, the name ' Glassye
" Borough ' occurs. At these woodland glass-
" houses, for many generations, the wandering
" pedlars, the ' glass men ' had been wont to
" renew the stock of ' vrynells, bottles, bowles,
" cuppis to drinck and such lyke ' that they
" hawked along the country side. ' You may
" send,' says Thomas Charnock in his Breviary
" of Philosophy (1557) ' to Chiddingfold to the
" glass-maker.

" ' And desire him in most humble wise
" ' To blow thee a glass after thy devise.'
" That is to say that the glass blower, as we have
" seen in other cases, worked from the patterns
" provided by his customers."

This short passage brings well before us the methods and manners of those primitive glass making times.

Much later we come to the coloured glass of Wrockwardine, Nailsea and Bristol. Nailsea has produced a charming variety of glass, not only green, and deep royal blue, but yellow and a peculiarly attractive kind of red, ranging from pale pink to a deep crushed strawberry. This is very frequently splashed and lined spirally with opaque white, which has a quaint and yet very pleasing effect ; the stripes were obtained in very much the same way as opaque and coloured spirals were introduced into the stems of drinking glasses. Of this process I gave a description in " Antiques and Curios."

At Wrockwardine, near to Wellington, there was a small " glass house " which produced a number of articles now much prized by collectors, such as spirit flasks, double and single, the double ones having the necks curving across each other, like the twin oil and vinegar bottles.

These flasks were used by travellers, whose chief mode of progress was on horseback, and so for safety they were made to fit into holsters hanging from the saddle.

I have always imagined it was Mrs. John Gilpin's penuriousness that prevented her setting up her husband with proper holster flasks, and allowing him to use the old fashioned and highly inconvenient stone bottles with " curling ears." If you remember we are told that " though on pleasure she was bent, she had a frugal mind."

> " Now Mistress Gilpin (careful soul !)
> " Had two stone bottles found,
> " To hold the liquor that he loved
> " And keep it safe and sound.

" Each bottle had a curling ear,
" Through which the belt he drew,
" And hung a bottle on each side,
" To make his balance true."

Disaster soon followed Mrs. Gilpin's ill-judged economy. The clattering of the bottles and the bad riding of poor Johnny precipitates a crisis, and the horse runs away.

" The wind did blow, the cloak did fly
" Like streamer long and gay,
" Till loop and button failing both
" At last it flew away.

" And now, as he went bowing down
" His reeking head full low,
" The bottles twain behind his back
" Were shattered at a blow.

" Down ran the wine into the road
" Most piteous to be seen
" Which made his horse's flanks to smoke,
" As they had basted been.

" But still he seemed to carry weight
" With leathern girdle braced ;
" For all might see the bottle-necks
" Still dangling at his waist."

A flask of the kind that Mrs. Gilpin should have possessed is to be seen in Fig. 41 in the centre of the lower shelf. These are now very rare, and I have only seen one which was still wedded to its holster. It was in Brittany in a château of one

FIG. 40.—NAILSEA GLASS.

FIG. 41.—ENAMELLED GLASS.

of the old nobility who had suffered much in the troubles of 1793. It was cracked but entire. The one seen in Fig. 41 is opaque white, and the looped lines are of brilliant blue, and the crushed strawberry I alluded to before. Nailsea and Bristol are close together, and so it is natural that the products of the two " glass houses " should have a family likeness. The small striped jug on the right of Fig. 40 is Nailsea, rather pale green with opaque white stripes, at the other corner another small jug—both of them for milk I should think—of brilliant dark blue. There is another of purple, but I thought it would crowd the picture too much to include it.

The central big jar was for strong waters, and is rather unusual, being black, splashed with grey instead of white.

During the 17th and early 18th centuries a large number of spirit bottles were made on Dutch lines ; probably the idea came to us from them in the mid 17th century. A good collection of these can be studied at the Guildhall Museum. They were usually globular in form, rather low in height and the sides squeezed somewhat flat. The later specimens have a glass seal applied on one side, with the name of the seller of the spirit.

Made both at Nailsea and Bristol, and indeed elsewhere, also were several curious and useless things, presumably done only to show how skilful the blowers were. For instance, a glass walking stick seems an absolutely unpractical idea, and

or another, the discomfiture of *some one*; there
was no fun unless some victim was made to look
a fool. This desirable end was easily attained
by the trick glass.

The difficulty of drinking out of these queer
glasses was caused by the bulb at the foot of the
yard, and when, on drinking, the unfortunate
performer had nearly reached the end, the outer
air somehow passed down the long tube into
this rounded knot or bulb, and pushed out the
remaining liquor, which flew all over the face
of the drinker.

This was considered a great joke, and it was
provocative of much rough horse play and
wrestling, in which usually the cause of quarrel
was broken. This accounts for the great scarcity
of glass yards.

We read in Evelyn's diary under Feb. 10,
1685, that " Being sent to by the Sheriff of the
" county to appear and assist in proclayming
" the King, I went the next day to Bromely,
" where I met the Sheriff, and the Commander
" of the Kentish troop, with an appearance I
" suppose of about 500 horse and innumerable
" people, two of his Majesty's trumpets, and a
" serjeant with other officers, who, having drawn
" up the horse in a large field neare the towne,
" march'd thence, with swords drawne, to the
" market place, where, making a ring, after
" sound of trumpets and silence made, the High
" Sheriff read the proclaiming titles to his

" Bailiffe, who repeated them aloud, and then,
" after many shouts of the people, his Majesty's
" health being drunk in a flint glasse of a yard
" long, by the Sheriff, Commander, Officers, and
" Chiefe gentlemen, they all dispersed, and I
" returned."

Somewhere about this time, or perhaps a little
earlier, must have been made the beautiful two
handled cup with cover shown in Fig. 42. It is
through the kindness of Miss Whitmore Jones
that I am able to show it to you ; it is truly a
beautiful thing and of most artistic design. Miss
Whitmore Jones told me that it has always been
thought to have been 16th century work, perhaps because the handles—alas ! one is broken—
are in the form of E, which at first sight might
point to Queen Elizabeth ; but although there
might be some colour to this theory given by the
fact that the first Mrs. Jones had been maid of
honour to the Virgin Queen, a close study of its
beautiful ornamentation dispels the idea, the
gophered edges to the handles and top of the lid
are an exact reproduction of the very decorative
slip ware of the early 17th century ; the bosses
and masks are also of that period and it seems
likely that it was made to order in Venice,
though on an English pattern, showing the
Tudor Rose. We read frequently in early
inventories of " Item thre glasses like pottes,
with two cases with covers to them," and again,
" Item foureteene other standing cuppes of

glasse diaper work of sondry fashions, some of
them lacking covers." It is curious to note that
in this inventory, dated 1542, the spelling is so
infinitely superior to that of a hundred years
later, when in reading the letters of Lady Sussex
to Sir Ralph Verney, the exercise is a sort of
guessing competition, helped out—at least in my
own case—by saying over the sentence as it
appears phonetically to be meant, when occasionally welcome light is thrown on our spelling
gloom.

In the 17th century English glass-making
seems to have received a severe check from the
successful competition of the glass makers of
Liège, but there must have been still a very
considerable trade, because Sir R. Mansel obtained the sole rights of glass-making, which
he retained for some thirty years.

At or about this time (there is some obscurity
about these dates), the Duke of Buckingham
obtained a grant to make glass ; owing to much
controversy and bickering between various as-
pirants to the same privilege, he could not secure
a renewal of his contract when he applied for it
in 1663, still he continued to own a factory,
which the ever useful Evelyn, in his Diary under
the date 1673 mentions, where he speaks of
" Vases of mettal as cleare, ponderous, and thick
as Crystal ; " certainly, too, the Duke—who was
as well able as any man in England to look after
his own interests—managed to get an order for-

FIG. 42.—THE CHASTLETON CUP.

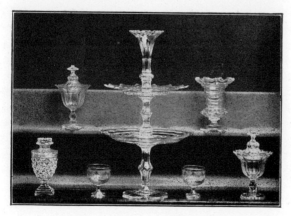

FIG. 43.—CENTRE-PIECE, ETC.
(By permission of Messrs. Gill and Reigate.)

bidding the importing of mirrors, etc., from the Continent.

At Hampton Court may be seen in perfection the splendid mirrors, with glass frames and enriched by sapphire stars and bosses, which were fixed there in William's short reign. Whatever our feelings with regard to his claim to the throne, we must at any rate render him due thanks for the great impetus and encouragement, aided by Dutch craftsmen, that he gave to our industrial arts.

The window panes themselves in parts of Hampton Court are quite mauve, due to the influence of light on the protoxide of manganese. I promised not to go into chemical matters, but that little fact may interest you when you look at the mauve windows belonging to some of the 18th century houses ; there are some still in Cranbourne Street in old-fashioned small windows there. The small panes in the lofty windows of William's gallery at Hampton Court are bevelled all round in the manner we associate with Vauxhall plates.

Before passing to the period of " cut " glass, which is the goal of this chapter, I want you to look at Fig. 41, which gives examples of a rare and charming kind of glass peculiar to Bristol, and which has been, one may almost say discovered by the researches of Mr. Hugh Owen.

This kind of glass, opaque white and painted

with great delicacy, was apparently intended as a close imitation of porcelain, and certainly the resemblance is very distinct. The flowers, extremely well drawn, are coloured after nature, and partake a little, I should say, of the character of those on Plymouth china.

The opaque ground is smooth and soft to the touch, and sometimes lined spirally, something in the manner of ribbed silk. The main part of the decoration, if not all of it, was done by one Michael Edkins, and it is the inspection of his ledgers which has thrown light on the subject. I find the following passage, among many others of equal interest in "Two centuries of Ceramic Art in Bristol," by Hugh Owen. This book will repay study, for it deals with both glass and china, and it is usually to be found in good libraries.

"Several firms about this period (1761) made "very large quantities of a translucent glass of a "peculiar softness and texture, very white and "closely resembling soft paste Sèvres or Derby "china. It is almost impossible to mistake the "genuine enamel glass of Bristol. . . . .

"Mr. Michael Edkins, after giving up painting "Delft ware, was chiefly employed by the makers "to ornament this enamel glass, and for this pur- "pose two methods were pursued. The com- "mon articles were simply painted with oil "colour, mixed with a desiccative and dried hard "by artificial heat. The more costly were enam-

" elled in the usual way with coloured frits, vitri-
" fied in a muffle or kiln.   Blue glass also was
" similarly decorated ; and judging by the quan-
" tity of both kinds painted by Mr. Edkins alone,
" the trade must have been considerable.

" Some extracts from the accounts will be read
" with interest."

1762 April 26.   To 5 long doz. Amell
              (enamel) Beakers 10   0

Jan. 19th.   To 1 Sett of Jars and Beakers,
              5 in a Sett 2   0

July 19th.   To 4 Blue Jars and Beakers
              with Mosaick Borders to
              match a large sett for Mr.
              Wilson 2   0

26th.   To 1 Pint Blue can ornamented
              with gold and letters   8

1763. Aug. 18.   To 6 Enamelled pt. canns
              wrote *Liberty and no excise*
              (a) 4d. 2   0

" The prices quoted from these old accounts
" for ornamenting both enamel and blue glass,
" certainly were for the cheaper mode, and not
" for the vitrified enamel painting. . . .

" The extreme fragility of the Bristol white
" enamel glass insured its early destruction, and
" considering the large quantity made, it is
" surprising how little has been rescued.

" Previous to the beginning of the year 1859,
" it was unknown to collectors, and, but for some
" few family memorials in the hands of Mr.

Q

" Edkins, the existence of it would have been
" forgotten."

In Fig. 41 the central figure is one of a " Sett
of Beakers," its height is 8½ inches, and the
flowers on it very brilliantly painted, all the designs being according to nature, in shape and
colouring, and not in any way conventionalized,
the oil and vinegar on each side are equally delicately painted, and the little wreaths are marvels of minute work.   The sugar and mustard
pair below are in exactly the same style, and all
four have metal tops, but they are not silver.

The gems of the collection, however, are to my
mind the dainty pair of candlesticks, which have
the groundwork which I likened to corded silk.

I have compared this delicate product to Swan-
sea china, and it certainly resembles it, but it
also reminds me of Battersea enamel, especially
the candlesticks.

The degenerate imitations of this beautiful
glass are familiar to all of us in the painfully
gorgeous vases, which we are called upon to study
on the mantelpieces of seaside lodgings.   Very
generally the groundwork is blue and the decoration runs to lilies of the valley and fuchsias !   And
now we come to considering " cut " glass ; this
variety has been brought to greater perfection in
England and Ireland than in any other country,
though it appears that in Liège they ran a close
race with us and called such glass " à l'Anglaise."
It was late in the 17th century when English glass

became so greatly esteemed in Europe, and it was owing to the discovery of working flint glass, which is really glass in which is a considerable quantity of lead and some potash. The terms flint glass and lead glass really represent the same metals as they are called.

The old kind of glass had been chiefly composed of silica from sand, chosen from parts where iron was present in large quantities, and alkali, etc., from the ashes of undergrowth and fern in the neighbourhood where it was made—hence the name *Verre à fougère* given to the same glass in France.

It seems quite uncertain at what exact period flint glass, or lead glass, was first made in England ; it appears that in 1680 glass was being made in Liège, which was described as flint glass "*à l'Anglaise*," which seems to prove that it must have been worked in England before that date. I will give you a few lines from the article on glass in the British Encyclopædia, which I think contains in very concentrated form the most lucid description of flint glass that I have yet met with.

" It is probable that the flint glass of that date " was very different from the flint glass of to-day. " The term flint glass is now understood to mean " a glass composed of the silicates of potash and " lead. It is the most brilliant and the most " colourless of all glasses. E. W. Hulme, how- " ever, who has carefully investigated the subject, " is of opinion that flint glass in its present form

" was introduced about 1730. . . . It is prob-
" able that flint glass was not invented, but
" gradually evolved, that potash-lead glasses
" were in use during the latter part of the 17th
" century, but that the mixture was not per-
" fected until the middle of the following cen-
" tury."

" It is the development of the craft of glass
" cutting in connection with the perfecting of
" flint glass that makes the 18th century the most
" important period in the history of English glass
" making. . . ."

Now as to the localities where the best cut glass
was made, I think we must give the palm to Ireland. Dublin, Cork, Belfast, Waterford and
Londonderry all produced beautiful glass of the
kind we are now considering, and that of Cork
and of Waterford take the first places.

Experts profess to be able to distinguish between the products of these two factories, but I
confess it is beyond my poor powers—they both
have the characteristic of a certain faint bluish
tinge in the metal, only to be seen in certain cross
lights. I fancy—but frankly, this is, perhaps,
only a fancy—that Cork glass shews a trifle more
green in the bluish tint than that of Waterford.

Waterford glass is immensely sought after, and
in the present day is valued before that made at
Bristol, Newcastle, Stourbridge and Birmingham,
etc., but I should not be surprised to hear that
some collector's pieces, labelled authoritatively

Waterford, would, could they speak, confide to us with a wink, that they were made at Bristol, or perhaps at Newcastle or Stourbridge.

However, these dark suspicions may only have been planted in our receptive minds by the sourly disappointed ones who have not secured such good specimens as they desired. Human nature being what it is, if we are unfortunate ourselves, it is at least some comfort to find others, who, pluming themselves on great successes and inclined to crow lustily, prove to be in reality no better off than ourselves, did they but know it.

It must always have been a pretty sight at the end of the 18th century when a well-ordered dinner table was set out with the beautiful cut glass of the time, all glittering and scintillating, and throwing out prismatic lights with all the brilliancy of diamonds.

At that time, when the cloth was removed in the fashion of those days, for the dessert to be arranged, how delightful the hobnailed bowls and dishes must have looked, sparkling, dancing, shimmering and reflecting in the deep toned old mahogany table, a table, perhaps, that had come from the inspiration of Chippendale and shining with the care and attentions of notable housewives.

Even to-day in some well-to-do houses, under the fine damask cloth, what do we find? Nothing but a meagre top of deal, masquerading on decent turned mahogany legs !

Here is a come down indeed, it does not really matter, everyone says, because the top is never seen. It is, indeed, a type of much of the meretricious display of the present day. The somewhat vulgar phrase, still sometimes heard amongst those not quite born in the purple, " come and put your legs under our mahogany," when an invitation to dinner is given, should be, " come and put your legs under our deal top."

On the tables of those days there were beautiful decanters—decanters seem now almost out of fashion—of every shape and form and decorated in every possible design. We had a very handsome pair, cut with what was called the thumb mark pattern, because all over the article there was a mark in rings, as if a thumb had been pressed symmetrically round and round, the marks becoming smaller as the circumference of the bowl or decanter decreased. This is a rare pattern and I have seen but very few examples. I remember how difficult they were to keep clean, I often had the job, and each individual thumb mark had to be wiped.

The following few lines from the encyclopædia will tell you all that it is necessary to know as to how the cutting is done.

" Cutting and engraving are mechanical pro-" cesses for producing decorative effects by " abrading the surface of the glass when cold.

" The abrasion is effected by pressing the glass
" against the edge of wheels, or discs, of hard
" material revolving on horizontal spindles. The
" wheels for making deep cuts are made of iron
" and are fed with sand and water.

" The wheels range in diameter from 18 inches
" to 3 inches. Wheels of carborundum are also
" used. Wheels of fine sandstone, fed with
" water, are used for making slighter cuts and
" for smoothing the rough surface left by the iron
" wheels. Polishing is effected by wooden wheels
" fed with wet pumice powder, and rotten stone,
" and by brushes fed with moistened putty pow-
" der. Patterns are produced by combining
" straight and curved cuts. Cutting brings out
" the brilliancy of glass, which is one of its in-
" trinsic qualities. At the end of the 18th cen-
" tury English cut glass was unrivalled for design
" and beauty. Gradually, however, the process
" was applied without restraint and the products
" lost all artistic quality."

The last few words are sadly true, decoration
has run riot and tortured patterns have replaced
the charmingly simple but effective varieties of
the hobnail group of patterns. Then again, cut
glass is now imitated in a cheap and nasty way,
by glass made in moulds, and so it has for many
resaons fallen somewhat into disrepute. Within
the last twenty-five years, however, cut glass
has come gradually into fashion, and happy are
those who have treasured a few old examples.

Owing to the courtesy of Messrs. Gill and
Reigate I am able to show you a great variety of
specimens. First, in Fig. 44 ; of all the treasures
displayed here I think the covered jam jar in the
centre of the middle shelf is the one I covet most.
The pattern is the hobnail, which in one form or
another is the basis of most of the old patterns.
The dish on which it stands curves over and the
whole thing, if it catches a ray of light, seems entirely to illumine a dark corner. The decanters
on each side, holding a quart, are very graceful, I
like so much the kind of close cut bands round
the neck. I think I prefer them to the splendid
pair of which you see one on the top shelf, though
I daresay most people would prefer the more pre-
tentious pattern. You will see it has elaborately
ornamented arched panels and the stopper is fat
and rounded.

On the lowest shelf you see a third pair, having
what are called mushroom stoppers. I like this
pair very much with the plain circles round the
shoulders, the band of hobnail design, and the
totally different pattern below.

Between them stands a Waterford jug of quite
another style. It shows the blue tinge supposed
to be typical of that factory very plainly, and its
owners very kindly had it photographed for me
on that account. It is entirely different in tone
from the one on the top shelf, which is English,
and has a likeness of the Duke of Wellington.
To the right of the top shelf is a very dainty

FIG. 44.—CUT GLASS.

(By permission of Messrs. Gill and Reigate.)

cream ewer, fluted diagonally and cut under the lip in kind of steps, which gives extraordinary brilliancy.

In Fig. 43 we have quite different specimens, the cutting being in broad effects. The large centre piece is a fine specimen, but I do not admire it much, the effect is a little top heavy. To the right, on the top shelf, is a celery glass, of these I am sure there must be a large number floating about somewhere, for in early Victorian times no household was considered to be adequately equipped without a celery glass. They are now usually dedicated to cut flowers. The two handsome covered jars seem to me to be for sweetmeats, or perhaps preserved ginger.

The deeply cut jar and cover to the extreme left of the lower shelf is a very handsome piece. I judge it to be early 19th century on account of the square plinth on which it is set.

Fig. 45 shows again a variety of objects quite different to those we have already studied.

The two handled jug in the centre is elegant, but of no especial interest, but above, to the left, is a really beautiful Waterford tea bottle, or tea poy as they were called. It is almost square, with a wide neck and broad squat stopper, a band of hobnail cutting is all round below the shoulders, and the rest is ornamented with kind of sharp vertical flutes, repeated on the neck and the stopper.

It is a most attractive piece and my soul

yearned for it directly I saw it, but the price of
Waterford glass is far beyond my modest purse,
moreover, it is sold already, which seems to settle
my longings. It reminds me of a very quaint
story connected with Henry IV. on a visit to one
of his provincial towns. Cannon not having been
fired off, as was usual on these occasions, the
mayor began to apologize. " *Sire, nous n'avons
pas fail lirer le canon en l'honneur de votre Majesté
pour plusieurs raisons : la première c'est que nous
n'avons pas de canons. . . . . 'Je vous dispense
des autres' interrompit aussitôt Henry IV.'* "

Next to this Naboth's vineyard, is a rather
uncommon shaped dish, deeply and fancifully
cut. On the top shelf to the right and at the
left on the lower one, are two sugar basins of the
kind that used to be placed between the two
divisions for black and green tea, in old fashioned
wooden tea caddies. These so often became
broken from constant lifting in and out, and but
seldom is it that we find them in proper position
now. They are always well cut, and worth
preserving. The covered jar is again evidently
a sweetmeat receptable, and the very handsome
piece immediately below is I think the lower half
of a decanter; from there being no border of any
kind, I think it is an indication that it has been
ground down from something else ; it is a beautiful piece of ornamentation and I rejoice that it
has been saved.

Now we come, in Fig. 46, to a set of very lovely

FIG. 45.—WATERFORD TEA-BOTTLE, ETC.
(By permission of Messrs. Gill and Reigate.)

FIG. 46.—SET OF LUSTRES.
(By permission of Messrs. Gill and Reigate.)

and perfect lustres, a centre, and one for each side.

There was a time, and that not very long ago, when lustres on the mantelshelf were considered as beneath the notice of "genteel" society, and only to be met with on lodging house chimney pieces, the last refuge of the unwanted ornaments, on a par with flowers executed in wool of fearsome tints, and fruit in wax, with a venomous wasp, or timorous butterfly hovering realistically over the tempting morsel.

But now our pride is hardly to be restrained within decent limits, if we possess a pair of really good lustres !

This is a remarkably handsome group, the double row of circular medallions from which the prisms hang was a very happy inspiration. The centre piece is uncommon ; how beautiful it must have looked in the centre of the mahogany table, and what hundreds of brilliant tints it must have thrown forth. There is no illuminant so charming as that of numerous wax candles, and when their radiance was intensified by the prismatic splendours of these lustres, both on the table and mantelpieces, and also from the central chandeliers, the effect must have been most soft and yet lustrous.

I have also an illustration of a very fine pair of mantelshelf lustres, but alas ! no room to insert it ; they are quite different to Fig. 40, but

though much larger are not, I think, so pleasing ;
they are mounted in ormolu and the feet are
sharply domed and facetted all over, which has
a very brilliant effect, but the long prisms
hanging from the neck, are not so long, nor so
numerous, and they lack the three charming
rows of glittering discs.

In America, where all these things are so
greatly valued, there is a large number of these
old-world lustres ; in proportion, a far larger collection than with us, whether, because they have
been taken greater care of, or because with their
usual astuteness, our transatlantic cousins saw
they were going to be much considered, I
know not, but it is assuredly a fact.

In collecting old glass, your ideas must at first,
at any rate, be a little modest ; there is still a
fairly representative number to be chosen from
of small articles if you take your time, and act
with caution.

Glasses (often on a stand to match) for jelly
and syllabub are desirable possessions. I have—
as I write—three before me, but unfortunately
only one is perfect, the two handsomest are
divorced from their glasses. The plainest one
which exists entire with its six glasses, takes
apart in the middle as is very frequently the
case ; so does a second one, which is most elaborately cut, in small and big hobnail design ; the
glasses to this one must have been charming,
but not one survives. Its owner can trace it

back over a hundred years to the year 1800, or
1801.

The third example is not so old, and though
very brilliant, belongs to the time when design
was going down hill. It also separates in the
middle, and makes into two dishes; it could
never have carried its glasses as it is quite in a
bowl shape.

A friend of mine possesses a small but very
perfect pair of Waterford "receptacles." I
cannot affirm what they are, so will prophesy on
velvet, and call them "receptacles." They
might possibly have been mustard pots, they
have silver neck bands and little nicks for the
spoons, but their size—5 inches in height—is
rather against that theory, moreover they have
no lids. Were they possibly little bowls for
clotted cream, or for pounded sugar. Their
pattern is the celebrated hobnail, and they show
a distinctly sea blue tinge. I say they, but alas!
there is only one genuine one, its twin is an
imitation, though a very perfect one. Sad to
say, it is the outcome of a tragedy; the pretty
little pair after surviving more than a hundred
years, fell a victim to a heavy-handed parlour-
maid, and one was shattered; that is another
and very disquieting quality of Waterford glass,
when it breaks, it does so with its whole heart,
shattering into minute pieces.

Having made a small and not expensive
collection of celery glasses, sugar basins, and

jelly, and syllabub glasses, turn your attention to old spirit bottles, these are comparatively easy to pick up ; one of a set having been broken, the remaining one or two were cast aside, and a new and more fashionable set bought, hence many derelicts are still to be found in dark corners of curiosity shops.

It is sad to think how the beautiful output of the Waterford glass workers came to an end, they cut their own throats, and closed the works on themselves.

It was after the great exhibition of 1852, when the Waterford glass shown was so beautiful that the firms were overwhelmed with orders, and the hands, thinking it a favourable moment to " better " themselves, demanded such increased wages that the masters could not make both ends meet, and after struggling in a moribund condition a short time, the whole industry came to an end.

As yet there is but little literature on the subject of glass ; but in the few books I mention I have as usual put a cross against the cheap ones, and there is a good deal of information to be found in " The Connoisseur " and the " Burlington." If I have aroused your interest in the direction of further study, I have realized my ambition.

CHAPTER VI

JACOBITE DECANTERS AND WINE GLASSES

I HAVE spoken of Jacobite drinking glasses before, but said nothing of decanters, for they are extremely scarce, and until recently I could not obtain an illustration of any, but now, through the kindness of Miss Whitmore Jones, of Chastleton, I am able to do so.

It is, of course, easy to understand that there would not be many, in comparison with the number of glasses used at Jacobite club meetings and private parties. It has been supposed by Mr. Hartshorne and other notable authorities, that the drinking glasses were individual property, and that at a convivial party the guests brought their own, reminding one of the direction issued to those about to join a school treat, " each child to bring his own mug."

It seems a little difficult to imagine this arrangement, because, owing to their fragility and shape, it would have been practically impossible to carry them in the pocket, but perhaps their real theory was that each member of the society, or club, to which they belonged, brought his own glass and deposited it at the club if convenient, or at the house of the member who usually entertained them. This seems to be natural, and there is a proof of it—more or less—to be found in the Oxburgh glasses, the property of Sir Henry Bedingfeld, of which I shall speak presently. I must very briefly review the causes that led to the feeling of semi-secretive Jacobitism, which took form in the birth of clubs and the making of Jacobite glasses.

There is something infinitely pathetic in looking at the frail glasses that have so long outlived the cause for which they were made, and the gallant lives that were freely given up on the scaffold and in exile, for the " cause."

A good many, doubtless, as in every political disturbance, were self-seekers, and many not untainted by an eager desire for personal aggrandisement, but side by side with this feeling was a nobler one, loyalty to the old race which had so long ruled the country, and fidelity to those who were on the losing side. There has always been in Englishmen the trait of wishing to help the under dog.

These gallant men, even if they were not absolutely disinterested, carried their lives in their hands and made no unmanly moan, when exile, ruin, and the headsman's axe, was their portion. Sir Walter Scott, himself a Jacobite in sentiment, depicted one of this class in a very masterly manner in " Waverley," in the character of Fergus MacIvor, and also showed the beautiful fidelity to a lost cause, untainted by personal ambition, in Flora, his hero's sister.

It must always be remembered that the decanters and wine glasses connected with the cult of Jacobitism do not (with a few exceptions) belong to a date as early as the first rising in 1715, nor indeed to the years prior to the " 45." Almost all date from after that year, when the high hopes of the loyal Stuart lovers were beginning to dwindle, and hope deferred which " maketh the heart sick," was sinking ever lower, with now and then a spasmodic leaping up of the flickering flame of enthusiasm. Those eager loyalists who had anchored all their hopes and aspirations on the Bonnie Prince Charlie of 1740 to 1754, now saw with unwillingness, but certainty, against which they fought in vain, that the cause had no chance against the indolence, incapability and indulged passions of that poor prince, who had indeed been the sport of fate.

But such a cause dies hard, and the north and west country squires and nobles kept their waning hopes alive by eager talk of the sure return of the Stuarts, and the rewards (so lavishly promised) which they would themselves reap, when the king should enjoy his own again.

Very naturally these meetings of the " disaffected," as they were rather quaintly called, could not in those hard drinking days, go on without conviviality, hence the glasses and decanters dedicated to the cult.

R

Mr. Hartshorne is of opinion that the drinking glasses and presumably the decanters were made at Newcastle, this would certainly have been a convenient spot, for, if trouble arose, the makers could slip over the border and lie low, till things settled down.

The whole subject is one that I, in my modest way, have studied somewhat closely, and the lives and deaths of the Jacobite leaders never fail to interest me deeply. They were—most of them—so loyal and hot-headed, so unselfish, so brave in a failing cause and, in most cases, were so cruelly neglected and forgotten, though, perhaps, that is hardly a fair judgment considering the lack of means at the little Stuart court.

It is, we must admit, an impossibility to explain the extraordinary fascination exercised by the Stuarts ; it is a thing not susceptible of prosaic explanation! For one thing they possessed "charm," that entirely elusive quality, with which an individual is born, or not ; it cannot be acquired, if in the personality it is not indigenous in the soil.

At any rate their personal influence has always been so great that no historic events have caused more controversy than have the virtues and vices of the Royal House of Stuart.

Even now, to embark tentatively on the question of the truth or forgery of the celebrated casket letters, so disastrous to the reputation of Mary Queen of Scots, is, not improbably, to bring a storm about one's ears.

Shortly after the publication of Andrew Lang's masterly book on the subject I was having tea in a prosaic A.B.C. tea shop, near to two elderly city gentlemen, of the sleek and rather rotund type, comfortably set up, with straw hats and white waistcoats, for it was a warm day. The whole affair and its sequel reminded me of the quarrel between the immortal Sarah Gamp and Betsy Prig. They began with great politeness, considering each other's tastes in the delicate question of buttered toast *versus* scones, but when all was arranged to their satisfaction, they started a discussion as to the last books they had read. As long as good manners reigned I did not hear much, as their voices were low. Presently, however, they began to be raised, and soon a heated discussion started, eyes sparkled, faces became red, and I heard confused exclamations of " Excuse me, sir, that *is* what he said, I have just read the book." Then a hollow calm reigned for a short time and I gathered that the casket letters were under discussion. Then I heard with angry emphasis " You will oblige me by not imputing such scandalous ideas to me," and from the other gentleman, who seemed literally to puff out with wrath, " She was no better than she should be, and so everyone knows, who is not blinded by prejudice." Then ensued tragedy, the defender of poor Mary was not so quick in word as his adversary, but in action nothing behindhand. Everyone was looking round at the disturbance, when the respectable gentleman, suddenly losing all control of himself, seized his plate with the neglected scone, all the primitive man in him rising unchecked, and he was about to hurl it at his enemy when 20th century prose reasserted itself, and he attempted to replace the plate, but such was the trembling of his hands that it fell on the marble, smashed in half, and the treacherous greasy morsel rebounded on to the enemy's knee, leaving a buttery trail on the immaculate grey trousers.

The sinner was so horrified and repentant that peace was restored, but somehow I think that city friendship was quenched for ever, and all because of a Stuart, dead more than 300 years !

One can well understand the loyalty and enthusiasm that reigned in the 17th century for Charles I. who, with many faults, had also many virtues, and of whom one may say " nothing in his life became him like the leaving of it "— and the clever and tactful Charles II., who had more than his fair share of the Stuart witchery, was beloved and forgiven time after time ; but it is difficult to understand much love being lavished upon the narrow, cruel disposition, and vindictive character of James II., and no doubt he was the least popular of the family, for, during his short and disastrous reign, he had tried his people too much. All the same they loved the family and hated the usurper, and as soon as his son was old enough for the loyal

English to regard him as a leader, they lavished enthusiasm upon him, and later on even more upon his son. The rising of 1715 culminating in disaster, in the flight of Prince James, and the execution of Derwentwater and Kenmure, for a considerable time quenched the hopes of the Stuart supporters. The cruel treatment meted out by the dour and hard-hearted George I., was deterrent for a time, but the sentiment existed as strongly as ever, and only awaited opportunity to display itself.

To this period belong a few glasses dedicated to the Old Pretender, which have verses inscribed on them, from paraphrases of what we now call the National Anthem, and which was written by Bull at the time of the scare concerning the gunpowder plot.

This is the song as arranged by the Jacobites—

God save the King I pray, God bless the King I pray,
God save the King,
Send him Victorious, Happy and Glorious
Soon to reign over us
God save the King.

God bliss the Prince of Wales
The Free born Prince of Wales
Sent us by Thee
Grant us one favour more
The King for to restore
As thou hast done before

THE FAMILIE.

> God save the Church I pray
> And bliss the Church I pray
>   Pure to remain.
> Against all Heressie
> Who strive maliciousslie
>   Her to defame.
>
> God Bliss the subjects all
> And save both great and small
>   In every station
> That will bring home the King
> Who hath best right to reign
>   It is the only thing
>   Can save the Nation.

One glass has the first lines inscribed with a border of scrolls and flourishes round, whilst in the middle is the crowned Cipher J. R. Underneath is Amen and a date 1749. This date would be confusing, but it is easy to see it was the year when it was presented to Prince Henry, for on the opposite side is

> To His Royal Highness,
>   PRINCE HENRY,
>   Duke of
>   Albany and York.

Mr. Hartshorne thinks all glasses with these verses were engraved by the same hand, for Bless is always spelt Bliss, and he thinks they were probably done in France.

If you have my former work, I should like you to refer to the chapter on Jacobite drinking glasses, for read in connection with this one it will be informing and enable me to avoid " vain repetitions."

We now come to the Chastleton glasses, Fig. 47, which, by the kindness of Miss Whitmore Jones, I am enabled to show you. Her ancestral home is full of treasures that take our thoughts back to the long distant past ; but first about the glasses.

There are eleven of the wine glasses all engraved with the rose and two buds in allusion to James II., his son and grandson, an oak leaf, and the word " Fiat " (that it be done). The oak leaf may refer to Charles II., and his rescue in the oak after Worcester, or it may be used simply as distinctive of the English Jacobites, as the thistle would be the peculiar sign of the Scotch loyalists.

The word "*Fiat*," which is so constantly found, is considered to be the " word " or " motto " of the Cycle club. Of this I shall speak more at length, presently.

The two decanters which are rather small, are still more interesting. They are much more elaborate, having as well as the rose and two buds, two oak leaves on a twig, and a fairly large compass, the indicator of which points to a star.

The beautiful allusion in this design is plain to the meanest capacity.

The photographer has shown the two sides of the decanters, so that you can see the complete design.

The glasses do not show the compass, or the star, and were in all probability made in accordance with the usual Cycle pattern, whereas the decanters were made to order for Henry Jones himself.

We know a little more about the Chastleton decanters and glasses than is usually the case with these elusive and mysterious treasures.

It seems that Henry Jones, who came into possession of Chastleton in 1738, belonged to a Jacobite club in Gloucestershire, and Miss Jones said—and no doubt she has family records that prove it—that the glasses for this club were made at Derby, at any rate theirs were.

Chastleton has the additional interest of having been the birthplace of the Gunpowder Plot ; most people know now that Guy Fawkes was only the agent of others, and that Catesby was the author of that fell design.

He originally owned Chastleton Manor, though not the present building. He sold the old house and land to Henry Jones, in or about 1602, who built the absolutely perfect structure, as it stands to-day.

Miss Jones, to whose able little book " The Gunpowder Plot and account of Chastleton," I am indebted for many of these particulars, has given us a very clear insight into the strange personality of Robert Catesby, who, despite his dreadful plot, seems to have been of so lovable and at the same time, so commanding a dis-

FIG. 47.—THE CHASTLETON JACOBITE DECANTERS AND
WINEGLASSES.

FIG. 48.—THE OXBURGH JACOBITE GLASSES.

position, that he dominated all who came under his influence.

The grandson of the Jones who built the house was an ardent Royalist, and followed the fallen fortunes of his master Charles I., and when, in 1651, Charles II. endeavoured, on the disastrous field of Worcester to retrieve his crown, Walter Jones, like the loyal gentleman he was, stood by him.

Well, as we know, things went badly, and whilst Charles was hiding here, there and everywhere, Walter Jones returned home, his horse dead beat, and himself a fugitive from the enemy.

No sooner had he begun to take a little much-needed food, then he heard the soldiers arriving on his track.

Now there is a secret room in Chastleton towards the front of the house, and opening from behind the bed's head in Mrs. Jones' room. Whilst her husband retreated there, she cleared away all traces of his presence, and on the thundering summons of the soldiers, opened to them.

They had already found the exhausted horse in the stable, and were sure they had come on Charles' tracks—" the young man " as they called him.

Mrs. Jones set about preparing supper and followed them in their search of the house, which, producing nothing, her dismay was great to find they were determined to have their supper

and to sleep in her bedroom, their suspicions
for some reason or another being aroused by that
room.

But the brave lady was not to be daunted,
she sent them up a tempting supper and herself
prepared the wine, adding to it a generous allow-
ance of opium, which she had in her medicine
chest ; the medicine chest of those days was
by no means a plaything !

Poor Sarah Jones, how her heart must have
beat, as she listened for the first sound of a snore !
At last they were all heavily asleep, and she
stepped over the prostrate forms, released her
husband, made with him the second perilous
journey, and saw him safe off the premises.

Imagine the rage of the invaders when they
awoke in the morning, especially as they were
allowed to think it was " the young man " who
had escaped them ! The Henry Jones of
Jacobite times planted three scotch firs in the
garden (still standing) a proceeding considered
to be a sign of loyalty to the absent Stuarts,
which no doubt it was, but Miss Jones gives a
quaint supplementary reason for the act, for
she says it was not alone loyalty that prompted
the deed, but also a desire to spite the Rector
with whom he was not on good terms, by shading
his garden !

This beautiful old house is full of Royal relics ;
it seems that in the old days Bishop Juxon, who
attended Charles I. on the scaffold, was an

intimate friend, and he lived after his retirement at Little Crompton, near to Chastleton. Miss Whitmore Jones owned King Charles' Bible, which he gave to Juxon on the scaffold, and the chair used on that grim occasion is now at the Moreton Cottage Hospital. Miss Whitmore Jones also owned one of those very singular miniatures of the Royal Martyr, which, itself executed with great delicacy on copper, has a number of supplementary subjects painted on transparencies, which can be placed upon the original miniature, and so represent different scenes in his life.

The following is the authoress's description of this singular relic.

" The miniature is beautifully painted on " copper, the painting on the talcs is more " roughly done, and the faces are evidently not " intended as likenesses.

1. Shows the King with his crown and sceptre.

2. The King with a sword instead of the sceptre.

3. The King in Armour.

4. In riding dress, with hat and red cloak.

5. In Cairsbrooke looking through the bars of a window.

6. The dress the King wore in prison.

7. The King with the hat he wore at his trial, with the green and white feather, hence the saying " green and white, forsaken quite."

8. The warrant for the execution being read to the King.

9. Bishop Juxon reading to him.

10. The King giving the order of the George to Juxon.

11. The King giving his handkerchief to his son, the Duke of Gloucester.

12. The King's hands being tied.

13. His eyes being bandaged, but he had the bandage taken off.

14. The King stripped to his shirt, with the executioner masked.

15. Holding up the head.

16. An angel's hand placing the crown of martyrdom on King Charles' head.

You will remember seeing in Fig. 1 the beautiful bed in Oxburgh Hall, and now in Figs. 48, 49 and 50, we have the celebrated Oxburgh Jacobite glasses. They were found a few years ago in such an interesting manner that I should like to quote the actual words of Mr. C. E. Jerningham on the subject. He wrote an account of the find in the " Connoisseur," and no words of mine can be so good as his article. I wish I could quote it at full length, but I give the most important part.

" In September, 1907, the present writer was
" on a visit at Oxburgh Hall, the ancient family
" seat of the Bedingfelds. Oxburgh came into
" the possession of that family in the 15th cen-
" tury at the death of the Lady Bedingfeld, who
" was a daughter of Sir Robert Taddenham, and
" descended from Sir William Grandison. On
" the occasion of the visit of the present writer,

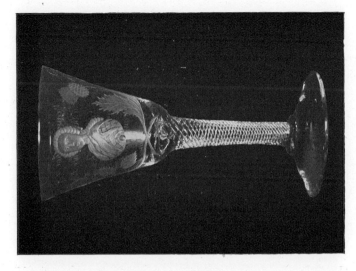

FIG. 49.—PRETENDER PORTRAIT GLASS.

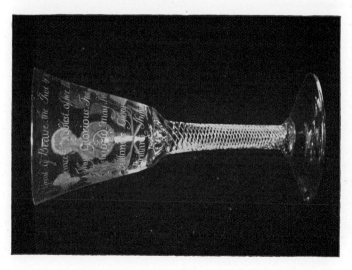

FIG. 50.—PRETENDER GLASS—THE OTHER SIDE.

" it was mentioned by Sir Henry Bedingfeld that
" it was thought there were still some old English
" drinking glasses at Oxburgh.

" The china closets having been searched, their
" glass contents were removed to the central table
" in the housekeeper's room, and, in the midst of
" this mixed collection of modern glass were—un-
" considered . . . . . eleven specimens of the
" Jacobite period. . . .

" Three of the specimens have special features.
" It has for long been the main ambition of col-
" lectors of old British glass to discover a speci-
" men associated with the Pretender, on which is
" engraved a new motto, an inscription which the
" tireless investigation of Mr. Albert Hartshorne
" had failed to find. The ' Pretender portrait '
" glass in the centre of Fig. 48, has the hitherto
" unknown inscription :—

" Charles ye great ye brave the just and good
" Britania's Prince ye noblest of her Bld
" Thy glorious Feats ye world may Pro^m
" Britania's glory and Brittane shame."

" Pro^m," presumably, is the abridgement of
proclaim. The glass is 8½ inches in height.

Before continuing Mr. Jerningham's account
I must point out to you that this glass seen in the
centre of Fig. 48 is the same of which both sides
are seen in Figs. 49 and 50.

The prince is represented in a somewhat overpowering wig, like an old woman's gophered

nightcap, from inside which his young face appears quite girlish. On his left arm the plaid is easily distinguishable.

The eight glasses seen each side of this central one bears the word " Fiat," which, as I told you, is considered to have been the motto of the Cycle Club. This seems to be additionally proved, because with the eight glasses is one not represented here which must have belonged to Sir Watkin Wynn, who founded the Cycle Club, so that it fits in very well that this glass should be found in such good company.

This is what Mr. Jerningham says about it, " The inscription engraved on it is :—

" ' Let no deceipt within your glass be found,
" But glorious Watkins health go briskly round.'

" It was a Sir Watkin Wynn who founded the
" ' Cycle ' Club, the members of which drank to
" the success of the Pretender in glasses which
" bore the inscription ' *Fiat*.' As the specimen
" has been found at Oxburgh in the company of a
" ' Pretender portrait ' glass and six glasses with
" the ' *Fiat* ' inscription, it may be supposed that
" the ' Watkin ' in question is the Sir Watkin
" Wynn who so ardently supported the Stuart
" cause. The remaining glasses, four of which are
" taller and larger than specimens of the kind
" that are occasionally found, bear the ' *Fiat* '
" inscription, and the four larger have the Prince

" of Wales' feathers on the upper surface of the
" base."

Unfortunately I have no room to give you an
illustration of the Watkin glass, or of another,
about which Mr. Jerningham tells us many interesting things, and which was found with the
others. I am greatly indebted to Sir Henry
Bedingfeld for so kindly allowing me to reproduce
his beautiful old glasses, as well as the unique bed
seen in Fig. 1. It is not possible to study Jacobite decanters and glasses without having one's
attention drawn to the mysterious clubs where
the Jacobites met, and which from their very
nature were shrouded in mystery. I gave a list
of these before and must not repeat, but I want
you to understand how impossible it is to get any
reliable information about them. The very few
records kept make not the slightest allusion to
politics, nor to the headquarters of the club as a
rule. It is to the researches of Mr. Hartshorne
that we are indebted for the principal facts that
are known about the Cycle and other clubs, and
as his beautiful book is, alas, very expensive, I
think you will be grateful to me if I quote one or
two paragraphs from it. He gives an account
of the mysterious " Loyal Brotherhood," whose
president was the Duke of Beaufort.

" There are at Badminton several old por-
" traits of gentlemen supposed to represent
" members of a Jacobite club, but their names
" do not appear upon the pictures, nor is there

" any record of them. . . . A letter exists at
" Wroxton addresed to Lord North by the second
" Duke of Beaufort as follows ; No date is given,
" but as the duke died in 1714, it must have been
" shortly before that.

" Dear Brother North—The Brotherhood hav-
" ing honoured me with their pictures, according
" to sketches prepared by Mr. Gouge, I hope you
" will favour me with sittings at a time most con-
" venient for yourself, and as Mr. Gouge can have
" opportunities to draw it. Mr. Sergeant Dewes
" is my solicitor on this occasion, wherefore I beg
" your answer and approbation either to him in
" person, or by letter directed to Jeremy Dewes
" Esqre., at the Cocoa Tree, in general, which is
" his office at present. The great honour the
" Brotherhood does me on this occasion shall be
" acknowledged by the pictures being entailed for
" after ages upon my ffamily, as memorials of the
" Loyal Brotherhood over whom I have the hap-
" piness to preside,
" This will infinitely oblige
My dear Lord,
Your faithful Brother and humble servant,
Beaufort, Prest. L.B.

" From information kindly given by the Duke
" of Beaufort, it appears that a tradition exists
" at Badminton to the effect that a spot at
" Hawkesbury Upton, now occupied by a
" monument to Lord Edward Somerset, was for-
" merly a bowling green, where the Jacobites

" held their meetings, under the cover of playing
" bowls."

The Cycle Club was started in 1710 and, as we
see, the Loyal Brotherhood was in working order
in 1714, so both must have been actively busy
before the first rising of 1715.   The minor clubs,
however, appear not to have come into existence
till much nearer the " 45 " rebellion, which was
the death blow to the Stuart cause.

It seems probable that the Cycle Club, of which
I have already given you an account (the headquarters of which were at Wynnstay, North
Wales, and which had very widespread influence
all round that part of the country), had also
supplementary meetings in quite distant parts
of the kingdom.   It naturally would be so, and
the club would meet at the different members'
houses, no matter where those members lived.
It has always been supposed—but without positive proof—that " *Fiat* " was the club's motto,
and this supposition is certainly borne out by the
number of " *Fiat* " glasses in existence.

Mr. Hartshorne says, " A characteristic of this
" club was that a new member was elected every
" month, and it appears that it was the custom
" to dine in rotation at each member's house
" within the compass of 15 miles, and that a
" general meeting was held as necessity dictated.
" Thus, if the number was unlimited, a point as
" to which we have failed to obtain information,
" by a process of dilatation, the Cycle must have

S

" formed in its political period a very consider-
" able body, and if we may assume that every
" member provided himself with glasses proper to
" drink ' The King over the water,' their number
" must at one time have been very great."

Therefore, though the club was originally
started in the west, there is no reason to be
surprised that the Oxburgh glasses found in the
extreme east should have belonged to it. The
Bedingfelds are an ancient Catholic family, and
were almost certain to be devoted to the interests
of the fallen Royal Stuarts, rather than to the
Protestant family, who at that time was far from
popular, and they would almost certainly have
joined hands with those held out to them in the
name of the exiled family living sadly in France.

Probably, when glasses could not at once be
obtained with the incriminating " _Fiat_ " on them,
or where perhaps the less heroic members were
timorous and inclined to see obstacles where none
existed, glasses simply showing the rose and buds
were used, which would explain the large number
of these less distinctive ones still to be found. I
have one myself which I reckon amongst my
greatest treasures.

You see in those days it was not possible just
to run round the corner and buy a wineglass when
it was wanted, more especially was it impossible
to get such a thing with a special mark on it, so
that even those whose courage was high, and
Jacobite spirit unquenchable, had doubtless

sometimes a difficulty in getting the danger signal engraved.

At Oulton there are six goblets and four glasses, engraved with the rose and two buds, the star, the oak leaf and " *Fiat.*" With them, for use at the same time, is a walnut wood cabinet, 14 inches high, with doors and a lock. It contains a portrait of Charles Edward in armour, but as at that time armour was gone out of general use and appeared only on state occasions, the artist, not being conversant with the use of it, has put the lance rest on the left side. Mr. Hartshorne it is who gives us these particulars, and he says that it was customary for the cabinet to be placed upon the table after dinner and unlocked with some ceremony.

Two cheap and very helpful books to the study of table glass are " English table glass," by Percy Bate, himself a collector, and " Early English glass," by D. Wilmer. These little books have numerous illustrations which are such a help to the beginner. Mr. Bate has a very good picture of the glass with the Old Pretender's portrait enclosed in a wreath and " *Cognoscunt me mei* " one side, and " *Premium Virtutis* " the other. The artists of those days, at least those working on glass, were not very successful with the wigs. Again, instead of a robust young man, we seem to see a hard featured woman, looking out from a most remarkable nightcap, which has the effect of being tied under his chin. There is something quaint in the timorous idea of some sitters on the hedge, to have the Jacobite emblems engraved under the foot, there are not many of these and they are valuable. It would be that kind of glass, I should say, that would appeal to the gentleman who, on being reproached for not praying for the king, confounded his questioner by saying, " For the king I do pray, but I do not think it necessary to tell God who is the king ! "

I forget the author of the four clever lines, known to most people who crystallized the whole situation in these few words.

" God bless the King, I mean the Faith's defender,
" God bless, no harm in blessing, the Pretender,
" But which Pretender is and which is King.
" God bless us all ! that's quite another thing ! "

I have given you Thornbury's charming old-fashioned ballad on the white rose before, but I think you will forgive me if I quote again just three verses, for they bring before us, so much better than my prosaic words can, the spirit of the time and of those devoted men who held on through good and evil report to a glorious dream.

" The old men sat with hats pulled down,
" Their claret cups before them :
" Broad shadows hid their sullen eyes,
" The tavern lamps shone o'er them,
" As a brimming bowl with crystal fill'd,
" Came borne by the landlord's daughter,
" Who wore in her bosom the fair white rose,
" That grew best over the water.

" Then all leap'd up and join'd their hands
" With hearty clasp and greeting,
" The brimming cups, outstretched by all,
" Over the wide bowl meeting,
" A health, they cried ' to the witching eyes
" Of Kate, the landlord's daughter ! '
" But don't forget the white, white rose
" That grows best over the water !

" Then hats flew up, and swords sprang out,
" And lusty rang the chorus—
" ' Never,' they cried ' while Scots are Scots,
" ' And the broad Frith's before us ! '
" A ruby ring the glasses shine
" As they toast the landlord's daughter,
" Because she wore the white, white rose,
" That grew best over the water."

In the first verse, the " brimming bowl with crystal fill'd," is in allusion to the custom of always having a bowl of water in the centre of the table, so that as the drinkers clinked glasses and gave the toast, " The King," it was " over the water " in the bowl, but if the company was doubtful and spies were suspected the difficulty was met by having water unobtrusively put into the goblets, which were usually on the table, as well as the wine glasses and served the purpose of our modern tumblers.

In my former book I much wanted to tell you the curious story of a man called Paynter, in connection with Simon Fraser, Lord Lovat, the last Jacobite executed for the rising of 1745. I had not space then, but I think I may venture now,

and it throws a strange light upon the lengths
that political enthusiasm can go, when allied to
a somewhat ill-balanced brain.

I have abridged the account from a history
of the Coger's Club, called " Cogers and Fleet
Street," by Peter Rayleigh.

It is much more amusing when not shortened,
and when given in the writer's own words.

It appears that when the Cogers Club was
founded in 1755, it was very largely, if not
exclusively, formed of Jacobites, and certain it
is that a special kind of handshake was instituted, called the " grip," and if a new comer,
or any person not well accredited, could not
respond to this mystic " grip," then things began
to hum !

It seems that a man named Paynter conceived a strange infatuation, almost amounting
to madness, for Lord Lovat, who was about the
least estimable of all the celebrated Jacobites ;
it is fairly proved in the light of research that
he was untrue to both parties, and always
engaged in the despicable game of sitting on the
fence !

Still for all that, however unworthy the
individual, we cannot but feel that it was a cruel,
and a very foolish thing, to behead an old man
of 80, and make into a martyr one who really
was a thorough self seeker.

Whatever his faults, he met death with all
the courage of a Highland gentleman, remarking

gaily, that it was wonderful to see so many people gathered together to see one old man's head fall !

The story of Paynter as told by Mr. Rayleigh is extremely amusing, but I can only give you the skeleton of it.

Paynter first met Lord Lovat at the time of the latter's arrest, in the neighbourhood of Lake Moran, and he joined in an attempt to rescue Lovat by drugging his guard at St. Albans, on the journey to London ; this, of course, failed, and on finding that the old man's execution was a settled thing, the eccentric Paynter offered himself as a substitute to the government.

It seems to me, this was a very cheap magnanimity, for he must have well known that the British government would not take the life of a mere nobody in exchange for that of the chief of one of the most powerful Highland clans.

Perhaps, however, in his cracked way, he was genuine in his offer, for there is no limit to the eccentricities of these hysterical cranks.

As he was not permitted to be a martyr, he solaced himself by visiting the object of his worship every day, and by accompanying him to the scaffold, since his desire to play the principal part had been frustrated. On the night preceding, Simon Fraser had solemnly presented Paynter with his pipe and a small oak chest, in which he kept the papers relating to his trial.

At the last moment he gave the executioner a canvas bag, and its contents. Immediately after all was over, the enthusiastic Paynter purchased the empty bag for a guinea ; he also gained possession of the victim's snuff box, but though he offered twenty guineas for the poor old man's cane he could not secure it.

Paynter joined the Coger's Club in 1755, and now comes the strangest part of all. In Mr. Rayleigh's early youth there was a constant member at the Cogers, by name Lomax, who was believed to be a great grandson of the " great Mr. Paynter," as Lomax grandiloquently called him.

On becoming acquainted with him, Mr. Rayleigh soon heard all the particulars of his ancestor's eccentricities, though Lomax was far from considering his conduct strange, or, indeed, anything short of inexpressibly noble. He always carried about in his pocket a number of the *North Briton* in which there was an article breathing fire and slaughter against the Stuarts, and as he seemed quite as singular in his ways as Paynter, was wont to read aloud—to anyone who would listen to the poor old bore—the hated passage ; then he regularly threw the paper on the floor, spat on it, and then (what an anti-climax) picked it up, carefully wiped it clean and returned it to his pocket for future use !

It is not difficult to conceive that a crank of this kind, soon developed into an intolerable nuisance.

The " great Mr. Paynter " had made a noble

present of the Lovat oak box, canvas bag, pipe and snuff box to the Cogers, on condition that they should be placed on the table on all solemn occasions, and that the rules of the club should be enshrined in the box.

At last, however (it was a hundred years since the execution) the landlord of the Tavern where the Cogers met grew irritated by seeing Lomax staring fascinated at the sacred box— it got on his nerves as we say—and the queer old man being rather unpopular with the members, a meeting was called, and a resolution passed that " Edwards (the landlord) be instructed to " light the kitchen fire with the chest, and to " throw the pipe and canvas bag into the dust- " bin ! Tableau."

No doubt the jovial Cogers meant no cruelty, but it was real cruelty, it was like dispossessing an old imbecile of a toy, and the poor half mad old devotee must have really suffered at the threat, and we cannot but be sorry for him, the treasures had become an obsession, and without the Lovat relics life was worth nothing.

The following night the landlord announced the disappearance of the articles under condemnation. They had been stolen, and it required no great acumen to spot the thief, especially as— conscience pricking him—he sent £10 to the Cogers, and never appeared again, his place knew him no more.

This strange little story seemed to me so curious, that I cannot resist giving it to you, as a proof, of the far-reaching influence of Jacobite interests.

CHAPTER VII

THE TEA TABLE OF THE 18TH CENTURY

Now as we sit comfortably at our afternoon tea and can make a supplementary cup at any hour we please, it is hard to realise that there was ever a time when tea was unknown in England. It was probably used in China many years before it penetrated to the West, and when it did so it was via Holland, where it was in use some time before it became generally known in England. The following few lines on the subject from the Encyclopædia Brittanica are, I think, of sufficient interest to quote. " The earliest mention of tea " by an Englishman is probably that contained " in a letter from Mr. Wickham, an agent of the " East India Company, written from Firando, in " Japan, on the 27th of June, 1615, to Mr. Easton, " another officer of the Company, resident at " Macao, and asking for ' a pot of the best sort of " *chaw* (the Chinese called it cha). How the com- " mission was executed does not appear, but in " Mr. Easton's subsequent accounts of expendi- " ture occurs this item : ' Three silver porringers " to drink chaw in.' "

It was about the middle of the 17th century

that tea began to be known over here, but at first it made its way slowly.   One of the small newspapers of the day, in 1658, issued the following advertisement :   " That excellent and by all " Physitians approved China drink, called by the " Chineans *Tcha*, by other nations *Tay, alias Tee*, " is sold at the Sultaness Head, a cophee-house " in Sweetings Rents by the Royal Exchange, " London."   At first the price was prohibitive, £6 to £10 per ℔.   A good many of us know our treasured Pepys, and so you may remember that in 1660 he tells us with his usual garrulity, of his first introduction to tea.   " I did send for a cup " of tee, a China drink, of which I never had " drunk before."

By 1664 we find tea fallen to 40 shillings the ℔., and by this time the " quality " had taken kindly to the " new drink."   In William and Mary's time the fashion made slow but steady progress, and by the accession of Queen Anne we soon come to the establishment of tea houses and tea gardens.

We have amongst us even now a house established at that time.   It was in 1710 that the famous Twining firm began its successful career.

By the kindness of the existing heads of the firm, I have been allowed to go all over the fine old house and see where Queen Anne and all the fashionable world from that time onwards got their " Tay," as they called it.

We should not be so sure how it was pronounced if Pope had not written his famous lines.

" Here, thou great Anna! Whom three realms
  obey,
" Dost sometimes counsel take—and sometimes tea."

Messrs. Twining celebrated the 200th year of
their establishment in 1910, and they then published a little booklet, with a fund of useful
information contained within its dainty white and
gold covers.

The house has perforce been a good deal altered
inside, to accommodate their machinery, which
in itself is worth seeing—the grinding wheels, the
roasting apparatus, the dynamos, etc.

As I was enjoying the study of the work-saving
apparatus now in use, to prepare the immense
output of the firm, not only for our own country,
but to supply the courts of all the Continental
countries, as well as the Paris branch of their
business, I could not but wonder what the
founder of this great house—Thomas Twining, who
in 1710 laid the first stone of its prosperity—would
think if he could walk through the old house now.

The family in those days lived there, as was the
fashion of the time, though not exactly " over the
shop," because the adjacent premises were
occupied by the Bank, also in the possession of
the Twining family, and it was in the upper
rooms of this portion that the family lived.

On the side of the court we may still read
" This is Devereux Courte, 1676." It was in
1711 that Queen Anne appointed Thomas Twining her tea merchant, or " purveyor of teas," as

he was grandly described, and Messrs. Twining have continued to be " purveyors of teas " to nine English sovereigns in succession.

There were once two coffee houses in Devereux Court : " Toms," where Twining's now is, and the " Grecian " commemorated in " Grecian " chambers. All the wits and literary men of the day met at these two fashionable houses, and " Toms," now Twinings, seems to have been rather the resort of those contented with the Hanoverian succession, because in an old news-paper of 1715, Addison speaks of someone—a lady—who had " a design of keeping an open tea table, where every man shall be welcome that is a friend to King George." This would, I imagine, be something in the nature of an " at home " with " tea and tattle " for those of approved political principles !

In 1710 Thomas Twining set up his sign of the " Golden Lyon," and prosperity followed his venture from the first beginnings, in spite of the outrageous prices paid for tea, 20 shillings and 30 shillings being quite a usual sum for a pound.

The first Twining of Devereux Court lived till 1741, and must have been a very important and wealthy citizen. Hogarth painted his portrait, and very vigorous and animated it is, as well as showing a most pleasing and benevolent expression.

The shop itself is but little altered, and has still the old world flavour of Queen Anne's time. On entering from the Strand side you find on the left a series of quaint little shallow cabinets of mahogany with glass doors, that would be ideal for the display of china and pottery.

These nice little cupboards cannot be co-equal with the starting of the business, for mahogany was not in use then. I should think—but this is pure conjecture—that very likely they were made on the death of Thomas Twining, in 1741, when alteration or improvements were undertaken.

The shop, being so little altered, is quite instructive, and one sees pass before one's mental eye the shoppers of two hundred years ago ; the ladies with the towering head-dresses which lasted from Queen Mary's time to nearly 1800, and the vast hoops, which, when the ladies condescended to order their own tea—preceded by a splendid footman, and followed by a negro page—must have pretty well filled the narrow precincts of the shop.

There is no record of where the tea drinking went on at Twinings. Very possibly it might have been in the room now used as a board room, and where all the interesting family portraits are hung.

I was told that at one time this was the tasting room. There is an illustration in the booklet that seems to suggest this as the tea drinking room, because there is the window in the same position as now, and you see the trees through it in the Temple gardens.

It is an illustration of 1750, and on a scroll

across the picture is written " The tea table."
The family have always personally supervised the
business.   In 1762 when David Twining died,
Mary, his widow, carried on the business, and in
the " London Directory " for 1763 we read,
" Mary Twining, Tea Warehouse, Devereaux
Court, Strand."

In 1783 Richard Twining was instrumental in
helping Pitt, who was Chancellor of the Exche-
quer, to arrange and pass the Commutation Act.
His advice, which was taken, was that the heavy
duty on tea should be removed, and that the
trade should instead pay a sum down to the
Treasury for four years, to make up the loss to
the revenue.   This arrangement brought down
the price of tea.

The bills form most interesting reading, Messrs.
Twining have kindly allowed me to show you one
in Fig. 51.

The prices varied enormously.   In 1714 the
cheapest was Bohea, from 9 shillings to 25 shillings
per lb., and the economical could buy tea dust
from 10 shillings to 12 shillings.   In 1776 Bohea
was 6 shillings ; in 1783 it was only 3 shillings
and sixpence ; in 1825 it was four shillings and
ninepence.   So, you see, there was a good deal of
fluctuation.

Now, with its present cheapness, it is difficult
to realize the expenses of the past, even in comparatively recent times.   I have an old servant
who tells me that she never tasted tea in her

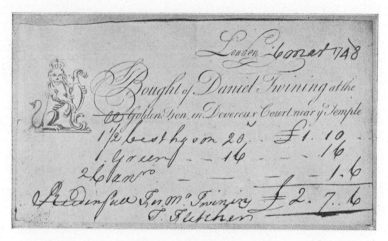

FIG. 51.—A BILLHEAD OF MESSRS. TWINING. OF THE
"GOLDEN LYON."

FIG. 52.—TEA APPLIANCES OF THE 18TH CENTURY.

childhood—seventy years ago—they drank milk
and water, much water and little milk, and it was
only the mother who, on rare occasions, infused a
pinch for herself. Perhaps it was better for them
on the whole than the black and stewed decoction
that is kept on the hob often the whole day.

Dr. Johnson was almost certainly a visitor and
tea drinker at the " Golden Lyon." His heart
was fixed in the Strand and Fleet Street, and all
the neighbourhood is full of memories of him.
His two homes, Gough Square and Bolt Court,
are within a stone's throw, and he must often
have taken his " dish of tea " in Devereux Court.

He probably took a cup there before going to
dinner at the " Cheshire Cheese," also near by.

He was a strange, provoking and yet very lovable man, and I cannot help thinking that his
extreme love for tea and coffee houses, and also
for taverns, was accounted for by the strange
constituents of his household.

There never was a man who better carried out
the Divine command to succour the needy and
distressed, his house was a veritable refuge for the
destitute, and after his wife's death he took in
(simply because they had no money, no home,
and were extremely disagreeable) a circle of can-
tankerous old women, whose continued presence
and perpetual bickering must, I think, often have
driven him from his home. " Williams," he
writes, " hates everybody ; Levett hates Desmou-
" lins and does not love Williams ; Desmoulins

T

"hates them both; Poll Carmichael loves none
"of them." This illuminating sentence occurs
in one of his letters to the Thrales !

He was an ardent tea drinker, and we hear of
sixteen cups being consumed at a sitting, though
we must always remember that they were probably very small ones. Not so his teapots. I
have seen one preserved at Pembroke College of
prodigious dimensions, and it seems to have been
quite suitable to one who—we have his own word
for it—was a shameless tea drinker, "whose
kettle had scarcely time to cool."

Kind, tender, loving soul, with all his eccentricities, it is not surprising that his memory is
affectionately enshrined in English hearts.

Co-existent with the tea houses were the tea
gardens—Bagnigge Wells—Marylebone Gardens,
then called Marybone—Vauxhall—Chelsea, and
many others.

It is curious to know that one of the most
famous and fashionable was where the "Adam
and Eve" public house now stands, at the
junction of Hampstead Road and Euston Road—
fancy the fastidious gentility of the 18th century
ever having been present on such a spot, if only
they could see it now !

Now I want you to consider the tea table and
its accessories in that 18th century. At first,
decidedly Chinese porcelain must have been
used from which to drink it and in which to
infuse it. China had not yet been made in

England, and silver was only for the very wealthy.

The teapots were very small ; I show you on the top shelf of Fig. 52, a small Chinese teapot, which presumably is such as were chiefly used at that time. Earthenware pots were made in imitation, and you have in our illustrations to the chapter on earthenware, the Whieldon Cauli-flower one, and the curious pot with the fortune telling group.

Silver we know was used, and by 1720, it was ousting the small and inconvenient Chinese teapots. In my first book, I told you of a silver one in my own family, that I never think of without a pang. It was stolen with other silver when I was a small child, but I remember it distinctly. It was perfectly round like an orange, and quite plain, but it owned an inscrip-tion and a date 1711. One of my forbears was maid of honour, or whatever they were called in those days, to Queen Anne, and as far as my memory goes the inscription was as follows, " To my deare waiting woman, Audrey Greene. Anna R, 1711."

Had it been in existence now it would have been of inestimable value. No doubt it entered the melting pot at once. As children it was our great delight to make tea in it, more especially as there was a tiny kind of stopper to the spout, suspended by a chain.

The whole thing is very firmly printed on my

brain, because my mother's ingenious plan was to allow us to make tea in this pot whenever we were a little bilious, or otherwise out of sorts, and the contents being, instead of the excellent herb from Devereux Court, where we, like bigger and more important folk bought our tea, was treacherously infused from senna leaves bought, alas! from the chemists.

We never found out the fraud, and what the eye does not see, the heart does not grieve at ; we associated the rather strange and not quite palatable taste of the " tea " with its being infused in our ancestress's sacred teapot, and should never have dared to suggest that such an aristocratic and, indeed, historic receptacle could possibly have made the tea taste oddly.

Therefore all went well, until a young brother of my mother's, with whom we loved to romp and play when he was home on leave, being unfortunately in the secret, could not refrain from a little questioning. " And so you children have " been so good that you are having tea in the " Queen's teapot, that must be nice !— " (taking it up and smelling it.) " Smells queer," " I suppose that is because it is so old ! " we eagerly agreed to this, and with self righteous exultation, explained how our extreme virtue had been rewarded with this coveted treat, to which we had looked forward for two days.

With great magnanimity we pressed Uncle to partake of the brew, but he refrained, " No

" thank you, chicks, I see it is nearly all gone and
" I must be off, but now tell me (with his head
a little on one side and a twinkle in his eye, which
I can distinctly recall), " when you have had
" tea out of this beautiful teapot, do you ever
" by chance have a little pain ? "

We could not at the moment recall that we
had, but somehow a serpent had entered into
our Eden, and though we should have found it
hard to give the exact reason, we never wanted
to have tea in Audrey's teapot again !

On the top shelf in Fig. 52, you will see two
small porcelain cups to the left in rather large
saucers ; they belong to a set I have of six cups
without handles, and six coffee cups ; with them,
you see a coffee cup of the same service next to
the teapot. The little cream jug in Willow
pattern with the cup and saucer and coffee cup
in the same design are of Caughley china ; they
are a deep full blue, with a good deal of gilding.
These handleless cups must have been very uncomfortable when the tea was hot ; they are the
kind with which I associate the expression " a
dish of tea."

To the left between the two oriental cups and
saucers you will see a very small cup without
a saucer, it is also Oriental, and I have been told,
whether correctly or not I cannot say, that these
tiny cups were used by the Chinese tea tasters
themselves, when employed by the great
growers.

Messrs. Twining own two very small Oriental teapots, not very much bigger than this cup, the only survivors from a large stock, which in olden days were used for tea tasting.

On the extreme right of the same shelf you see a little cane coloured cream jug of earthenware, made by John Turner, it is a very dainty little piece, with a fine mask of Bacchus under the lip. On the lower shelf is a tea cup and saucer with coffee cup of a later date, somewhere about 1790. They do not photograph well, being of a peculiar kind of pale turquoise blue, the design again Willow pattern. This set was made for my great-great-grandmother and the set is still intact.

The sugar basin to the left is Irish ; the date letter is effaced with much rubbing and cleaning, but other marks prove it to have been made between 1730 and 1785. From its shape I should not think it can be older than 1775.

The little cream jug on the right is of George III. date.

Miss Esther Singleton has written two very instructive and interesting books—see names in the Bibliography ; if you can get hold of them they will teach you a great deal. Apparently in America, many old bills and chronicles and inventories of all kinds have been kept, which in our country have in most instances been destroyed, and these records give us a good insight into many things, of which, without them, we should know nothing.

This is a short extract concerning the tea table. " The ' tea-board ' and furniture are nearly " always mentioned in company. One of these " belonging to Peter Cunningham (1748) is " typical of the most fashionable equipment in " vogue. It was set with ten china cups and " saucers and five handle cups, a slop-basin, and " plate beneath, milk pot, teapot and plate and " a boat for spoons . . . . . it will be noticed that " ten of the cups had no handles and the five " that had no saucers were therefore more like " mugs in form."

I should like to know a little more about this inventory, whether for instance the " plate beneath," was really the silver stand for the tea-pot, which I omitted to place under the tea-pot in Fig. 53, but which is seen in the chapter on Sheffield plate in " Antiques and Curios," and what could " a boat for spoons " have been ? this is most puzzling ; I can only think of some thing to keep them hot, as we do for a gravy spoon.

Miss Singleton also gives particulars of several tea sets where " dishes " for tea are spoken of, which seems a confirmation of my theory of the origin of the expression " a dish of tea." Dr. William Crook owned a tea table ; " forty one dishes with saucers and three basins, all china, costing £36," she adds, " In many southern houses these dishes, which are simple little bowls, or cups without handles, have been preserved."

In her book on " Dutch and Flemish furniture,"
I commend to your notice her account of the
Dutch tea table, or rather tea room, for it seems
one apartment was solemnly dedicated to the
rite of tea making. Her description of the
pomp and ceremony attending the whole performance is most curious. It is too long to
quote, but well worth study.

Now let us look at the kettle or urn stand
shown in Fig. 53. As far as wood and style go
it might have had birth in Queen Anne's time,
but I think it is perhaps more likely to be a
George I. piece. You see it has a convenient
little slide which pulls out, and on which the teapot sits, to be filled from the kettle or urn.

This is one of the prettiest little stands for the
purpose, and one of the oldest, I have ever seen ;
it has been long, perhaps always, in our family,
it is in walnut wood of the golden type, and has
the graceful cabriole leg of the time.

There are several good examples of kettle and
urn stands to study in the Victoria and Albert
Museum, though none so old as this one.

In furnishing a house, two or three of these
little conveniences would be most useful ; you
certainly do not want more than one as an urn
stand, but they are small and invaluable to hand
about at afternoon tea, and with their aid you
may hope to save your Indian, or Axminster,
carpet, from having crumbs embedded in it.
I am sure many have felt with me, how thankful

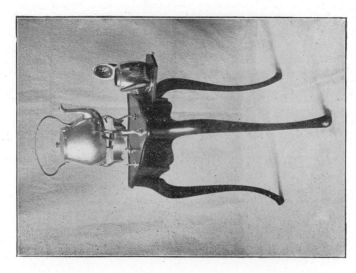

FIG. 53.—KETTLE, OR URN TABLE.

FIG. 54.—TEA-CADDY, SPOON-BOX, AND
WATCH-STAND.

they would have been to have some island of refuge for their cup, when, in one hand a succulent tea cake, in the other a cup of tea, a genial friend comes up, eager to shake hands—we hastily deposit the greasy morsel in the saucer, the friend shakes hands vigorously, and in a prolonged manner—result—the tea cake, a sodden mass from the upsetting of the tea, falls in our lap, and cannons off on to the carpet, leaving behind it a trail of tea—milk, and butter ; our feeling towards the genial friend it is as well not to analyse.

These little tables are positive godsends, I have two, and am keeping a searching eye open for one of the Sheraton period. I must tell you that the term urn stand can only apply to these little tables of the later kind, for urns did not come into use until the second half of the century, so that kettle stand is the correct term for such as mine.

Caddy spoons and sugar tongs photograph badly, so I give you no examples. It is difficult for people of small means to collect old silver, but if you limit yourselves to caddy spoons and tongs, it is not very expensive, and it makes a charming little collection.

It will not be easy and it will take you a long time for these little treasures are quickly snapped up. Sugar tongs are often not marked, the reason for this I do not know unless, being small, they were sometimes overlooked.

The form I like best of all are those like scissors ; they are scarce, because the mechanism being delicate, the work of long years proved too much, and they gave out at the joint.

Another pretty kind are those that pretend to be birds, such as cranes and storks with long bills, but they, too, being fragile, are not often found genuinely old ; and then as charming as any are the flexible kind, pierced down the two arms. Caddy spoons show many varieties, you must be careful about these, as frauds are numerous. The plan is to make a new bowl and cut off the handle of an old tea spoon so as to have the Hall marks ;   the two are then welded together, but a little experience and care will teach you the difference between the true and the false.

In the latter the handle is generally too big, or has not the right sweep, as, though it joins the bowl perfectly, there is something odd about the junction of the pattern round the edge.

I have a very pretty one with a heart in the centre of the bowl, probably a sweetheart's gift, it belongs to my old mahogany tea caddy ; another one, not so old, but quite as taking is like a miniature fire shovel with a tiny discoloured ivory handle.

In Fig. 54, the items of which chiefly belong to the next chapter, you will see the tea caddy of which I speak.   I said a great deal of tea caddies before, but I cannot quite pass them over, for they were very important adjuncts to the tea tables of those days.

They are not so much used now because our degenerate custom is to have tea made in the kitchen and ignobly kept in a vulgar tin canister. In olden days when tea was such a huge price, it was naturally kept under lock and key, and the mistress of the house herself infused it, if in winter from a copper kettle simmering on the hob on a brass footman, and in summer with the aid of the kettle stand and kettle, as you see in Fig. 53. I dare say, if she was " house proud," as the Germans say, she liked even in winter to display to admiring and, perhaps, envious friends the glories of the urn or kettle stand.

I hope she kept the water really boiling. I observe with misgiving many friends of mine, who, using dainty little swinging copper kettles, do *not* keep them boiling, with the result of a tepid and absolutely tasteless liquid, only to be eclipsed in nastiness by tea made in the kitchen with water which has probably " been on the boil " for hours, and a teapot only big enough to serve one comfortably, but is made to do for three, the supply being constantly augmented from a so-called hot waterjug, which was never heated before it was filled, and from which the hostess teems in supplies of tepid water, and this she calls tea ! For a nation of tea drinkers we can certainly show many specimens of lamentable makers.

The first tea-caddies, or tea-poys as they were

called, came from the East and were of Oriental
china ; they were quickly imitated in pottery,
and later on in china ; then came silver and
Sheffield plate caddies, and the infinite variety
of wooden boxes, the most usual being those with
divisions inside for black and green tea, with lids
on hinges, or sliding in and out. These were also
made in shagreen ; it was of two kinds, elephant
grey and also green. We had one of these in
elephant grey, but it disappeared long ago, and I
rather think it went with the tea-pot, for I do not
remember seeing it after nursery days. Tortoiseshell was often used for the purpose, clamped
and ornamented with silver, ivory, inlaid and
plain, all of different shapes—round, octagonal,
square, rectangular and oval, etc.

At the last quarter of the 18th century very
delicately inlaid wood, in the style we connect
with Sheraton's name, came into great favour,
and a good number of these still exist. During
the first thirty years of the 19th century the
general form was oblong, and the shape frequently
inclining to that of a sarcophagus ; there were two
divisions for green and black tea, and in the centre
a cut glass sugar bowl.

You will say the boxes of the early 19th century
have nothing to do with the tea table of the 18th,
and that is true, but as I am considering the collector
of small means, he or she may have to be content
with a caddy of only one hundred years in age.

The boxes most likely to be picked up now are

plain mahogany, or rosewood, and occasionally satinwood. Sometimes they are inlaid with mother-of-pearl, and more rarely with brass ; these latter are especially desirable. The more expensive boxes are lined with velvet or brocade. I possess one lined with lemon coloured brocade, which, though the box must certainly be as old as 1800, is quite unfaded and in perfect condition. The boxes inside seem to be of a kind of zinc, and have domed and hinged lids.

The commoner makes of the same period were lined with a scarlet or emerald green embossed paper, but scarlet is the more usual. They have also little brass ball feet, and, for handles, rings depending from lions' mouths. I have seen one in which the lions, of ferocious aspect, are holding innocent baskets of flowers, which form the handles ; the effect is very quaint.

In Fig. 54, to the right of the spoon box, is a caddy—owning the little spoon of which I speak, with a heart—which I like to think is a Chippendale—no harm in thinking at any rate. I know it was in our family in 1780, and might have been some time before that. It is square, with the lid rounded concavely at the edges, of plain mahogany, the hinges and ring to the lid are of silver and very solid. It has its original lining of faded green velvet, and the two divisions have sliding lids with silver plates, respectively inscribed green and Bohea. I have drawn one half out, to show you how it works.

When you are hunting round for an early 19th century or late 18th century tea caddy, and you want one of the kind with the cut glass sugar basin, I fear you are very unlikely to find one perfect, at least, not without paying rather a large sum, but buy one without the basin, and sooner or later you are pretty sure to find one that has been divorced from its box among the queer odd and end corners in some dealer's shop. So much patience is required to collect, but then that is half the pleasure ; collecting would be a dull affair if we simply paid down whatever was asked and had no trouble at all to find our treasures ; it is the continual hunting with an occasional and unexpected find that makes our joy, and oh ! the pleasure when we take home our gem and display it with pride. Naturally, with the advent of tea all kinds of convenient tables came into use, and though we never practised such ceremonies over it as the Dutch, it seemed to be a very common custom to keep the tea table ready prepared. The prevailing fashion was for the tea things to be displayed on a " toilet," as it was called, and this " toilet " was what we now call an afternoon tea cloth.

As early as the time of William and Mary we find in Celia Fiennes' journal allusions to the permanent tea table. She was a great traveller, and was here, there and everywhere perpetually. She is describing Hampton Court and the so-called improvements there.

" Here was a white marble table behind the
" doore as a sideboard and a clap table under ye
" large looking glass between. The windows ;
" nex this was a drawing roome ; both these rooms
" were hung with small Image tapistry very
" Lively and fresh, here was Crimson, Damaske
" window curtains, chaires, and stooles. . . . .
" There is a back doore in ye dressing roome, to a
" little anty roome with presses, a little Wans-
" coate table for tea, cards or writing, so to a
" back stairs."

Fortunately for us Celia Fiennes was of the in-
quisitive order ; she goes on to give a discreet
account of the sanitary arrangements of the
Palace, and then we come to tea again.

" Over right the entrance of the dressing roome
" was another little closet with the tea equipage,
" and under that was such a little tea roome
" within ye drawing roome."

I should very much like to know what a " clap "
table was. I know about clap cakes, but a table
for making them on would hardly have been in
the state apartments at Hampton Court !

The " little tea room " sounds as if Dutch
William had introduced the custom from his own
country.

We do not know much about his liking for the
herb, but his successor, Queen Anne, was a devotee of the tea table, and we know how often in
the summer she used to have tea in the orangery
at Kensington Palace. Now it stands empty,

without a scrap of furniture, but it is easy to
fancy poor Anne sitting in the two circular ends,
chosen according to the direction of the sun, and
there taking tea with the self-willed Sarah.
Alas! poor Anne, it was a fatal move of hers
when she instituted the " Mrs. Freeman " and
" Mrs. Morley " business.

The variety in the shape of tea tables was endless. When mahogany began to be generally
used we have the small circular table with a move-
able top, which, when not in use, turned down
and the whole thing could be placed against the
wall. A pin secured by a chain effected the
junction of the table top and bottom when needed.

This table was of a convenient form for houses
of small pretention, where the tea equipage was
not always in evidence on the " toilet."

These round tables were made in such numbers
that you can certainly find one if you take a little
trouble. The handsomest ones are already appropriated, but those with hoof, or snake feet,
and a very little spiral carving on the centre pillar
are still to be had, and are convenient for small
rooms.

They are only big enough for the tray though.
A more convenient and practical table is the
Pembroke, which, with its two flaps, will make
into a square of three feet six inches, or, with one
flap down, agreeably contract itself in a very
handy manner. If you use a kettle on the hob,
a footman, as it was called, is a convenient thing.

It was made of brass and so constructed with hooks and legs that it could attach itself to the bars, or stand immediately in front of the fire.
- These have never really gone completely out of fashion, and are still made. The old ones, of which there are still a good number, are generally found to have shed their original handles. From their position close to a hot fire, the handles cracked and perished and new ones were perforce supplied. I have one, a genuine elderly gentleman, rather tottery on his iron legs, and the handle is distressingly vulgar and robust, and instead of being of polished oak, as it should be, it is of unabashed birch, painted black and varnished.

The brass part is handsome and quaint. I can never make up my mind whether it is meant to represent a thistle or a pineapple, but it matters not. " You pays your money and you takes your choice."

With these footmen it was very easy to keep the buttered tea cakes, muffins and crumpets hot close in front of the glowing fire, an arrangement far superior to our inadequate basin, with a gill or so of tepid water at the bottom. In company with the footmen there was always a copper kettle, with a copper handle. The glass handles belong to a later date and came in, I fancy, about 1840. The old copper kettles and coal scuttles of the same period show a beautiful rose colour tone, which does not seem to belong to new specimens. I have a very fine 18th century

U

copper and brass coffee pot of the urn like shape beloved of Robert Adam. It has a band of brass round the neck, a brass ornament to lift the lid, a brass foot and brass fittings to secure the basket-covered handle to the body of the piece. This mixture of copper and brass is very pretty and effective, and when freshly cleaned, the copper is a beautiful rose pink. On the title page you will see an incense burner of fine bronze sent to Messrs. Twining from the East, which they kindly allow me to show you as well as their billhead.

CHAPTER VIII

THE FLOTSAM AND JETSAM OF OLD LUMBER ROOMS

THE idea of naming this chapter as above came to me from an exhaustive hunt I once undertook through two old French country houses.

I have always been addicted to these rummaging excursions, if my friends permit me ; sometimes the search yields richly, sometimes nothing of much interest rises to the surface, but there is always something, I have never quite drawn a blank. English country houses have not quite the same possibilities in their lumber rooms as there are in French *greniers,* because the French are more conservative than we are, they dislike change, and they never throw away anything.

Some of the things I mention in this chapter did not come from a lumber room, or a *grenier,* but I put them in here because they are of interest to the collector of the small things and are too numerous to have chapters devoted to them, and in most cases would not yield sufficient information.

There are so many small things that the true lover of the past likes to hear about, and even perhaps to collect, so I bethought me of lumping them altogether, with the genuine finds from various lumber rooms, extending over several years.

I think on the whole I have certainly found the larger number of treasures in a *grenier* of a Louis XV. house in the Pyrenees, and in a still older house in Brittany.

The *grenier* in the Pyrenees was very large and extended round the three sides of the house, which surrounded a vast courtyard. In this entrancing place I was allowed to investigate to my heart's content, unattended and un-watched.

I dare say I have now forgotten much that I saw, but fortunately I made notes and spent many wet days making sketches of the old bed-steads, etc.

The house is very large, having 59 bedrooms, so it is easy to see how many beds, and how much furniture, must at one time have been required. Now the fine old house is only partially inhabited, and much of the furniture is hidden away in the spacious loft.

There were several handsome Empire beds, and others, which I preferred, of an earlier date with large and handsome brass rosettes as ornaments. One of these latter was a child's bed, though of a fair length, and I persuaded the owners to use it in one of their vast drawing rooms as a sofa. As many of you are aware,

French beds of that period and of the present day are something in the form of a box ; the spring mattress, wool mattress, and all the bed clothes, being tucked neatly in at the sides. The head and foot are of equal height, and the wooden sides slope gracefully down from each end to the level of the lower mattress in the middle.

You can judge then, how easy it is to make a charming sofa out of one of them if narrow, and intended for a child. We found in the drawer of an old *escritoire*, some golden coloured woollen damask in the form of a pair of large curtains, so there was plenty of material in spite of a quantity of moth holes in parts. The top mattress was in fairly good condition, so we covered it with the yellow damask, and then set to work to improve the box spring arrangement.

It was a very hot and hard job, but in the end was accomplished satisfactorily. We made two firm, round bolsters, one for each end, supplemented by two square feather pillows and in the end it looked beautiful. The wood, being the warm yellowish brown of old chestnut, toned well with the material. Another bed with beautiful brass bosses the owners offered to me, and I should have loved to have it, but I remembered in time the " commodious residential flat," and regretfully left it behind.

You are not in the least likely to meet with a cot bedstead, like the one we transmogrified, in England, but I saw something of the same idea carried out a short time ago, with a child's railed cot of mahogany, not very old, about ninety years I should think.

The railing on one side was removed, and thus became a settee. The mattress was covered with old fashioned chintz and so were four fat pillows, one for each end, and two in the middle ; it was really very pretty, and the wood and workmanship sufficiently old to be thoroughly good.

In the Pyrenean *grenier*, I found some entrancing pieces of needlework. Alas ! in these days we shall not hand down much of this kind of treasure to our descendants.

First came three pairs of curtains, of white linen, with a design all over them of pieces of beautifully patterned old fashioned chintz, or printed calico.

The flowers and arabesques were cut out of the fabric and *appliqué* to the white linen, the edges being covered with a tightly twisted cotton cord.

These, though still in good condition, were faded from much washing and from the ardour of the Southern sun, but the effect was still very pleasing. Next came a large bedspread very curiously worked. It consisted of a kind of minute quilting between layers of linen ; the quilting material, or perhaps stuffing would be the more correct term, was formed of quantities of coarse, rather soft cotton cord, which was fastened on each side by minute stitching with white silk ; as the cord was only about an eighth of an inch wide, you may faintly conceive the labour expended.

Besides the quilting, there were at rather wide intervals, conventional flowers in peacock shades of blue and green silk, executed in chain stitch.

When we found it, the needle was still sticking in one of the flowers, and many were traced ready for work. I looked at this tracing with interest and wondered how it had been done. The lines were very delicate and clear, and looked like Indian ink, but that could hardly have been so for it would have run.

There was something sad in looking at that old unfinished task, long laid by in the chestnut wood bureau in the dark *grenier*.

What caused that abrupt interruption ? Was it death that stepped in and laid his cold hand on the worker, or was it a sudden emigration at the time of the great terror in 1793, the worker hastily leaving her embroidery and flying the country and perhaps—who knows—never being able to return. The work is in style rather too old for that period, but modes and fashions change slowly in provincial France, so that does not tell us much.

And then again my thoughts began to work on another line, was the worker a prospective bride, who, full of happiness and joy laboured in eager and joyous anticipation at the furnishing of her new home, and then perhaps something happened—was that golden future never realized, did the bridegroom die, or prove faithless, and was the work thrust into a drawer, with a bitter desire never to look upon it again ?

No voice from the long buried past comes to tell us these things, and the thoughts we weave about these forgotten treasures, give us a tender interest that we could never feel about commonplace things, however beautiful, prosaically bought in a modern shop.

In Fig. 55 you see a piece of Jacobean embroidery, such as dear kind Doll Leeke helps the afflicted Mary Verney to make—see page 21. This is a fine piece, though it has none of the " birds and flyes and other crepers " in it. The foundation looks like thick linen, but is really a mixture, the warp of linen and the weft of cotton.

This special material is now made again for the purpose, for good workers are imitating the Jacobean embroidery. The chief colours were green and blue greens of different tints, all inclining to the peacock shades, a few tones of yellow and brown and an occasional red or dull blue for the " birds and flyes and other crepers."

The leaves that you see looking like small chess boards are managed by leaving the groundwork and executing the dark dice in brown. There are some especially fine examples in the Victoria and Albert Museum. One valance has an ambitious

FIG. 55.—JACOBEAN EMBROIDERY.

FIG. 56.—QUEEN ANNE EMBROIDERY.

design comprising snakes, parrots, squirrels, hornets and grasshoppers all living amicably together.

I am pretty sure if people instituted a search in most really old houses they would often find interesting pieces of work. Look at Fig. 57. It was worked by my great, great grandmother, somewhere about the year 1800. It is all done in ribbons of different widths and kinds, and is one of the most beautiful examples of that kind of work I have ever seen.

I gave it to a dear American friend, who loves these old treasures, and she has done it great honour. First, with a great deal of trouble and considerable cost, she found a frame of the right date, then some old pale blue brocade and, crowning triumph, a piece of tarnished narrow galon as a beading, between the work and the brocade.

I have the portrait of the worker and very striking it is, and has considerable interest attached to it. She was in Paris in 1793 and imprisoned in the Conciergerie. I think no one could have looked death nearer in the face than she did, she was brought out for execution, she got into the tumbril, but it was over-crowded and the gaoler told her to get out and wait till it came back. How one can fancy the poor woman braced up to meet death bravely, and then put back, she was probably then sorry for the delay, but it saved her life, for ere the tumbril could return,

Robespierre was dead and the counter revolution had set in. I think I spoke of her near execution before, but the circumstances were so strange that I may, perhaps, be pardoned for mentioning them again.

In her picture she looks, and I believe she was, a very beautiful woman. Her hair became white during her imprisonment and she never entirely recovered the shock. Fig. 56 is a piece of work of Queen Anne's time, though it continued to be done much later ; it is on linen of a kind of un-bleached tone ; it is, I should imagine, a portion of a bedspread or coverlet, as it was then called, but when rescued from oblivion in the top drawer of a " tall boy," it had been cut up into chair covers.

The work is very fine, done in crewels of a thin make, in the crewel stitch of the present day, not chain stitch, which belongs to a different kind of work. The colours (unlike those of Jacobean embroidery which are chiefly greens, blues and browns) imitate as closely as possible those of the flowers they represent. The design is no longer conventional, but realistic, with roses, peonies, convolvulus, etc., depicted after nature, though in a very stiff manner.

The worsteds of those days must have been wonderfully good, for there is but little fading.

The owner of the work, herself a beautiful embroideress, determined to save the old work by cutting it from its worn foundation and plant-

FIG. 57.—OLD RIBBON WORK.

FIG. 58.—FRENCH CLOCK OF THE 18TH CENTURY.

ing it on another of the same kind. She began
by pasting thin cap paper over the back of the
work, ironed it dry and then cut it out, the great
danger being to cut through some of the stitches.
Having the eye of a hawk, my humble contribu-
tion to the noble work was to do the cutting out,
at the cost of some thumb blisters, for it was like
cutting cardboard. She then put it in position
on the new material, well stretched in a large
frame and fastened each petal and leaf down
by imitating exactly the stitches and the colours
round each one. It was a serious difficulty to get
the faded tones right, but the clever creature
managed that by leaving the new crewels in the
sun on the lawn, for a few hours several days in
succession, till they were faded to exactly the
right tint.

In the near neighbourhood of the quilted coverlet there was a bundle of pieces of needlework of
various kinds, which I think must have been
stored for mending. Amongst other curiosities
were portions of several nightcaps, some uninteresting and comparatively modern, but one
was a little gem (only a portion remaining) of the
rare old black silk embroidery of the 17th century.
The ever illuminating Verney records tell us
something about this. In 1651 Sir Ralph, still in
Blois, where he remains in a kind of honourable
exile, writes out an order for what he wishes sent
to him in the matter of supplementary clothes,
and it is surprising what an infinite number of

night caps he requires, of varying degrees of grandeur. " 6 Fine night capps Laced marked V in black silke, and 2 Fine night capps plaine." No doubt these were necessary after the heat of the periwig, but how funny those bearded men must have looked, with their moustaches and peaked beards emerging from a " Fine night cappe laced." You may now see good examples of these " cappes laced," and some worked in black silk, in the Victoria and Albert Museum. In good Sir Ralph's list of necessaries are one or two things, the uses of which quite beat me. What could a " Dimothy wastcoate " be ? I think, perhaps, it meant " dimity," and what can be meant by " fine Holland handkerchers buttoned " ?

He orders altogether 59 night caps for himself and his little son, and one marvels more and more as the list rounds off with " 2 night Periwigs." He also desires to have sent as he is a widower, " 2 Black Taffaty night cloathes," as well as " black night cappes." Fancy the gloom of this, he could not repose according to the fashion of the day (see page 22) in the mourning bed, but, at any rate, he would do his " Deare Hart " the respect of sleeping in " Black Taffaty night cloathes."

The times of mourning were always times of great ceremony, servants and all retainers, and even the family coaches, were clothed in the all pervading gloom.

There are so many words and expressions of which, unfortunately, we lack the explanation. For instance, on one of these mourning occasions, the coachman, whom it is hinted is somewhat obese, is to have two specially large " wastcotes " at 10 shillings, " and a Pair of mild serge breeches at 11 shillings," this is most puzzling, what can *mild* breeches be ?   I can only fancy it refers to moderately thick clothes, a kind of *demi saison* garment.

Next to the ribbon embroidery you will see in Fig. 58 an old French hanging wall clock.   Of its history I do not know much.   A very elderly relative, then living in one of the fine old London houses of Queen Anne's reign, found it hidden away in her lumber room.   She had it cleaned and set going, and it is still in working order, but requires a good deal of humouring and attention, like a querulous old human being.

There is no date, but judging from the style of ornament I do not think it can be older than 1780. One of the hands has evidently been renewed, though probably quite a hundred years ago. You will see the two are quite different, the ornate one I take to be original and the plainer one a reparation.

This clock, though not in itself a beauty, has a very pretty and dainty effect on the wall, hung between some 18th century engravings.

We now come to Fig. 59, a " herb " or " physic " chest.   He who would know something

of the domestic arrangements of the 17th and 18th
centuries must always bear in mind the important
part home doctoring played in those days. Every
mistress of a house was bound to know something of drugs, and be able to combat simple
ailments, because doctors were few and far
between, and as travelling was difficult, if a doctor
was called in, he usually had to be kept in the
house till the malady abated, so it was no trifling
expense and trouble to call in the faculty, and
small wonder that the ladies became expert in the
manipulation and administration of home-made
physic.

We learn from Lady Brilliana Harley's letters,
in 1641, something of these difficulties. She
writes, " Mr. Ballam is very sicke ; I think it is
" an ague, but he eates and so makes his fits
" violent ; he will take nothinge of Wodowes, nor
" Morgan, but is resolved to send to-morrow for
" doctor Rwit, but he feares that he will stay
" longer with him then £3 will hoold out ; that
" he is willing to give, but he can spare no more
" as he says ; this 2 dayes he has bine debating of,
" as they tell me ; but now in his fitte he resoulfes
" to send for him and dous not recken the
" charges."

One has to remember all these curious little
side facts, for they explain much that would
otherwise be dark to us.

For instance, without this light we should be
somewhat mystified by the enormous number of

FIG. 59.—HERB CHEST.

FIG. 60.—MINIATURE HAIR TRUNK.

drug pots and pill slabs that were made at the time, but, you see, as all well-to-do families wanted at least two or three drug pots, and one pill slab, the mystery is explained.

We had in our family at one time no less than five medicine chests, they were for different purposes, some smaller, some bigger, some for bottles, some for herbs. This one, I think, must have been for herbs chiefly. It was discovered in an attic many years ago and appropriated by our valued housekeeper as a cotton box.

One of the smaller chests was for bottles only, a few of which remained, sunk in holes in the shelves, and a shallow drawer at the bottom lined with velvet must have been for simple instruments. A third one, still smaller, had a number of tiny drawers and a miniature set of weights and scales.

Miss Singleton has got together for our instruction and certainly greatly for our amusement, various inventories concerning the past, one of 1653 concerning the possessions of a certain captain, records among many amusing items of an intimate nature, a " Phisick chest," " 2 old Plaister boxes," " six lancets." It makes one shiver with apprehension to imagine the gallant captain operating on his household with the aid of the " six lancets." I can fancy them lying in my little velvet lined drawer. Miss Bradley's book, too, which is to me a continual pleasure, contains many quaint items which she has discovered in old records of this kind and kindred sorts. For a " pimpled and saucy face " an ointment of copperas and roasted eggs is prepared, and one to cure deafness is truly horrific. They are to have the oil which will come out of a gray eel, which has been buried a fortnight in an earthenware pot, in a dunghill !

Again we have a receipt for curing the bite of a mad dog. " The patient must be blooded " at the arm, and a mixture of ground " liverwort and black pepper must be taken " every morning fasting for four mornings in half- " a-pint of cow's milk warm. The patient must " then go into the cold bath fasting for a month. " He must be dipt all over, but not stay in (with " his head above water) longer than half a minute " if the water be very cold. After this he must " go in three times a week for a fortnight longer."

This is very funnily expressed, for it appears on a cursory glance that the sufferer is to be in a cold bath for a month and fast all the time, but fortunately, instructions are given to " keep his head above water."

This receipt is in " The Art of Cookery made plain and easy," by Mrs. Glasse, though Miss Bradley says that Mrs. Glasse, like the immortal Mrs. Harris, never existed at all, but was *in propria persona* an apothecary named Hill from St. Martin's Lane.

Besides the actual physic making, pomander balls, wash balls and perfumes of all kinds had to

be compounded.   Another of Miss Bradley's
finds is an old receipt for the special kind of
perfume with which to scent gloves.   " For this
" purpose the gloves were actually boiled in musk
" and rose water and a mixture of herbs.   They
" were then to be partially dried and rubbed with
" some stuff called Benjamine, amber grease and
" musk ground up with oil of almonds, after which
" they must be hung up to dry, or better still ' —
run the instructions—" let them dry in your
" bosom."   This last advice seems to invite
pneumonia.

As I write I have before me a delightful old
book, the " Herbal," of John Gerard, written at
the end of the 16th century.   I wish I had space
to give you several of his remedies, but they are
rather involved, and also a little too plain spoken.
One is for unpleasant breath (only it is described
less guardedly) when the trouble is caused by
" a naughty stomach."

In the Verney memoirs we learn about many
different remedies passed round the family.
When in Venice Sir Ralph is anxious that his
relatives should benefit by any good medicines
he can get them, so sends Aunt Isham some
Venice " Trekle."   This was a most ornate and
horrid receipt made of vipers, opium and white
wine, etc., but to be at its best " a dozen vipers
" should be put alive into white wine."   Mrs.
Isham receives it with gratitude, but says, " I see
" by your sending of me Venice Trekle, as you

x

" thinke I still deale in Phisicke, but my travils
" hath binne so aboute in Inglande as I have
" almost forgote all Phisicke."

Mrs. Westerholt, the much valued housekeeper
at Claydon, was no doubt strong in the matter of
drugs and medicine, and we read in volume three
that " She kept various potent mixtures going,
" to be administered as the Doctor wrote her word.
" He refers admiringly to that ' purginge drinke,
" as she made for the maids and the upholsterer,'
" and suggests that some Burdock seeds or root
" might be added to it with advantage.   The
" upholsterer as he worked in the house, was
" admitted to share the household privileges. Did
" he abuse the housekeeper's kindness and help
" himself too greedily ?   We know not ; we only
" hear that the upholsterer is ' like to make a dye
" of it,' but then it is added, ' he was always a
" delicate man ' ! "

They had courage in those days to venture upon
some of the remedies—in the same volume we
read, " Sir Ralph being troubled with an eruption
" on his leg was deluged with advice by his lady
" friends. Doll wished him to drink Asses' milk,
" while he sat in a bath of it up to his neck for
" two hours twice a day ; a less tedious remedy
" is lotion, ' so violant a drop would fetch of the
" skin wher it touched and a dreadful old woman
" is recommended, who has an infallible ' oynt-
" ment for yumurs.' "

I could quote many pages from these charming

memoirs, but must content myself with only one more remedy against the plague.

Sir Ralph is in town in 1665 and Aunt Isham exhorts him to " ware a quill as is filed up with " quicsilver and sealed up with hard waxe and " soed up in a silke thinge with a string to ware " about your neck, this is as sartine as anythinge " is to keep one from taking of the Plage if one is " in the house with them . . . . iff you let your " horse ware it about his head, he will never have " the desese . . . . then follows a caution, ' the " quicsilver must be corked up fust and then " seled, itt tis nitty (what can nitty mean ?) for " one's teth and eies, so without one is in danger, " one would not ware it.' "

It was more in the 18th than the 17th century, that so many face washes and cosmetics of all kinds were compounded, beauty culture was then as assiduously carried on as now, but entirely at home, and without the assistance of specialists.

The " pimpled and saucy face " was considered and the unpleasant effects, inimical to beauty and charm of " a naughty stomach." Perhaps some of you may remember the catastrophe to Sophia's and Olivia's cosmetic preparations when on the fire in " The Vicar of Wakefield." " Washes," said the vicar, " I " had a natural antipathy to ; for I knew that " instead of mending the complexion they spoilt " it. I therefore approached my chair by sly

" degrees to the fire and grasping the poker, as
" if it wanted mending, seemingly by accident
" overturned the whole composition and it
" was too late to begin another."

In Fig. 54, you will see in the centre an old
spoon box ; it was not found in a lumber room,
and has always been treated with respectful
solicitude by its owners. I included it here,
because it is one of the many oddments that
interest us in the things of the past, and yet
are not sufficient in themselves to stand alone.
I have put in some spoons to show you how these
boxes were used.

This is a fine specimen, and is probably of the
period of George II. It is beautifully inlaid
inside, the outside being of dark walnut. Many
of these boxes—especially those of late Chippen-
date and Adam date have fine brass, or silver
keyplates, and massive handles. The spoons,
as you see, are inserted with the bowls upwards,
but in the case of knife boxes, the blades are
naturally downwards.

Those of a later date are still to be picked up.
I have seen some Sheraton ones stripped of their
insides, and used as stationery cases, but what
a pernicious idea, why try to turn one thing
into another, it is a silly and vulgar idea to my
mind.

By the side of the spoon box you will see a
very rare and unusual treasure ; it is an old watch
stand ; this, too, came from the same lumber

room as the clock and the herb chest. A relative married a German about 1810, and this belonged to him. It is old Flemish work, and on the top is the coronet of the Counts of Flanders. It would probably have been made rather early in the 17th century ; except that wood worms have devoured the insides of the *amorini,* the thing is in good condition and all carved out of one piece.

In Fig. 60, you see a nice little possession of quite another family. We cannot trace it beyond about 1800. It is a well made and daintily finished miniature hair trunk, with lock, handle, and brass nails intact. What was its original use I cannot say, but my idea is that it was a cap box ; the caps and turbans of those days were formidable structures, and if a lady went out to spend the evening, she took her cap with her as now, and I think this was a receptacle for the purpose.

Sometimes the cap was left on, and a calash was put over it. I am sure very few, if any, of my readers have ever seen a calash. I remember as a child seeing one that was hidden away in a deep drawer ; the structure was always of silk, generally green or blue, in the form of a hood primarily, but in front, was a kind of second part also of silk gathered on to a collapsible whalebone frame ; you put it on, pulled this front edifice forward, and held it over the face by means of a string attached to the middle of the front, the end being held in the hand. The mechanism was almost exactly like that of the hood to a motor car that we call the " cape cart " hood. The face of the wearer appeared dimly at the end of the tunnel ; fancy what a horrid thing to wear when the wind got inside, it must have been like a balloon.

On our discovering it my father told me a quaint story of its owner. It seems it belonged to his great aunt, who was an extraordinarily plain woman, so much so, that just at first people were repelled, the more so that she was terribly marked with small pox ; she had, however, a fine figure, and owned that invaluable gift—charm. Her plainness did not prevent her marriage, she was the adored wife of a smart naval officer, and at his death she had more than one chance to marry again of which, however, she did not avail herself.

But to my story, it was in the days of the " Charlies," and the old oil lamps few and far between. She was coming home very late at night from some errand of mercy to her home in Panton Square, near St. James, and most probably in the calash, when a set of rowdy young men ran after her, and one catching her round the waist, tried to kiss her—rather difficult I should think with the cape car hood. Great-great-aunt Andress never lacked humour, and never lost her head, so she said, " Not yet, not yet, take me under the lamp." He obeyed,

and did *not* kiss her, but I think more because
he was ashamed of himself than on account of
her plain face ; he apologised, and explained
that he had foolishly made a bet to kiss the first
woman he met ; but now instead he most respect-
fully saw her home in safety, lest other gay
sparks should molest her.

Suiting very well in company with the calash
is a big and beautiful crimson silk umbrella,
which, as a boy, my husband found in their
grenier ; it is of vast proportions, the ribs of
sturdy whalebone, like the carriage umbrella
of to-day, each rib tipped with ivory, and a
carved ivory handle turning a warm yellowish
tint. The silk is of the richest description
without a crack, none of the flimsy machine
pressed stuff which in the umbrella of to-day, we
expect (and we are never disappointed) will very
soon develop pin holes down every fold, and if
we neglect this warning, will one gusty day
slit from top to bottom, and leave us treacherously exposed to the elements.

Well I could tell you about many other finds—
for I am always hunting—but I must leave them
for another day, when I hope we may chat
together again about the interests of the past.

INDEX TO PART I

PART I.—FURNITURE

PART II AND III—EARTHENWARE, GLASS, THE TEA TABLE, ETC.